A GUIDE TO ROMANS

TEF Study Guides

This series was first sponsored and subsidized by the Theological Education Fund of the WCC in response to requests from Africa, Asia, the Caribbean, and the Pacific. The books are prepared by and in consultation with theological teachers in those areas. Special attention is given to problems of interpretation and application arising there as well as in the West, and to the particular needs of students using English as a second language. More advanced titles in the list are marked (A).

General Editors: Daphne Terry and Nicholas Beddow

IN PREPARATION:

TEF Study Guide 11

A GUIDE TO ROMANS

Roger Bowen

First published in 1975
SPCK
Holy Trinity Church
Marylebone Road, London, NW1 4DU

Seventh Impression 1990

© Roger Bowen 1975

The photographs in this book are reproduced
by courtesy of Camera Press Ltd.

ISBN 0 281 02822 2 (net edition)

ISBN 0 281 02823 0 (non-net edition for Africa, Asia, S. Pacific and Caribbean)

Printed and bound in Great Britain at
The Camelot Press Ltd, Southampton

Contents

v

Preface

The appearance of this book is due very largely to the help and encouragement I have received from many people, to whom thanks are due, especially:

Miss Daphne Terry, whose tireless editorial comments and stimulating queries have made this book as much hers as mine, and Miss Lorna Gage of the TEF office who typed much of the final version for the printer;

The Reverend John Baker, in whose fellowship I first explored the treasures contained in the Letter to the Romans;

Dr J. I. Packer, of Trinity College, Bristol, to whose teaching I am greatly indebted, and who will readily recognize much of his material in the pages which follow;

All the authors mentioned in the Bibliography on p. xi, together with many other authors too numerous to mention by name;

Dr Leon Morris, of Ridley College, Melbourne, and the Reverend W. B. Harris, of the Tamilnad Theological Seminary, both of whom gave special help by their careful reading of and detailed comments on an early version;

My students at Kongwa, who will be modestly unaware of their part in this project, but on whom all the material has been tried out, and whose response to it has determined the final form in which it appears;

Above all, my wife, who has for many months been on the receiving end of all the most teasing questions connected with Romans, has borne them cheerfully, and has offered unfailingly constructive suggestions.

Kongwa, Tanzania 1974   ROGER BOWEN

Using this Guide

In planning this book much the same pattern has been followed as for earlier biblical guides in the series. There is a preliminary note on the background to Paul's Letter to the Romans, and on ways of studying it. Then the letter itself has been divided into fairly short sections for study. The treatment of each section consists of:

1. An *Outline* of the Bible passage itself.
2. An *Introduction* to the passage, summarizing what Paul was trying to say and his reasons for saying it, and showing how it fits into the rest of the letter and Paul's teaching as a whole.
3. An *Interpretation* of the passage as it applied to Paul's hearers at the time, and as we should understand and apply its teaching to our own lives as Christians today. *Notes* on particular words and points of possible difficulty are included as part of the interpretation, so that readers can make sure of understanding them as they arise.

SPECIAL NOTES

Separate Special Notes deal in more detail with some of the main themes and problems which Paul was wrestling with. They explain some ideas of his time which we may find helpful in order to understand his teaching more fully, and apply it to our own situation today. They are, however, not essential, and readers with limited time may skip them.

ADDITIONAL NOTES

These are provided at the end of the book, to help clarify the meaning of 26 important words or ideas which Paul used in this and other Letters and which appear elsewhere in the Bible. They are an essential part of the Guide, and all references to them should be followed up as they occur.

STUDY SUGGESTIONS

Suggestions for further study are provided at the end of each section and for most of the Special Notes. Besides enabling students working alone to check their own progress, they provide topics for group research and classroom discussion, and will help all readers to understand Paul's teaching more clearly. They are of four main sorts:

1. *Words:* These are to help readers check and deepen their understanding of specific words and phrases;

2. *Content:* These review questions will help a reader to ensure that he has fully grasped the ideas and points of teaching studied;
3. *Bible:* These relate Paul's teaching in Romans with that in other parts of the Bible. The additional Bible references they contain will enable readers to complete their study of the theme under discussion.
4. *Application, opinion, and research:* These will help readers to clarify their own thinking on the themes Paul was discussing, and relate his teaching to their own situation.

The best way to use these Study Suggestions is: first, re-read the Bible passage; second, read the appropriate section of the Guide carefully once or twice, and then do the work suggested, either in writing or in group discussion, without looking at the Guide again except where instructed to do so.

The *Key* on p. 225 will enable you to check your work on those questions which can be checked in this way. In most cases the Key does not give the answer to a question; it shows where an answer is to be found.

Please note that these are only *suggestions*. Rather more numerous questions have been provided here than in other Guides, because of the complexity and importance of the truths which Paul was discussing. But some readers may not wish to use the study material at all. And some teachers will probably wish to select those questions which are most relevant to the needs of their particular students, or to substitute questions of their own.

INDEX

The Index (p. 233) includes only the more important proper names and the main subjects which occur in Paul's Letter or which are discussed in the Guide.

BIBLE VERSION

The English translation of the Bible used in the Guide is the Revised Standard version (RSV); the abbreviation 'mg' in RSV references stands for 'margin', i.e. the marginal or foot notes given in some editions. Reference is also made to the New English Bible (NEB) where this shows the meaning more clearly.

FURTHER READING

The Bibliography (p. xi) lists some books which readers may find useful for further study of Romans and of Paul's teaching generally.

Bibliography

Readers may find the following books useful for further study of the Letter to the Romans.

INTRODUCTORY BOOKS
Reading through Romans, C. K. Barrett (SCM Press, London)

MORE ADVANCED BOOKS
Romans, A. Nygren (SCM Press, London, and Fortress Press, Philadelphia)
Romans, F. F. Bruce (IVP, Leicester)
Wrestling with Romans, J. A. T. Robinson (SCM Press, London)

ADVANCED AND TECHNICAL
The Epistle to the Romans, C. K. Barrett (A. & C. Black, London)
Romans, C. E. B. Cranfield (T. & T. Clark, Edinburgh)

SERMONS ON ROMANS
Romans, D. M. Lloyd-Jones (Banner of Truth, London). A series of expository sermons, in several volumes.

Notes on Studying Paul's Letter to the Romans

Paul's letter to the Romans is important for three chief reasons:

1. It brings a message which comes from God to us, as it came long ago to the Christians at Rome, through His servant, Paul. In it we read of 'the gospel' (i.e. the good news) which comes from God and which is about His Son Jesus Christ (see Rom. 1.1–3). We read the letter, therefore, because we want to hear God's message and to know more about Jesus Christ. As one scholar has written, it is 'a letter from God to us today'.

2. Many people in the history of the Church have had their lives changed as a result of reading this letter. Here are four examples:

(a) North Africa, 386: *Augustine*, whose theological teaching has influenced the whole Christian Church, had been seeking God for a long time, but was in despair because evil desires continued to defeat him. Then he heard a voice say, 'Take and read.' He picked up a book containing this letter, opened it at Romans 13.13, 14, and read, 'Put on the Lord Jesus Christ . . .' As a result, he came to know God through Jesus Christ.

(b) Germany, 1513: *Martin Luther*, who became one of the leaders of the Reformation, was afraid that God, who is perfectly just, would condemn him for his sin. He tried hard to please God, but still knew that he was guilty of many evil thoughts and actions. But one day he had to explain to his students in the University the meaning of Romans 1.17. After puzzling over it for a long time, he at last saw its meaning, and explained it as follows: 'God's righteousness is like a garment with which He clothes us, with the result that He regards us as righteous.' From that time Luther stopped trusting in his own efforts; he trusted Jesus Christ instead, and found peace.

(c) England, 1738: *John Wesley* was a famous preacher, but felt that he himself had not yet received God's forgiveness. But 'one evening,' he wrote, 'I went very unwillingly to a society in Aldersgate Street, where one was reading Luther's preface to the letter to the Romans.' God spoke to Wesley through that reading, with the result that he at once felt sure that Christ had died, not for the world only, but for him, John Wesley, personally.

(d) Japan, 1910: *Taisei Michihata* was a Buddhist priest who had accepted all kinds of suffering in his efforts to find the true God. Then Jesus spoke to him through the Bible. But still he could not trust Jesus enough to take the step of baptism until, one evening, he read

Romans 8.32: 'He who did not spare his own Son, but gave him up for us all, will he not give us all things with him?' At once Michihata and his wife left the temple and were baptized. For twenty-five years he worked as an evangelist, and wrote that God supplied all his needs in that time.

God still changes people's lives today in order that they may do His work in the world, just as He changed the lives of Augustine, Luther, Wesley, and Michihata. These four men found that their study of Romans changed not only them, but many others also. This letter has been good for the Church as well as for individuals. Studying it may have a similar effect on you and, through you, on the lives of others also. All who read the Bible should be ready for God to change their lives through its message.

3. Many Christian thinkers have found that Romans is the key to understanding the rest of the Bible. John Calvin called it 'an open door to understanding all the treasures of Scripture'. William Tyndale, the English Bible translator, said that it shone 'a light on to the whole Bible'. J. B. Phillips, in his translation of the New Testament, called it 'The Gospel according to Paul'. And Luther, after seeing the meaning of Romans 1.17, wrote: 'The whole of Scripture took on a new meaning.' He called it 'the chief book of the New Testament and the clearest Gospel, so valuable that a Christian should not only know every word of it by heart, but should take it about with him every day as the daily bread of his soul'.

If we find parts of the Bible difficult to understand, a study of Romans will probably help us. In it Paul explained, step by step, what man's real need is, and how Jesus Christ is God's answer to that need.

WHO WROTE THIS LETTER,
WHERE, WHEN, AND TO WHOM?

Most introductions to Paul's letters deal with these questions, and when we study other letters, e.g. Galatians, Colossians, 1 John, it is helpful if we try to answer them in advance. We shall not do so here, however, partly because we can understand this letter without knowing the answers, and partly because we shall consider these questions as we study the text of the letter itself. It will be sufficient now if we assume that Paul wrote this letter to the Christians at Rome, whom he had never met, whilst he was staying at Corinth, just before he set out to take a gift of money to the poor Christians at Jerusalem (see Acts 20.3 and Rom. 15.25).

WHY WAS THIS LETTER WRITTEN?

The important question is not 'Why did Paul write a letter to the Romans?' but 'Why did Paul write to the Romans a letter *of this kind*?'

In other words, why did he send them this careful statement of the Gospel which he preached?

Scholars have suggested many different answers to this question. For example:

(a) Paul hoped that the Roman Christians would help him in the new work which he was planning to do in Spain (see Rom. 15.24). So he wrote to tell them the Gospel which he preached, in the hope that they would approve and give him the help he needed.

(b) Until that time, the centre of the Church's mission had been Antioch, in Syria. Now it was time to extend the Church's mission to the West, so a new centre was needed in the West. Perhaps Paul hoped that Rome might be that centre. If so, the Christians there would need to have a good understanding of the Gospel.

(c) In those days Rome was the world's greatest city. If Christians there held the faith strongly, then that same faith was likely to spread throughout the world.

(d) Paul wanted to preserve in writing a clear statement of Christian doctrine for the benefit of all Christians. So this is a 'Handbook of Christian Beliefs', sent to the chief city in the world. (Some scholars think that Paul sent another copy of the same letter to Ephesus, another great city.)

(e) One of the most likely answers, and one which is particularly helpful when we try to understand Romans 9—16, is that Paul wanted to remind the Roman Christians about their unity with one another and with the whole Church of Christ. Perhaps some disagreements had arisen between Jewish and Gentile Christians in Rome. Romans 14.10 and 16.17 may indicate such disagreement (see also p. 12). For this reason Paul showed in this letter: (i) that everyone has the same real need (3.22, 23); (ii) that God's good news is meant for everyone (10.12); (iii) that Gentiles and Jews are indebted to one another (11.30, 31); (iv) that all Christians need one another's help (12.4–8); (v) that Christians ought to care for one another in practical ways (13.8–10).

Perhaps all these suggestions have some truth in them. We shall be better able to consider this question after we have studied the teaching of the letter itself. See Special Note, p. 200.

WHAT IS THE PLAN OF ROMANS?

Before we look at the details of the letter, it will be helpful to try to see its general plan. This will not be difficult, because Paul himself made it clear how his thought was moving on step by step. He was like a man who puts up signposts to show travellers which way to go. In this letter there are two kinds of signpost:

1. Sometimes, near the beginning of a paragraph, there is a signpost showing what the whole paragraph is about. We could call this a *Theme*

Signpost. It is like a signpost set up at the entrance to a large town, to announce the name of the town. The chief signpost of this kind is 1.16, 17:

'For I am not ashamed of the gospel: it is the power of God for salvation to everyone who has faith, to the Jew first and also to the Greek. For in it the righteousness of God is revealed through faith for faith; as it is written, "He who through faith is righteous shall live." '

This is a summary of 'the gospel', which Paul was about to explain in detail. Thus 1.16, 17 provides a Signpost to show the theme of the next eight chapters. But usually the Theme Signpost is a short phrase of a word or two, giving the theme, not of many chapters, but of just one section. The Plan on p. 5 lists most of them.

2. We can call the other kind of signpost a *Link Signpost*. This is like a signpost pointing the way to a distant town. Sometimes Paul mentioned a new idea, which he did not explain in detail until a later section. One good example of this is 'you are not under law' (6.14). This is a difficult phrase which needs some explanation; the explanation comes in chapter 7, especially vv. 4–6. Therefore the words 'you are not under law' point forward to the next chapter. These Link Signposts are indicated in this Guide, as we study the passages where they occur.

This Guide provides two ways of getting a clear idea of the plan of this letter; as follows:

(a) Work your way carefully through the Plan on p. 5. Notice how Paul's thought moved on. Use your Bible to see where the main divisions come, and to notice the Theme Signposts.

(b) Read quickly through the Outlines given at the beginning of each section in this Guide. If you do this you will have read a summary of the whole letter by the time you reach the end. But you will want to turn back to the Plan, and certainly to the Bible itself. In any case, you should have your Bible open in front of you whenever you read any part of this Guide, so that you can at once look up each word and passage discussed.

PLAN OF ROMANS

		Theme Signposts
Part 1: Introduction and Theme		
1.1-15	Paul and his Readers	
1.16,17	Theme of the Letter	'the gospel'
Part 2: 'He who through faith is righteous ...		
1.18-32	Man's Need: Unrighteousness of the Gentiles	'wrath of God'
2.1–3.20	Man's Need: Unrighteousness of the Jews	
3.21-31	God's Gift: Righteousness from God	'righteousness of God'
4.1-25	God's Gift: The Witness of the Old Testament	
Part 3: '... shall live.'		
5.1-11	Free from Wrath	'peace with God'
5.12-21	The Two Families (of Adam and Christ)	
6.1-23	Free from Sin	'died to sin'
7.1-25	Free from Law	'died to the law'
8.1-39	Free from Death	'the Spirit of life'
Part 4: The Nation of God		
9.1-5	The Problem	
9.6-29	God's Sovereignty and Freedom	
9.30–10.21	Man's Responsibility	
11.1-36	God's Plan	
Part 5: The Behaviour of God's People		
12.1-8	Basis of Christian Behaviour: Life in the Body of Christ	
12.9-21	The Life of Love	
13.1-7	Christian Citizenship	
13.8-10	Brotherly Love	
13.11-14	The Coming Day	
14.1–15.13	The Weak and the Strong	
15.14-33	Paul's Ministry and Future Plans	
16.1-27	Greetings and Hymn of Praise	

PART 1

CONTEXT AND THEME OF THE LETTER

1.1–15
Paul and His Readers

OUTLINE

'Since I have never met you personally, I should first introduce myself. My name is Paul. God has given me the job of telling men His good news. This good news is about Jesus Christ, His Son, and my aim is that all men should obey Jesus as Lord. I am so glad to hear from all sides about the strength of your Christian faith. I have been praying for you, and am looking forward to meeting you all personally. It will do all of us good!'

INTRODUCTION

When one person writes a letter to another, he usually (a) gives personal news of himself, (b) makes some comment on the latest news he has received about the other person, (c) explains why he is writing the present letter. Paul did all of these things at the beginning of his letter to the Romans. And he did more. A sick man wants to be sure that his doctor has the basic knowledge necessary to treat his sickness. Before a man starts to read a book, he often asks, 'Who is this writer? Is he qualified to write about this subject?' Paul imagined his readers asking the same sort of questions about him, so he showed them how he was qualified to write to them about the Gospel of Jesus Christ. He also gave them a short summary of his message in words with which they were familiar.

INTERPRETATION AND NOTES

PAUL, AND HOW GOD CALLED HIM (ROM. 1.1)

Paul described himself in three ways:

1. The first word he used was *servant*. Long before, when Paul was on a journey to Damascus, he had been a servant of the Jewish High Priest, and had obeyed his master's orders to arrest any Christians he could find. But on his journey Jesus appeared to him, with the result that he became the servant of Jesus Christ (see Acts 9.1–6). 'Servant'

is a true description of anyone who has become a disciple of Jesus Christ. The Greek word actually means 'slave', and the main idea is that he belongs to his master and obeys not his own will, but his master's—just as Jesus obeyed His Father's will in His life on earth.

2. The second word which Paul used to describe himself was *apostle*. Although every disciple is a servant of Christ, only some were called to be His apostles. The word 'apostle' means 'one who is sent out' for a special purpose. Those whom Jesus sent out in this way received His authority, fulfilled His commands, and reported back to Him on what they had done. Jewish leaders sometimes sent out apostles, and so did some local churches, but Paul was an apostle sent by Jesus Christ. For him, this meant that:

(a) He had met Jesus, risen from the dead (1 Cor. 15.8).

(b) He was commissioned by Jesus to be a witness to the resurrection (Gal. 1.16).

(c) He received his message directly from Jesus, and this message was the same as that preached by the other apostles (Gal. 1.11; 1 Cor. 15.11).

(d) As a result, he was a missionary, sent to plant Churches in new areas (Acts 9.15).

(e) He was also one of Jesus's special representatives within His Church, and had been given authority to teach the truth which Jesus had revealed to him (2 Cor. 13.10).

3. The third description of himself which Paul gave was *set apart for the gospel of God*. The important thing for Paul was not himself or his rank, but his message.

Before Paul met with the risen Christ, he had been a Pharisee, i.e. one who is 'set apart' from ordinary people. The Pharisees thought of themselves in this way because their chief aim was to fulfil the Jewish law in every detail. But Paul's life was now devoted to fulfilling his commission from Christ, which was to proclaim not his own ideas but God's Gospel. This was Christ's will for him, and he, as a servant, had to obey.

Paul therefore wanted his readers to think of him, not as a great or gifted man, but as one sent by Jesus Christ, with His commission, His authority, and His word.

PAUL'S MESSAGE (ROM. 1.2–5)

The message was more important than the messenger, so Paul at once gave a summary of that message. And because the Roman Christians had never met Paul, he used words which would be familiar to them, in order to break down the feeling of strangeness between them. Some scholars have suggested that vv. 2–4 are a simple creed, or saying, which was much used amongst the early Christians. They would find

'Paul showed how he was qualified to write about the Gospel...as one sent by Jesus Christ with His commission, His authority, His word' (pp. 7, 8).

A British diplomat presents Letters of Commission as credentials to the President of Tanzania. What 'credentials' do ordinary Christians have which authorize them to write or speak about the Gospel?

it easy to remember because of the way the lines balance in poetical
fashion:

the gospel of God
Which he promised beforehand through his prophets in the holy
scriptures, the gospel concerning his Son,
Who was descended from David according to the flesh
And designated Son of God (in power) according to the Spirit of
holiness
By his resurrection from the dead Jesus Christ our Lord.

Other scholars divide up this 'creed' in different ways, but most of them
agree that Paul probably borrowed the words from a worship-service
of the early Christians. Their origin does not much matter to us now,
but it is important that we should carefully consider their meaning.
The gospel was the message with which Paul had been entrusted. It
was the 'good news' which comes from the one and only God, and must
therefore be proclaimed to all men.
Which he promised beforehand . . . One of the most important points
made by the first preachers of the Gospel was that it was the fulfilment
of the hopes and prophecies contained in the Jewish Scriptures. The
Gospel was not a new idea which God had just thought of when He
sent His Son.
Concerning his Son: The Gospel is an announcement of what God has
done through His Son—therefore it is good news about Christ for men.
In v. 9 it is called the Gospel *of* His Son, i.e. it comes from His Son and
is about His Son. Paul at once went on to make three parallel statements about God's Son:
1. **Descended from David:** The first statement concerns the Son's
human life. It is possible to trace the ancestry of Jesus, through Joseph
and probably through Mary, until one reaches the name of David
(Luke 3.31; Matt. 1.1). God's Son lived a truly human life as a descendant of David. The Jewish people were looking forward to the coming
of a great King who would rule them well and lead the nation to great
prosperity under God. They believed that he would be of David's
family, but even greater than David.
2. **Son of God in power:** This second statement concerns the Son's
divinity. The unusual phrase, 'the Spirit of holiness', probably refers
to the Holy Spirit, and is in contrast with 'according to the flesh'. The
probable meaning is that although Jesus, from a human point of view,
was a man descended from David, yet the fuller truth about Him,
looked at from the point of view of God's Spirit, is that He is God's
own Son. This was true right from the beginning of His life. But it
was especially emphasized at His *baptism* (see Luke 3.22), followed by
the works of *power* which He did during His ministry, and also at His

9

resurrection (see Acts 5.31), followed by His reign of *power* in heaven. Both these great events showed forth the work of the Holy Spirit. The word 'designated' may appear to suggest that there was a time when Jesus was not the Son of God, but this interpretation would be different from Paul's usual teaching, and so is unlikely to be correct.

3. **By his resurrection from the dead Jesus Christ our Lord:** This last statement sums up Paul's meaning. It was the resurrection which revealed Jesus as He really is—Jesus Christ our Lord, which was Paul's favourite way of speaking of Him. There are three separate ideas contained in the one name:

(a) *Jesus:* He is a true man, who lived in Galilee and was well known to His neighbours. His name 'Jesus' means 'Saviour' (Matt. 1.21), but perhaps the meaning of the name had no special significance for Paul.

(b) *Christ:* this is a title which means the 'Anointed One' of God. The Jews looked forward to the 'One who should come' from God and who would rule God's people as God's own representative. They called Him 'Messiah' (i.e., the Anointed, the Christ) because kings were anointed in the name of God. So this title, which came to be used by Christians as the usual name for Jesus, has a similar meaning to 'Son of David'.

(c) *Our Lord:* this was the confession of the first Christians, which marked them off from other people who served other lords, as the new people of God. The risen Jesus Christ is more than a historical person, more than an appearance of God—he is *our* living Lord.

PAUL'S READERS (ROM. 1.6–8)

Paul had been sent by God to take His Gospel especially to the non-Jewish nations (v. 5). Therefore he felt a responsibility for the Christians at Rome, as well as those of other non-Jewish cities. Just as we are interested in the news that comes from the capital city of our country, so Paul was interested in the Christians who lived in the chief city of the world at that time. He greeted them warmly (vv. 6, 7), and described them in three ways:

1. When they first heard the Gospel concerning Jesus Christ, it was accompanied by a *call to belong to him* as His obedient disciples.

2. Jesus is God's beloved Son, and those who belong to Jesus share His relationship with God. They too have become *God's beloved* sons. Paul did not mean that God does not love all men, but simply that at Rome, as in every place, those who belong to Jesus Christ have this *special* relationship with God, and can enjoy, understand, and accept His love.

3. The word *saint* means a 'holy person'. It is not, in the New Testament, used of specially good Christians, but of *all* Christians. There are two main ideas in the word:

(a) the idea that Christians are *different from* others who do not belong to Christ—just as God is 'holy', i.e. *different from* all that He has created;

(b) the idea that they are *set apart for* God—just as the Israelites were brought out of Egypt to be a people *for* God (see Exod. 19.5, 6). Notice that writers in the Bible almost never use the word 'saint' in the singular. A man cannot be a saint by himself. As soon as he belongs to Jesus Christ he enters the company of God's people—the saints.

Vv. 6, 7. Called: Paul used the word 'call' in two chief ways:

1. It can have the ordinary sense of an *invitation* (1 Cor. 10.27), which may be accepted or refused. In this sense, 'many are called, but few chosen'. God calls all men everywhere to believe the Gospel, but many refuse His call.

2. Paul normally used the word to mean *God's call which is accepted*. This meaning is seen clearly in Romans 8.28, 30. In this sense God's call is powerful and effective. God's word carries power with it, it has results (see Gen. 1.3; Isa. 55.11; John 11.43). All those whom God calls in this way respond to His calling. This is Paul's meaning in Romans. 1.1, 6, 7. The Roman Christians were not simply 'invited'—they *became* saints.

V. 7. Grace to you and peace: The custom in Paul's time was to start every letter with a greeting, just as people do today. Paul took the customary Greek and Hebrew words of greeting, i.e. 'Good health' and 'peace' (*shalom*), and gave them a truly Christian meaning: (a) *Grace* from God—this is the source of all the blessings we receive (see Additional Note, p. 209, *Grace*); (b) *Peace* from God—this is one of God's greatest gifts to us which we only truly experience through the Gospel (see p. 64).

We know very little about the Christians at Rome, and this letter does not give us much certain information. Scholars have made many different suggestions about the Church at Rome. Here are some of them:

(a) The first Romans to become Christians were probably Jews who were baptized on the Day of Pentecost in Jerusalem (Act 2.10). When they returned home, they spread the Gospel to their Jewish friends.

(b) Rome, like Nairobi or Hong Kong today, was visited by many travellers. Some of these were Christians, who brought their new faith with them. This faith quickly spread among the inhabitants of Rome, many of whom were longing for a better way of life.

(c) The new faith was the subject of a lot of argument, especially in the Jewish synagogues. Sometimes these arguments became violent (see Acts 14.4, 5; 17.5–8). They even led to rioting, so that the Emperor Claudius ordered all Jews to leave the city (see Acts 18.2). A Roman

11

historian named Suetonius wrote: 'Claudius expelled the Jews from Rome because they were causing disturbances at the instigation of Chrestus.' Suetonius knew little about the Jews, and even less about Christ, whose name he may just have heard mentioned. He probably wrote 'Chrestus' by mistake for 'Christus' (which is Latin for Christ).

(d) Probably, for some years after that, the only Christians in Rome were Gentiles, i.e. not Jews, but people of other nations. The history and teaching of the Jewish Scriptures would have been strange to them, so they developed customs and teachings which were different from those of which Jewish Christians would have approved. For example, they might forget the Jewish background of Jesus's life, and the importance of what we now call the Old Testament for the first Christians. They might reject the Jewish Christians' habit of observing certain rules about their food and about certain days of the year. This did not matter while the Jewish Christians were away from Rome; but after a few years they came back—and then perhaps disagreements and misunderstandings arose between the Gentile Christians and the Jewish minority in the Church. This may have been one of the reasons why Paul wrote this letter (see p. 3(e)).

(e) By the time that Paul wrote to the Christians in Rome, the Church there was strong. Everybody was talking about how Christianity had spread in the capital city (v. 8). Another Roman historian, Tacitus, wrote that by the year AD 64 there was a 'very great multitude' of Christians in the city.

PAUL'S PLANS (ROM. 1.9–15)

These verses teach us a great deal about Paul's ministry and his attitude to other people.

(a) He prayed for other Christians, even though he had never met them (v. 9).

(b) He wanted to visit Rome. We should not imagine that Paul's aim was to preach the Gospel himself to as many unconverted people as he could find. His chief aim was to plant Churches in the big cities—Corinth, Ephesus, Thessalonika—from which the Gospel would spread round about. For this reason he was concerned for the welfare of the Church at Rome, the most strategic city of all (vv. 10, 11).

(c) He was humble enough to realize that his fellow Christians could encourage him, just as he hoped that he could strengthen them (v. 12).

(d) Paul's intention of preaching to others was much more than a personal desire. It was his obligation as an apostle. God had entrusted him with something which belonged to other people. It belonged to everyone, because it came from the one God who created everyone. Therefore Paul had to spend his life giving to men what he owed them: the Gospel (vv. 13–15).

(e) Paul did not divide people into different sorts or classes. The people of Greece and Rome thought of the world as divided into two main groups: (i) the Greeks (i.e. cultured, educated people); (ii) the barbarians (uncivilized people outside Rome's influence). But Paul knew that *all* men needed the Gospel of God. There were none so cultured that they had no need of it, and none so uncivilized that they could not receive it. The word *gospel*, used in v. 15, is Paul's first Link Signpost (see p. 4), and points forward to the main idea of the next section, vv. 16 and 17.

STUDY SUGGESTIONS

WORD STUDY

1. Which *two* of the following words mean almost the same as 'apostle'?
   priest   missionary   ruler   preacher   ambassador
2. For each of the words in list (a) below, choose one of the words in list (b) which the Greeks used with the same or nearly the same meaning.
   (a) servant   Gospel   anointed   Gentiles   saint   barbarian
   (b) good news   Christ   holy   uncivilized   slave   nations

REVIEW OF CONTENT

3. (a) What sort of man was the writer of this letter?
   (b) In what ways was he qualified to be a teacher of the Christian faith?
4. (a) What sort of people were the Christians in Rome?
   (b) What were the chief points of Paul's message to them?
5. How does Paul's description of himself in vv. 1 and 5 help to explain why Christians have put his writings, with the rest of the New Testament, in a different class from all other literature?
6. Which of the following events in Jesus's life showed Him as (i) truly man; (ii) Son of God in power?
   (a) He forgave sins   (b) He was tempted   (c) He slept   (d) He ascended into heaven   (e) He did not know the time of His second coming   (f) He raised the dead.

BIBLE

7. Which of the five points about Paul's apostleship noted on p. 7 is mentioned in each of the following five verses?
   (a) Acts 26.16   (b) Rom. 15.18–20   (c) 1 Cor. 9.1   (d) 1 Cor. 14.37   (e) Gal. 1.12
8. Romans 1.2–4 may be a simple creed.
   (a) In what ways is the teaching of Romans 1.2–5 like that of 1

Timothy 3.16? (b) What other short creeds of this sort can be found in 2 Timothy?

9. In Rom. 1.2–5, Paul emphasized (a) the Old Testament prophecies of the Gospel; (b) Jesus's human life and ministry; (c) Jesus's resurrection; (d) the witness of the resurrection; (e) the need to turn to Jesus in faith. Read the following passages which record the earliest Christian sermons, and list the references to these same five points.
Acts 2.14–36; 3.12–26; 10.34–43

10. 'Paul used the word "call" in two chief ways' (p. 11). What are those ways, and in which way is it used in each of the following verses?
(a) Acts 2.39 (b) Acts 5.40 (c) Acts 20.17 (d) 2 Tim. 1.9 (e) 1 Pet. 2.9

APPLICATION, OPINION, AND RESEARCH

11. 'The new faith was the subject of a lot of argument, sometimes violent' (p. 11). Give examples of conflicts arising in people's lives as a result of the coming of the Gospel, either from your own experience, or from what you have heard or read.

12. Paul thanked God for the Roman Christians. Look for similar thanksgiving in the first chapters of Paul's other letters. What do we learn from these examples?

13. As in the ancient world, so today we tend to divide people up into groups or classes and judge them according to which they belong to. Name some of the groups and classes into which people are divided today. Why do such divisions arise? Do you think it is right to classify and judge people in this way? Give reasons for your answers.

14. The early Christians used poetical forms to help in teaching and learning basic Christian doctrine. In many parts of the world Christians who cannot read have learned Bible stories by singing songs about them. What songs and poems, if any, are used for purposes of teaching in your own country, either by Christians or by those of other faiths? In what other ways, if any, and for what other purposes, do you think the Church could use these methods?

1.16–17

The Theme of the Letter

OUTLINE

'I have a good reason for talking so much about this good news. For hundreds of years men everywhere have been wondering about God, and how they can meet with Him in friendship and love. The Gospel of Christ tells us how: this life of fellowship with Him is a gift which we simply receive from Him. This is no new idea—Habakkuk taught it long ago.'

INTRODUCTION

Four times already in this letter Paul had used the word 'Gospel'. For Paul, there was nothing so important as this, and the whole letter is his attempt to give the Roman Christians a full explanation of this Gospel. His explanation begins with this short paragraph of two verses. It is his *Theme Signpost*, because it points forward and says briefly what the next eight chapters of the letter are going to be about.

It is not easy to give a brief summary of the Christian Gospel. Many people have tried, but in doing so have often raised further problems. This is also true of Paul's summary here. He used the three most important words of this letter—*righteousness, faith, live*—as well as two words of lesser importance—*power, salvation*—without explaining what they mean. Paul's own explanations come later on in the letter. But we shall find it helpful to consider now the chief points which he was making in these two verses (see Notes below).

The first thing to notice, before coming to the Notes, is that Paul took the words of Habakkuk 2.4 as his theme for the next eight chapters:

'He who through faith is righteous shall live.'

He divided Habakkuk's sentence into two parts, with the result that
    (a) Part 1: **'He who through faith is righteous . . .'** is the theme of Romans 1.18—4.25, where Paul explained *how* a man becomes 'righteous', i.e. through faith.
    (b) Part 2: **'. . . shall live'**, is the theme of Romans 5—8, where Paul explained what the *life* of the 'righteous' man is like.
We can therefore summarize Paul's thought in this way:
    Faith leads to *righteousness*: *righteousness* leads to *life*.

INTERPRETATION AND NOTES

I am not ashamed: This fact was certainly clear to all who knew Paul. Far from being ashamed of the Gospel, he seemed unable to talk about anything else! But in this he was different from most people of his time, who despised the foolish religion of the Christians. For Jesus had been rejected by the Jewish religious leaders; and He had none of the learning which the Greeks admired. Finally He was put to death like a criminal who seemed to be under God's curse. How could such a man have any message for mankind? One Roman soldier laughed at his Christian friend, Alexamenos, and drew a picture of him kneeling down in front of a man with an ass's head who was hanging on a cross (the ass was regarded as the most stupid of animals).

Paul was different from this soldier; he was proud of this Gospel of the crucified Christ. Paul knew that, whether you were a Jew or a Greek, the Gospel had power to 'save' you in a way that neither Jewish religion nor Greek wisdom ever could.

The power of God for salvation: See Additional Note, p. 217, Salvation. Men have always wanted power of different kinds. Today some call for 'black power', others struggle to preserve the power of European rule, others long for economic power which will enable them to defeat poverty, ignorance, and sickness. Many people are conscious of needing power in their own lives. They find that they lack the power to follow what they know to be right. Many new nations aim at high standards, pass good laws, and acquire wealth. Yet many find that their people, even the leaders, seem to lack the power to maintain those standards in their own lives and to use the national wealth honestly and faithfully.

When Paul wrote to the Romans, the most powerful man in the world was the Roman Emperor. A Roman writer, Epictetus, said of him, 'While the Emperor has power to give peace from war on land and sea, he is unable to give peace from passion, grief, and envy. He cannot give peace of heart, for which man longs even more than outward peace.' Although human power can achieve a great deal, it can never bring men to salvation. Only God's power can do this, because only God is stronger than the powers of evil from which men need to be saved.

This power of God was at work in the ministry of His Son here on earth. It is at work now to an even greater extent throughout the world because of His resurrection (see p. 10, 3). It is particularly connected with *the Gospel*. Men have no power to save themselves through their own activity—*God* saves, and He does so through this Gospel. But whom does God save? The answer is contained in the words which immediately follow.

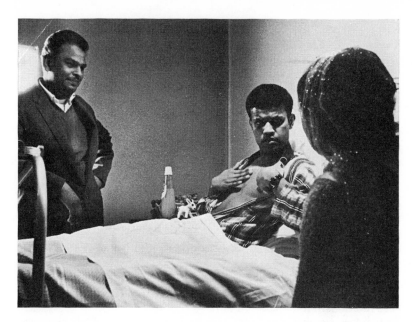

'Salvation is for everyone who believes: "he who through faith is righteous shall live, ... We must first accept the bad news of how serious our sickness is' (pp. 18, 22).

When doctors told Mohan Gharu that only a heart transplant could save his life, he believed them, though relatives who visited him in hospital thought he would die. Mohan's faith was justified. The morning after the operation he was well enough to eat from a spoon, and five days later he was walking about the ward. In what chief ways does 'salvation' differ from restoration to physical health?

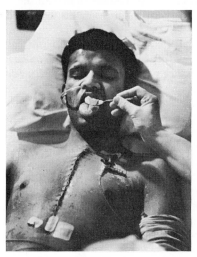

Everyone who has faith: In Paul's time it was thought that only certain classes of people could ever attain salvation. The Greeks thought that salvation was for the wise, the Jews thought it was for religious people. In the same way, in some countries today, only people of a certain race have full rights of citizenship, or only those of a certain educational standard, or those with a certain amount of property, or members of a particular party. But Paul said that Christian salvation is not reserved for any one class of people at all. It belongs to every class, and none is excluded. In this sense salvation is *universal*. No one can ever say, 'Christ cannot (or will not) save me.'

But this does not mean that everyone *will* be saved. In this sense, salvation is *not universal*, because it comes to *everyone who has faith*. Paul repeated this idea in v. 17, when he wrote 'through faith for faith'. Scholars have suggested different ways of translating these words, but if we follow the RSV, they seem to mean the same as those in 3.22, 'through faith for all who believe', i.e.:

(a) Salvation comes *only* to those who believe (unbelievers miss it);

(b) Salvation comes to *all* those who believe (no believers miss it).

See Additional Note, p. 206, Faith.

To the Jew first and also to the Greek: The word 'Greek' here means 'Gentile', i.e. anyone who is not a Jew. It does not mean here the same as in v. 14 (see p. 13). Everyone in the world is either a Jew or a Gentile. Paul meant that the Gospel is for everyone.

But why is the Jew 'first'? Part of the answer can be discovered by answering question 13 on p. 20. Paul discussed this question fully in Romans 9—11. He showed that the Jews were God's chosen people, and it was fitting that Christ and His Gospel should come first to those people who had been prepared for His coming through the laws and prophecies of their own Scriptures.

In it the righteousness of God is revealed: Righteousness is one of the most important words which Paul used in Romans, and it shows *how* the Gospel can have such a revolutionary effect on a person's life. See Additional Note, p. 215, Righteousness.

These words probably contained for Paul two main ideas:

1. Isaiah closely linked the words 'salvation' and 'righteousness', and taught that God reveals His righteousness when He saves His people (see p. 215, 4b). This idea was probably in Paul's mind here: in saving men through the Gospel God shows His righteousness.

2. But it is likely that Paul meant more than this, for two reasons:

(a) Writers in the Old Testament spoke of God saving His *righteous* people (Isa. 51.7; Ps. 24.4). Therefore man *needs* righteousness *in order* to be saved.

(b) Paul's quotation from Habakkuk at the end of v. 17 says that a man *becomes* righteous through faith.

18

It seems likely, therefore, that Paul meant that God *gives* righteousness to a person who has faith. It is this *gift* of God which is revealed in the Gospel, and which brings people to salvation. This is the good news which Martin Luther discovered with such joy as a result of puzzling over this verse (see p. 1). 'Thereupon,' he wrote, 'I felt myself to be reborn and to have gone through open doors into paradise.' Paul gave a fuller explanation of his meaning in Romans 3.21–26.

He who through faith is righteous shall live: Paul supported his teaching with a quotation from the prophet Habakkuk. The next eight chapters are like a long exposition of the meaning of this quotation. Paul saw in it a summary of the Gospel which he himself preached (see also Gal. 3.11), and he used it to form the basis of this letter.

Shall live: Many writers in the Bible used the word 'life' to describe a right relationship with God. See Additional Note, p. 211, Life. In Romans 5—8, Paul described how Christians experience this life now, and said a little about how they will experience it perfectly in the future. This experience, both now and in the future, comes from being right with God through faith.

STUDY SUGGESTIONS

WORD STUDY

1. Which *two* of the following words or phrases meant, for Paul, the same, or almost the same, as 'salvation'?
   life   slavery   fellowship with God   independence   happiness
2. In the following sentences the word 'believe' is used with different meanings. In each sentence substitute another word which also means 'believe', so that it gives good sense:
   (a) Even the demons believe that God is one—and shudder.
   (b) Believe in the Lord Jesus Christ and you will be saved.
   (c) The football captain believes that his team will win the Cup.
3. In the Bible 'righteousness' can mean: (i) God's own righteousness, seen in His character and acts; (ii) the righteousness which God demands from men; (iii) God's righteous act of saving His own people; (iv) God's gift to those who have faith. Which of these four meanings does the word have in Romans 1.17 and each of the following verses?
   (a) Matt. 5.20   (b) Psalm 103.17   (c) Eph. 4.24   (d) Acts 17.31

REVIEW OF CONTENT

4. (a) What is the main theme of Romans 1—8?
   (b) Use a Concordance to help you to count how many times the words 'faith', 'believe', and 'trust' occur in (a) Rom. 1.18—4.25, and (b) Rom. 5—8. Then count how many times the words 'life'

and 'live' occur in the same passages. What do you learn from this study about the main theme of (a) Rom. 1.18—4.25; and (b) Rom. 5—8? Do its results support what was said on p. 15?

5. (a) Why was the Gospel the most important thing in the world for Paul?

(b) In what ways was Paul's message 'good news' for men?

(c) What sort of people receive the benefits of this good news?

6. Place the following words in the order in which they are normally experienced in the life of a man who becomes a Christian:
life   Gospel   righteousness   faith

7. Which of the following statements about faith is the nearest to Paul's teaching?

(a) God cannot save us by Himself, but He waits for us to help Him by believing.

(b) God draws out our faith through the Gospel, so our salvation comes entirely from Him.

(c) It is too difficult to obey God's law, so God has offered us a much easier way of salvation—the way of faith.

(d) Through Christ God has enabled us to save ourselves if we have faith.

Give reasons for your answer.

8. After he came to understand the meaning of Romans 1.17, Luther wrote, 'Whereas before the "righteousness of God" had filled me with hate, now it became to me wonderfully sweet.' Why did Luther at first hate God's righteousness? Why did he later change his opinion?

BIBLE

9. 'The word of the cross' (i.e. the Gospel) has a different effect on different sorts of people. What three different sorts of people are mentioned by Paul in 1 Cor. 1.18–25? What did each one think about the Gospel and why did they think as they did?

10. 'The power of God was at work in the ministry of His Son' (p. 16). In what ways did Jesus show His power on earth? Give references from the Gospels to support your answer.

11. On what did Paul rely for salvation, before he became a Christian, and on what did he rely afterwards? (See Phil. 3.3–11.)

12. 'Faith is called into action by God's power . . . through the Gospel' (p. 207, 3). What evidence for this statement do we find in the following passages?

(a) Acts 8.5–12   (b) Acts 16.11–15   (c) Rom. 10.14–17
(d) 1 Thess. 1.4–9

13. 'The Jew first.' Read the following passages. In what four ways did the Jews have the first chance of hearing the Gospel?

(a) Luke 24.25–27 (b) Acts 10.36–39 (c) Acts 2.5, 10 ('from Rome') (d) Acts 13.43–48

APPLICATION, OPINION, AND RESEARCH

14. For what reason might a Christian today be 'ashamed' of the Gospel?
15. 'Men aim at salvation', i.e. they want the greatest good. What are the chief aims of the people amongst whom you live? Do you consider that these aims are good. If so, do you think they are 'the greatest good'?
16. 'It is not easy to give a brief summary of the Christian Gospel' (p. 16). Write a short summary of the 'good news', in language that would be meaningful and relevant for ordinary Christians today.
17. Imagine that you have been invited to preach one sermon during a week of mission in a small town. Which method will you use to bring your hearers to faith in Christ; (a) to explain fully the nature of faith; (b) to show the people that they are sinners; or (c) to tell the people about Jesus and what He did; or (d) to define the meaning of repentance? Give reasons for your choice.

PART 2

'HE WHO THROUGH FAITH IS RIGHTEOUS ...'

1.18–32
Man's Need: The Unrighteousness of the Gentiles

OUTLINE

'But how can there be friendship and fellowship between men and God? Consider what men are like, think of the evil all around us—there at Rome or here in Corinth. Yet we all know that God is good—so how can He be friendly with human beings as they are? People's chief trouble is that they just do not want to know God. They prefer to put other things first in their lives, but this is the sure way to misery and chaos (which is in fact what we see all round us).'

INTRODUCTION

A 'right relationship' with God is God's gift to human beings when they turn to Him in faith (v. 17). This is certainly good news, but it cannot be properly understood until we have understood the 'bad news' about ourselves. A doctor may be able to heal us of a dangerous disease, and this is good news; but before the good news of the cure can be of any use to us, we must first accept the bad news of the 'diagnosis', that is, the news of how serious our sickness is. Like a good doctor, Paul made his diagnosis of man's problem in 1.18—3.20. Only then (3.21–31) was he ready to explain the good news of God's cure.

Paul's description of mankind is a gloomy one. It falls into three main parts:

1. The Gentiles (all non-Jews) and their relationship with God (1.18–32).

2. The Jews (God's people) and their relationship with God (2.1—3.8).

3. The conclusion—all men alike are in a wrong relationship with God (3.9–20).

The first part shows men as Paul saw them at Corinth. We may think that some of the details are not true of the people whom we know. But if we concentrate on the main points which Paul made, we shall probably find that it is an accurate picture of people as they are today. His thought seems to have progressed like this:

Men know God—men reject God—men worship other 'gods'—God leaves men to live as they have chosen—men get further and further from the knowledge of God—men's relationships with one another are spoiled—men live in misery.

In this process, Paul saw 'the wrath of God' at work in the world.

INTERPRETATION AND NOTES

V. 18. Is revealed: These words occur in both v. 17 and v. 18. Paul was saying that:

(a) *In the Gospel*, righteousness is revealed from God to men. This is good news.

(b) *Apart from the Gospel*, wrath is revealed from God to men. This is bad news. Paul was here contrasting the good news of God's righteousness with the bad news of God's wrath.

The wrath of God: This phrase occurs many times in the Bible, and was used by most writers of the New Testament. Here it contains the following thoughts:

1. Because God is righteous, He is opposed to all unrighteousness, wherever it is found.

2. God's wrath (or anger) is good and righteous, not evil as ours often is, and it ensures the final triumph of goodness.

3. God is always loving, and His wrath is only revealed when people reject His love. Those who will not have faith in the Gospel which leads to salvation, experience, not God's salvation, but His wrath.

4. Although God's wrath against evil will be fully revealed only at the end of the world (see 2.4–9), it can even now be seen in the world, particularly in the disorder of society (1.24–31). Paul was here describing people as they are apart from the Gospel, i.e. without Christ. See Additional Note, p. 221, Wrath.

We now consider first Paul's teaching, and secondly, human beings as they are today.

PAUL'S TEACHING

In these verses Paul was making four chief points:

1. *Man's knowledge of God:* Paul was not here thinking about the Jews, who had received God's 'Special Revelation', as scholars call it, in their history and the teachings of their Scriptures (Rom. 9.4, 5). He was thinking of the Gentiles, who have God's 'General Revelation', which is given to all men alike. Although the Gentiles of Paul's day had no Bible, they had the 'Book of Creation', through which they could

learn about the Creator. God has shown Himself to the Gentiles in two ways:

(a) Men see something of God outside themselves (v. 20). Read Psalm 19.1–4 for a clear Old Testament statement of the same idea.

(b) Men see something of God within themselves (vv. 21, 32). In their minds, men know that there is a Supreme God and that He is the Righteous Judge.

2. *Man's duty to God:* Men should (a) honour and serve the Supreme God as He deserves (vv. 20, 21); and (b) do what they know to be right in His sight (v. 32; see 2.15).

3. *Man's response to God:* Men refuse to worship God and to obey His will, although they know that they should. Paul saw three separate stages in man's rebellion against God:

(a) People ignore God and His love (v. 21), and do not want to think about Him (v. 28).

(b) They pervert their knowledge of God (see 1, above) into something which is foolish (vv. 21, 22) and untrue (vv. 23, 25).

(c) They do unrighteous deeds (vv. 24–31). The words 'therefore', 'because', 'for this reason', 'since' (vv. 24, 25, 26, 28) all show clearly that people behave in the evil ways mentioned *as a result* of refusing to honour God.

Paul called all this *ungodliness* and *wickedness* (i.e. unrighteousness) in v. 18. He was saying that man's basic trouble is not all his sins, nor his ignorance; it is his rebellion against God and his refusal to honour God. Therefore men are 'without excuse', i.e. they *know* what is right and true, but they 'suppress the truth' (see v. 28a).

4. *God's wrath:* 'God gave them up . . .' (vv. 24, 26, 28). Perhaps these are the most terrible words in the Bible (see Hosea 4.17). It means that God leaves men to walk in the path which they have chosen. If men choose to live without God, then they shall be free to do so—and their lives will become increasingly unhappy and disorderly. This is part of the meaning of God's wrath.

But even here we can see God's mercy and love. Pain is often a warning that we should go to the doctor for treatment before we fall seriously ill. In the same way, God's wrath now is really a loving warning to men that if they do not return to God in this life, then they will suffer the full extent of His wrath at the last Judgement. God leaves us free to set up wrong relationships with other people, in order to show us that our relationship with Him is wrong. God abandons us a little now, as a warning against being separated from Him for ever. God lets us be a little miserable now—as a way of saving us from eternal misery.

These four points represent the main teaching of this passage about the Gentiles. 'This is what human beings are like,' said Paul. This teaching is so important that we shall give more thought to it later. But here are some practical points to remember when we take the Gospel to others. They all arise from this teaching:

1. We should respect all men without distinction, because all have been created by God in such a way that they think about Him. This means that we should:

(a) always *reason* with people, and not assume that they cannot understand God's truth;

(b) never despise or laugh at the religious beliefs of others.

2. We should try to build on people's basic knowledge of God. This may often mean reminding them of what they really know—though they may not realize that they know it.

3. As we discuss with them beliefs about God, we should be ready to point out how their thinking has gone wrong, and even perhaps ways in which they may have 'exchanged the truth about God for a lie'.

4. We should always feel compassion for human misery and ignorance wherever we meet it, remembering that 'Man' isn't 'them', 'man' is *'me'*. See Special Note, p. 29. Paul himself followed all these principles in his own missionary work (see question 9 on p. 28).

HUMAN BEINGS AS THEY ARE TODAY

We must now ask whether Paul's picture of human beings in 1.18–32 is true of people today. We shall first consider a few traditional beliefs, taken for the sake of example from various parts of Africa and from an island group in the Pacific.

1. *People know that God exists.* They have different names for Him. Here are some examples:

The **Yoruba** (Nigeria) call the Supreme God 'Olorun' (the heavenly one), Creator, Almighty, all-wise, Life-giver, and Judge.

The **Chagga** (Tanzania) call Him 'Ruwa', who is greater than all, and from whom all things came in the beginning. God loves men and, unlike the spirits, does not punish them for their minor errors.

The **Gilbert Islanders** in the Pacific believe in 'Nakaa', who gave men His law long ago.

2. *People believe that God is now far from men.* They have various stories to explain this.

The **Vaasu** (Tanzania) say that men built a tower to reach heaven, but 'Kiumbi', the good Creator, in His anger went far away, with the result that men cannot come near Him now.

The **Dinka** (Sudan) say that God left the earth because a woman hit Him with her hoe. He sent a blue bird to cut the rope which joined earth and heaven.

The **Gilbert Islanders** say that when men disobeyed Nakaa's law, He sent them far from Him and punished them with sickness and death.

(A few scholars think that these peoples only pretend to believe that God is far away, because they really know He is near and want to escape from Him. We should, however, accept what they *say* they believe. See Acts 17.27.)

3. *People worship gods which are less than the Supreme God.*

The **Ashanti** (Ghana) say: 'Why should we worship Him, for He has never done us any harm?' Therefore they worship the spirits in the storm, the earth, springs, snakes, trees, mountains, leopards, etc., for they need to protect themselves from these things.

The **Vaasu** do not normally think about Kiumbi, but about the spirits of nature and the ancestors who can trouble them with drought, famine, sickness, and death. In many homes there is a secret room where they keep a skull as a kind of 'family god'. It is to these things that they pray, so that they may not be troubled by them.

The **Gilbert Islanders** honour the spirits rather than Nakaa, because the spirits are concerned with men's daily offences.

4. *People do not entirely forget God.*

The **Chagga** turn to Ruwa for help in a great crisis, after the spirits have failed to help them.

The **Vaasu** often mention Kiumbi in a final, formal prayer at the end of the prayers to the spirits.

The **Gilbert Islanders** recognize that Nakaa, who is pure spirit, will be their final Judge.

5. *People want deliverance from the power of the spirits.* In many parts of Africa, prophets have arisen from time to time who have offered deliverance from the things which people fear. In the Maji-maji rising in Tanganyika in 1905, for example, Kinjikitile Ngwale offered deliverance not only from the bullets of the Germans but also from witchcraft and the oppression of evil spirits. He was welcomed as a saviour. People are aware of the misery of their present condition.

So far in this section we have considered traditional beliefs. Some people today despise such beliefs, calling them 'primitive', 'uncivilized', or 'pagan'. They think that simple uneducated people may hold such beliefs, but not educated ones, not the followers of the 'higher' religions, not Westerners. For the question of education and of other religions, see the Special Notes, pp. 29–32. But what about Westerners? In many ways their beliefs and attitudes are similar to those of people who follow traditional religions. Here are two examples:

(a) In 1939 most English people called themselves Christians, but the majority did not worship God regularly. In 1940, when they thought their country was going to be invaded by the Germans, many went to church and prayed to God for protection. But when the danger was over, they returned to their old habits.

(b) Today in England, also, most of the people still believe in a

Supreme God. But few honour Him, or give Him the first place in their lives. Some try to make contact with spirits, some believe the stars control their lives, some think money, or comfort, or pleasure, or success is the most important thing. There are many 'gods' which people worship, but few worship the Supreme God as they ought.

STUDY SUGGESTIONS

WORD STUDY

1. In the following sentences, which of the three alternative words is correct?
   (a) In diagnosis, the doctor treats/heals/ examines his patient.
   (b) In a cure, the doctor advises/heals/criticizes his patient.
2. (a) What is the difference between 'ungodliness' and 'unrighteousness'?
   (b) Which of the Ten Commandments describe unrighteousness, and which describe ungodliness?
   (c) What is the relationship between the two ideas?

REVIEW OF CONTENT

3. (a) 'Men see something of God outside themselves' (p. 24).
   What three truths about God which people can see outside themselves, are expressed in Romans 1.20?
   (b) 'Men know that there is a Supreme God and that He is the Righteous Judge' (p. 24).
   Which phrases in Romans 1.21 and 32 support this statement?

BIBLE

4. The following passages of Genesis describe occasions when God showed His wrath. Find words in these passages which show His love.
   (a) Genesis 3.8–24   (b) 4.1–16   (c) 6
5. (a) In Psalm 78, which verses describe God's wrath, and which describe His mercy, love, or kindness?
   (b) What do you think is the writer's chief theme?
6. 'Those who will not have God's love have nothing left to them but wrath' (p. 222). How is this truth illustrated in the following parables of Jesus? (a) Matt. 18.23–35   (b) Luke 14.16–24.
7. Which of the following passages refer to (i) God's General Revelation to all men alike, and which refer to (ii) His Special Revelation to His chosen people? (a) Exod. 3.2–4   (b) Psalm 19.1–4   (c) Psalm 103.7   (d) Acts 14.17   (e) Heb. 1.1, 2
8. How does Amos 4.6–12 show that God's wrath is often meant as a loving warning to men?

9. Read Acts 17.1–4; 17.16–34. In his ministry in Thessalonika and Athens, how did Paul (a) show respect for his hearers; (b) build on their basic knowledge of God; (c) show them their errors; (d) show compassion for them?

10. What similarities, if any, do you notice between the traditional beliefs described on pp. 25, 26 and some of the early stories in the Book of Genesis? What are the chief differences between the traditional stories and those in Genesis?

APPLICATION, OPINION, AND RESEARCH

11. 'In the New Testament human anger . . . is almost always said to be wrong' (p. 222; see 1 Cor. 13.5 and James 1.20). But we are told to imitate Jesus (1 Cor. 11.1), and He was sometimes angry.
    Is it ever right for a Christian to be angry? If so, give examples.

12. Notice how Paul described men's behaviour (1.22–32). This was an accurate picture of life at Corinth.
    Is it an accurate picture of life where you live? What differences, if any, do you notice? If you can, say why you think there are differences.

13. (a) If Rom. 1.23 is not true of some peoples, does this mean that they are not guilty of idolatry?
    (b) What is idolatry? (See 1 John 5.21; Eph. 5.5.) Give some modern examples of idolatry.

14. Ancestors are very important in the life and thought of most peoples in the world.
    (a) Among the people you know best, do you think their attitude to their ancestors is right or wrong, and in what ways?
    (b) Walk round the interior and exterior of any church building you know. What, if anything, do you see there which shows the congregation's belief about their ancestors?
    (c) As Christians, what should we say to people on the subject of their ancestors?

15. According to Paul, men knew certain things about God. To what extent do people of today know these things about Him? (Remember that people can often 'know' something without being ready to admit that they know it.)

16. 'People worship gods which are less than the Supreme God . . . they worship spirits' (p. 26). Do you think it is right to use the word 'worship' in this passage? Can you think of a better word to express men's attitude to the spirits?

17. Many peoples traditionally worship at one particular place, e.g. under a certain tree. Whom do they worship there? If you know any followers of traditional religion, find out whether they are conscious of worshipping the Supreme God, or Creator,

18. What are the traditions of your people, or any others you know, on the five points mentioned on pp. 25, 26? Write them down, including names and descriptions of God, and stories about Him.

SPECIAL NOTE A:
THE SOCIAL GOSPEL

In the past Christians have often led the way in putting right the wrong things in the world. In doing this they have been following the example of Jesus who loved those who were poor and despised (John 9.35–39), and had pity on those who were suffering (Mark 1.41). Disciples of Jesus will always want to bring healing where there is sickness, understanding where there is ignorance, relief where there is poverty, peace where there is war and fear, love where there is hatred. There is always going to be plenty of work for Christians to do in the world! This kind of activity has often been called 'the Social Gospel'.

But we ought not to think that these good deeds will actually change the nature of human beings. Health, education, food, and clothing can never make a bad person good. In Romans 1.18–32 Paul explained why this is so. People's basic need is to return to God. Until they do so, their relationship with God will be wrong, and as long as their relationship with God is wrong, their relationship with their fellow men will be wrong also. Uncleanness, hatred, envy, and the other wrong thoughts and actions listed in vv. 28–31 are like sores on the outside of a person's body which show that there is poison in the blood. The doctor must treat the blood condition before the sores will disappear. It is therefore good to try to correct the outward evils in the world, as Jesus did, but perhaps it is even better to proclaim to men the Gospel of the righteousness of God which can heal our relationship with Him. It is best of all to follow the example of Jesus and do both. Tom Skinner, who led race riots in America, was filled with hatred for white people—until he came into fellowship with God through Jesus Christ, when his attitude to his fellow men was completely changed. People who truly love God will care for their fellow men *because* they love Him.

Many people today sincerely think that education is the real answer to most human problems. But in 1930 the most highly educated nation in the world was Germany, and within 15 years that nation had destroyed and oppressed so many people on racial grounds that almost the whole world was forced to fight against her.

'Men just do not want to know God . . . this is the sure way to misery and chaos'
(p. 22).

In the slum areas of Callao in Peru, as in many other cities today, there is no water,
no sanitation—and no work. The people have no power to improve the conditions
in which they live. What connection, if any, is there between their misery and God's
wrath?

SPECIAL NOTE B:
THE WORLD'S RELIGIONS

Human beings are religious. Most people who live in India and Africa accept this as a fact. President Nyerere of Tanzania has said, 'Tanzanians believe in God'. In Romans 1, Paul took the same view—he was talking about ordinary people, and ordinary people are religious (Rom. 1.23; Acts 17.22). Paul's teaching seems to mean:

1. God has shown men many truths about Himself, and the world.

2. In their rebellion against God, men have 'suppressed' (Rom. 1.18) or 'changed' (Rom. 1.25) the truths they know, and their religion has become full of falsehood.

3. God Himself, through religious beliefs and in other ways, preserves something of His truth in the minds of men (Acts 14.17; 17.23, 28) so that they do not lose it entirely.

4. Every religion is different, e.g. there were differences between what the Athenians believed and what the Lystrans believed (Acts 14.17; 17.29).

5. When a man turns *to* Jesus Christ in faith, he finds he must turn *from* his old religious ideas (Acts 14.15; Gal. 4.8; 1 Thess. 1.9), and from anything else he used to rely on (Phil. 3.7–9). Many of these things may have been good, but they must no longer be the most important things in his life. Everything of his past must be judged by Christ and, if necessary, changed by Him. 'Jesus is Lord.'

Many readers may want to ask, 'How do the points just mentioned apply to the faith of Islam, or any other religious system?' Here are some suggestions:

(a) It is impossible to answer this question, because writers of the Bible had no knowledge of most of the great religions which are today practised all over the world.

(b) If the above points are true, then we shall expect to find both truth and falsehood in each of the world's religious systems.

(c) Christianity is, itself, a religious system. So it, too, comes under the judgement of Christ.

(d) In the Gospel of Christ, which comes from God, there is only truth. But Christians have often misunderstood this truth, and should be ready to correct their mistakes.

(e) Some of the truth and falsehood in the religions can be set out as overleaf.

(f) Men's religions, therefore, do not properly represent God's truth, although parts of His truth may be seen in them. In the religions we see men's rebellion, foolishness, and idolatry. Paul calls them 'a lie', and God's wrath is revealed against them.

Islam stresses that God is in control of all events which take place in the world.	This truth has often become 'fatalism', so that people think that suffering and evil must be God's will and cannot be resisted. All that happens is 'God's will'.
Hinduism stresses that God is present every-where in the world.	This teaching has sometimes failed to distinguish between God and the world, so it seems that God is the same as the world.
Communism stresses that man is a social being who should live in communities where all are equal.	This truth has been overemphasized, with the result that the rights and dignity of individual persons are often forgotten.
Jews in the time of Jesus stressed the importance of keeping every detail of God's law.	Overemphasizing this truth, they forgot that the righteousness which pleases God consists of loving our fellow-men (Luke 11.42).
Christianity stresses the fatherhood and love of God.	Christians have often forgotten that God is just and that we see His love most clearly in the death of His Son, through whom alone we can become His children.

(g) Men's religion is part of their need, not the answer to their need. All people—pagan, Muslim, Jewish, Christian—need Jesus Christ and the Gospel of righteousness.

This Special Note is only an introduction to a very big subject. The Study Suggestions below are intended to encourage further discussion.

STUDY SUGGESTIONS

REVIEW OF CONTENT

1. God's intention for men is 'that they should seek God' (Acts 17.27). In what sense, if at all, do men seek God? Illustrate your answer from Romans 1.

BIBLE

2. Read the following passages and say in each case:
    (i) what true beliefs did the 'pagans' there mentioned hold?
    (ii) in what ways were their religious beliefs false?
    (a) Isa. 44.9–20   (b) Acts 14.11–18   (c) Acts 17.22–31

APPLICATION AND OPINION

3. 'Human beings are religious' (p. 31).
    In many developed societies today this does not seem to be true. In such societies, what do you think has happened to men's religious instincts, and why has it happened?

4. Some people think that the way in which people live during this life is not very important, as long as they have eternal life through faith in Jesus. Others think that the important thing is to improve the conditions of men's life now, and leave everyone to follow God in his own way. What is your opinion?

5. 'They did not honour him as God' (Rom. 1.21). But Muslims worship God.

(a) Do they worship the true God? (See John 1.18; 4.22–24; 14.6; but also Acts 17.23.)

(b) Should Muslims and Christians join together in worship?

(c) Should Christians try to persuade Muslims to become Christians? (This question is for group discussion. If there are few Muslims in your area, change 'Muslims' to the name of some other religious group.)

6. Some scholars have distinguished between local 'tribal' religions and the 'higher' religions (e.g. Islam, Hinduism, Buddhism, Judaism) which are more widely practised, with, perhaps, Christianity as the 'highest' of all.

(a) Do you think it is useful to classify religions in this way?

(b) Discuss whether or not Communism should be classed as a religion.

2.1—3.20
Man's Need: The Unrighteousness of the Jews

OUTLINE

'Jews, I know, will agree with what I have just said about mankind. But are they themselves any better? They "know" God, but knowledge is not enough. Like everyone else they resist His rule in their lives. It is no help to point to people's good deeds. The fact that we, Jews and Gentiles alike, often do good only shows that we recognize the difference between right and wrong, and so cannot plead ignorance as our excuse. Some people may follow false religions, some (like the Jews) follow a religion which God Himself has revealed. But God is concerned not with our religion but with our deeds—and we all do wrong, and cannot change ourselves. The Jews' Scriptures made that perfectly clear in words addressed to Jews. God says we are all "guilty". He rightly condemns us all.'

INTRODUCTION

Having described the Gentiles, Paul next went on to describe the Jews. He needed to consider the Jews separately, because any Jew reading 1.18–32 would have thought as follows: 'Yes, Paul, what you say about the Gentiles is terrible, but true. It makes me thank God that I am not one of them. How glad I am that I am one of God's chosen people! I know Him and belong to Him!'

Therefore Paul needed to explain to the Jews that there is 'bad news' for them, too. His purpose was to show that no one, Jew or Gentile, is good enough to satisfy God.

In this section Paul reminded the Jews of four truths about themselves:

1. They had many privileges and blessings from God (2.17–20, 25; 3.1, 2).

2. These privileges were intended to guide them to do what is right (2.4, 21–24).

3. God judges people according to what they *do*, not according to their religious privileges (2.6–13, 26–29).

4. The Jews, like everyone else, had failed to do what God requires (3.9–20).

In making these four points, Paul was saying nothing new. The prophets had said it all before, and so had Jesus Himself, who taught that righteous deeds were more important than outward religious practices.

Some readers of this Guide may think that Paul's words to Jews long ago cannot be important to Christians today. But we should remember that in Paul's day the Jews firmly believed that they had a religion which was superior to everyone else's, and many modern Christians think in the same way. What Paul says here to Jews is therefore likely to be very relevant to us today.

The chief sections into which this passage is divided are indicated in the Notes below.

INTERPRETATION AND NOTES

SECTION A. 2.1–11:
GOD WILL JUDGE JEWS AND GENTILES ALIKE,
ACCORDING TO THEIR DEEDS

In this section it is not quite clear whether Paul was thinking of Jews or of Gentiles. There are three possible interpretations: (1) Some scholars say that Paul was speaking to Gentiles still, because he did not mention Jews until v. 17. (2) Others think he was referring to anyone, Jew or Gentile, who thinks that for some reason he is better than other people in the sight of God, because vv. 9, 10 refer to 'every human being'. (3) Others say he was speaking to Jews, because they were particularly aware of the special blessings they had received (2.4), and believed themselves to be superior to Gentiles (2.1). In this Guide we shall follow the *third* interpretation, remembering at the same time that these words are often as true of Gentiles today as they are of Jews.

V. 1: You condemn yourself: Paul first persuaded his Jewish readers to agree with his judgement of the Gentiles. Then he showed them that the same judgement is true of them: (1) Gentiles know God's decree—so do Jews (2.2); (2) Gentiles do wrong—so do Jews (2.1); (3) Gentiles have no excuse—nor have Jews (2.1); (4) Gentiles are under God's wrath—so are Jews (2.5).

People are often quick to see faults in others, but slow to see the same faults in themselves. One national Church joined the World Council of Churches, saying that all Christians should try to live and work together, whilst at the same time opposing the work of a small group of Christians in its own country.

V. 4. The riches of his kindness: Although all men share in God's blessings, the Jews had experienced His kindness in a *special* way. Some examples of this can be found in Exodus 6.6–8; 34.6, 7. The Jews often thought of their relationship with God in this way:

'God has shown us His love in a special way; therefore He will never condemn us.' But they should have thought: 'God has shown us His love in a special way; therefore we have a special responsibility to serve and obey Him.'

They often thought:

'God does not punish us for our evil deeds as we deserve; this must be because He loves us so much that He forgives us.' But they should have thought: 'God does not punish us for our evil deeds as we deserve; this must be because He is giving us a chance to repent and turn back to Him.' This is what Paul was trying to show them in vv. 3, 4.

Repentance: This word means 'change of mind', and refers to the action of turning away from a way of life which is displeasing to God. It is often used in close connection with faith (see Mark 1.15). *Repentance* emphasizes the action of turning *away from* something; *faith* emphasizes the action of turning *to* something.

V. 5. The day of wrath: This idea was used by the prophets, who called it sometimes 'the Day of the Lord', sometimes 'that Day'. In Paul's time, most Jews thought of it as follows:

1. It will be a day of judgement when all God's enemies will be punished (Zeph. 1.14ff).

2. It will be a day of joy and final salvation for God's people (Joel 3.18).

3. Many of those who look forward to it confidently will find that it will be a day of judgement for them because of their unrighteousness (Amos 5.18–24).

35

4. But those who preserve and honour God's law during their lives (see Deut. 4.6–8) are storing up for themselves a great reward which they will receive on 'that Day', when all their present sufferings will be over.

Paul was telling the Jews in v. 5 that what is in fact in store for them is not a reward, but God's wrath, because God is concerned not with whether or not men know His law, but with whether or not they obey it (vv. 6–13). By not repenting, they are *choosing* wrath for themselves. See Additional Note, p. 222, Wrath, 4–6.

Vv. 6–11: Paul next reminded his Jewish readers that God judges men according to their works, i.e. their actions. God will judge 'righteously' (v. 5) and 'by Jesus Christ' (v. 16). These expressions show that God has a definite standard of righteousness, and that everyone will be judged by that standard. God will not 'forget' the wrong which men have done, nor 'pretend' that they are righteous if they are not. But many Jews of Paul's day thought that He would, as did the writer of the Wisdom of Solomon:

'But Thou, our God, art kind and true, patient, and ruling all things in mercy. For even if we sin we are Thine, knowing Thy power; but we will not sin, because we know that we are accounted Thine. For to know Thee is complete righteousness, and to know Thy power is the root of immortality. For neither has the evil intent of human art misled us, nor the fruitless toil of painters' (15.1–4).

The Jews did not claim to be better than other men, but to have the Law and to know God. Paul's reply was, 'God judges men not by their knowledge and privileges, but by their *works*.' This is true of Jew and Gentile alike.

Later on in this letter, Paul taught that *no one* will be counted righteous by God through works (3.20). We may ask, was Paul contradicting himself? Will God judge men by their works or apart from works? As we try to answer this question, we should be guided by the following points:

1. No one succeeds in fulfilling God's will. Therefore, although God will reward the righteous with eternal life (2, 7, 10), in fact no one is righteous (3.10), and so no one will earn the reward (3.20).

2. Paul taught repeatedly that men will be judged by their works (2 Cor. 5.10; Gal. 6.7–10; Eph. 6.8), but will be saved only by God's mercy (Titus 3.5; Gal. 2.16; Eph. 2.8, 9).

3. Although men are saved only through God's mercy, by means of faith and not through works, yet we should not think that this salvation has nothing to do with good works. On the contrary, the Gospel, which offers salvation through God's mercy, upholds the law, which demands good works (3.31). See Notes on p. 53, and Additional Notes on Glory, p. 208; Judgement, p. 209; Life, p. 211.

SECTION B. 2.12–16:
THE STANDARD OF JUDGEMENT IS GOD'S LAW,
AND EVERYONE WILL BE MEASURED
BY WHAT THEY KNOW OF THAT LAW

2.12, 13, Sinned . . . law . . . justified: These three important words occur here for the first time in this letter. Paul first used them when he was thinking about the Jews. Jews well understood the meaning of these words, but they might have been strange to Gentile readers. Most Christians are familiar with them because they appear so often in the Bible, but it will be helpful to recall what Paul meant by them, by reading the Additional Notes on pp. 210, 218. In these two verses Paul was saying:

1. *The Jews* were chosen by God to receive the written law. So they know God's will, and they will be judged (and condemned for their sin) by that law.

2. *The Gentiles*, who have not God's law, will be judged and condemned apart from that law. This means that God will not act unfairly —he will not judge Gentiles as if they were Jews, by the laws revealed to Moses. God does not expect people to obey laws which they do not know.

3. The important question is whether or not people obey what they *do* know (v. 13), and Paul then went on to show that in fact no one is completely ignorant of God's law.

2.14, 15: It is important to read these verses 'in context', i.e. as part of Paul's whole argument in this section. If we take them completely by themselves, we might think that Paul was here teaching that there are some people who fulfil God's will, please Him, and will not be condemned by Him. This cannot have been his meaning, because the aim of all his teaching in 1.18—3.20 was to prove that 'None is righteous, no, not one'. Paul was certainly not here saying something which contradicts that conclusion. He was in fact making the following points:

1. Jews should not imagine that they are the only people who know God's will.

2. Gentiles, although they do not know Moses's law, have an inward understanding of God's will in many matters. For example, most tribal peoples honour the elders of their families. In doing so, they probably keep the fifth Commandment better than many Christians, although they have never heard of the fifth Commandment. In this way they 'are a law to themselves' (v. 14).

3. This fact shows that everyone knows something of the difference between right and wrong. This knowledge is called 'conscience'. By means of his conscience a man can stand away from himself and consider his own thoughts, words, and actions.

37

4. When people do right, they are ready to defend their actions. When they do wrong, their thoughts accuse them of the wrong (v. 15). Some people call conscience 'the voice of God in the soul of man'.

5. This passage suggests that there is no one who *always* does evil. People's good actions are a proof that they know right from wrong.

6. But it also shows that there is no one who *always* does right. People's wrong actions are a proof that they are sinners. The conscience needs to be trained and encouraged. If it receives false instruction, or is too often ignored, it can go astray and give wrong guidance (see 1 Cor. 8.7).

2.16: This verse should probably be taken closely with vv. 12, 13. Paul was referring again to the coming day (see v. 5), when God will judge all men not according to what they appear to be, but as they truly are. See Additional Note, p. 209, Judgement.

SECTION C. 2.17–29:
THE TRUE PEOPLE OF GOD ARE THOSE WHO OBEY HIM,
NOT THOSE WHO HAVE KNOWLEDGE AND PRIVILEGES

It sounds in these verses as though Paul was preaching a short sermon to a Jewish friend. Perhaps he had preached like this on many occasions. The Jews, said Paul,

(a) believe they have a special relationship with God (v. 17);

(b) rely especially on their knowledge of God's law (vv. 18–23);

(c) believe that they can teach others the right way (vv. 19–21);

(d) rely also on their circumcision, the sign of God's love for the Jewish people (vv. 25–29).

Paul's aim was to tell the Jews that what matters to God is not what they know, but what they do. He advised them to think more about their own behaviour and less about their religious advantages. See Additional Note, Circumcision, p. 203 (where vv. 25–29 are explained).

SECTION D. 3.1–8:
FOUR QUESTIONS ANSWERED

Paul then went on to forestall any objections which his Jewish friends might have to make. Probably he had had to deal with many questions like these on his preaching journeys. The first question is a very reasonable one. The second is also quite sensible. The third is a little foolish. The fourth is so foolish that Paul refused to answer it.

Question 1. Paul had said that neither the law nor circumcision can guarantee God's favour. What, then, was the advantage of being a Jew? (v. 1).

Paul answered that all these things were part of God's special revelation to the Jews, i.e. His 'oracles', or His word. They cannot save the Jews, but they do point the way to salvation (v. 2; see 2.25). Paul gave a fuller answer in Romans 9—11.

Question 2. But is God not going to fulfil His promises to His people? Does this mean that human beings, by disobeying God, can stop Him from doing what He has promised? (v. 3).

Paul answered this question, like the first, in detail in Romans 9—11. Here he simply said:

1. God's promises are always trustworthy, although men are not.

2. God is true to His promises when He justly judges those who break His law. Paul quoted Psalm 51.4 to show how God did this in the case of David. It is the same for everyone. All are sinners, and this fact shows up God's righteousness (v. 4). (In chapter 11 Paul showed how, in spite of the Jews' unfaithfulness, God had not completely rejected them. Perhaps this thought was in his mind here too—for David was not rejected by God even though he was judged for his unfaithfulness— but it is not clearly explained.)

Question 3. This question arises from v. 4: 'If our sin shows up how righteous God is, then surely we are doing Him a favour when we sin, and He must be wrong to punish us?' (v. 5).

Paul answered that this righteousness (or, justice) of God is seen in His judgement of sin. If God did not judge and punish sin, then His justice would not appear (v. 6).

Question 4. This is like question 3, but it goes further, suggesting that we really *ought* to do evil, for God's benefit. The idea is, 'If we see how great God's love is when He forgives a great sinner, then let us sin more, so that the wonder of His love in forgiving us may be more clearly seen.' Some people did in fact say that Paul himself taught this (vv. 7, 8a).

Paul answered that people who talk like this are rebelling against God and deserve to be condemned by Him. He dealt with this problem again, at length, in chapter 6.

As we read these 8 verses, we may feel that Paul did not answer his own questions very well. Some big problems are involved, which cannot be dealt with in a sentence or two. But he did answer them properly later in the letter. Perhaps he thought that at this point he ought to show that he realized the problems exist, before moving on to his conclusion in vv. 19–20.

SECTION E. 3.9–20. THE CONCLUSION:
ALL MEN ARE UNRIGHTEOUS AND GUILTY IN GOD'S SIGHT

Paul made five chief points in this section:

1. He gave a list of Old Testament passages to confirm his teaching that everyone sins. These passages speak of sin in (a) men's deeds—

'Paul had considered the most cultured, civilized, and educated people, and those who were most ignorant. And he had found no difference in their relationship with God, the power of sin ruled them all' (p. 41).

Daughters of upper class families at a finishing school near Calcutta are extremely well educated and well brought up. But too many children, like these (below) in a refugee camp, because of war or poverty get no education at all. What sorts of sin — and whose sin — rule each of these groups of young people?

and what they fail to do; (b) men's words; (c) men's thoughts and aims; (d) men's attitude to God (vv. 10–18).

2. Since these passages come from the Jewish Scriptures, they refer particularly to Jews (v. 19a).

3. Therefore Jews must admit that it is not only the Gentiles who are guilty before God, but they themselves also, God's own chosen people (v. 19b). In this matter, Jews are no better than Gentiles; both are in the same situation.

4. The law cannot help anyone to get out of this situation (see Additional Note, Law 3, p. 210). It can only prove that we have in fact gone against God's will and are guilty. So far from justifying us, it confirms that we are sinners (v. 20).

5. But why are people like this? The answer lies in the one word 'sin' (vv. 9, 20; see Additional Note, Sin 2, p. 218). Sin is like a king which rules over human beings. From its reign in their lives come the actual sins which people do.

So Paul came to the end of his description of man, especially man in his relationship with God. He had considered the most cultured, civilized, and educated sort of people. He had considered the followers of the world's greatest religion, who had the most complete knowledge of what God is like, because God had revealed Himself to them during hundreds of years. He had considered those who were most ignorant of these things. He had looked back into history, and he had considered men as they were in his own days. And he had found that despite all the outward differences that exist between men, there is no difference in their relationship with God. All people, everywhere, at all times, have turned against Him. Men cannot get themselves out of this situation, because the power of sin rules them. They stand guilty before Him who is perfectly just and true in His judgement. There does not seem to be any hope for men in this picture of sin, wrath, and punishment. There were many others in the ancient world who agreed with Paul's gloomy picture—and there are many thinkers who agree with him today. Here are some examples:

Seneca, a philosopher who lived at Rome about the time of Paul, wrote: 'We must say of ourselves that we are evil, that we have been evil, and that we shall be evil in the future. The human mind is by nature perverse, and strives after what is forbidden. Nobody can deliver himself. Someone must stretch out a hand to lift him up.'

Professor C. E. M. Joad, an English philosopher, as a result of observing the world, the people who live in it, and himself, found himself compelled to accept the biblical view of mankind: 'My eyes were gradually opened to the extent of my own sinfulness in thought, word, and deed; so that, finding that it was only with the greatest difficulty and effort that I could restrain myself to even the most modest degree of virtue, and that very rarely, I came whole-heartedly to endorse the account of me given in the English Prayer Book' (*Recovery of Belief*, chapter 3).

Dag Hammarskjold, Secretary-General of the United Nations until 1961: 'I see no hope for permanent world peace. We have tried so hard and we have failed so miserably. Unless the world has a spiritual rebirth within the next few years, civilization is doomed.'

Abdal-Nasir, President of Egypt, had high hopes for his people after the Revolution, but found that personal and persistent selfishness was the rule of the day: 'The word "I" was on every tongue. . . . Endless crowds showed up, but how different is the reality from the vision. . . . If I were asked then what I required most, my instant answer would have been: "To hear but one Egyptian uttering one word of justice about another, to see but one Egyptian not devoting his time to criticizing wilfully the ideas of another, to feel that there was but one Egyptian ready to open his heart for forgiveness, indulgence, and loving his brother Egyptians" ' (*The Philosophy of the Revolution*, pp. 33–36).

STUDY SUGGESTIONS

WORD STUDY

1. An old Roman proverb said, 'Every man carries two sacks—one in front for his neighbour's faults, and one behind for his own.'
   (a) Which of the following sentences is saying the same as this proverb?
   (i) All men are burdened with the world's evil;
   (ii) Men are more ready to see the faults of others than their own;
   (iii) All men alike have their faults.
   (b) Does any proverb in your own language say the same?
2. The following words are slightly different from one another in meaning. Show the difference between them by placing the correct word in the blank spaces in the sentences below:
   repentance   regret   remorse   sorrow
   (a) Judas hanged himself because he felt . . . . at betraying Jesus.
   (b) The children expressed . . . . that it was too wet for them to play football.
   (c) The old man spoke of his . . . . that he had not studied harder at school.
   (d) John the Baptist told the people to show their . . . . by doing good works.

REVIEW OF CONTENT

3. (a) On what grounds will people be judged by God?
(b) Of what value is human goodness in God's sight?
4. (a) In what sense are the Jews God's own chosen people?
(b) In what ways are Jews different from Gentiles, and in what ways are they alike?
(c) For what reason did the Jews think they were superior to Gentiles?
5. What is 'the Law' and what is its function?
6. In what ways do the following passages support the teaching of Rom. 2.4, 5?
Amos 3.2; Luke 12.48; 1 Pet. 4.17
7. The three different aspects of sin mentioned on p. 218 are: (i) sinful actions, (ii) the power of sin, (iii) the guilt of sin. Which of these three aspects is stressed in each of the following verses?
(a) 2 Sam. 12.13   (b) Matt. 3.6   (c) John 8.34.
8. 'God judges the secrets of men' (2.16). What do you think these 'secrets' are? Give examples from the teaching of the New Testament.

BIBLE

9. Paul reminded the Jews of: (i) their blessings, (ii) God's intention that these blessings should guide them to do right, (iii) God's judgement of men's *deeds*; (iv) their failure to do God's will.
Which of these four points is emphasized in each of the following passages?
(a) Ps. 78.5–8   (b) Isa. 1.11–17   (c) Hos. 11.1–4   (d) Amos 2.1–8.
10. Read Genesis 17.10; Exod. 6.7; 19.5, 6; Jer. 31.33; Matt. 1.23; 28.18–20.
(a) When God gave Abraham circumcision, what laws did He give Abraham to keep, and what promises did He give to Abraham?
(b) What was the *chief* promise of God's covenant with Abraham, which He later gave to Israel, and which is true for Christians today?
11. 'Those who obey God's will are counted as circumcised and as real Jews' (p. 204). How is this idea taught in the following passages?
(a) Gal. 6.15, 16   (b) Phil. 3.2, 3   (c) Rev. 3.9.
12. 'Paul, like Jesus, distinguished between the outward "letter" of the law and its inward meaning' (p. 204).
(a) How do the following passages show this distinction? Matt. 23.23   John 7.19–24.
(b) Which rules of the law, if any, did Jesus say a Jew was free to break?

(c) What ceremony has taken the place of circumcision for Christians?

(d) In what way, if any, does Paul's warning to the Jews about their attitude to circumcision apply to Christians today?

13. The Jews thought that those who 'honour the law of God are storing up for themselves a great reward'. What did the Jews who are described in Jeremiah 7.1–15 honour? What 'reward', if any, could this bring them?

14. 'What the law requires is written on their hearts' (Rom. 2.15): 'I will write my law upon their hearts' (Jer. 31.33). What is the difference in meaning between these two sentences? (Look carefully at the 'context' in which each occurs.)

15. 'We may offend our fellow men, but we *sin* against God.' How does Psalm 51.4 show this to be true? Whom had David wronged, and how?

APPLICATION AND OPINION

16. 'Men are often quick to see faults in others.' Isaiah was using this fact when he sang a song about a vineyard to help the Israelites recognize their own faults (Isa. 5.1–7). Compare Nathan's story in 2 Sam. 12.1–9. Then give an example of a story which a pastor could use in the same way today.

17. 'Paul first used the words "sinned", "law", "justified", when he was thinking about the Jews. These words might have been unfamiliar to Gentile readers' (p. 37). What does Paul's example here teach us about the sort of language we should use when explaining our faith to others?

18. In many parts of Africa, preachers who want to explain the power of sin in a person's life, use the illustration of the power of colonial governments before independence. In what ways do you think this is a good illustration, and in what ways is it a bad one?

19. 'God does not expect people to obey laws which they do not know' (p. 37). In what way, if any, does this help us to answer the difficult question of whether God will condemn for their unbelief those who have never had the chance of hearing about Christ (see John 3.18)? Will He condemn them for *anything*?

20. The law is God's will revealed to us, and it condemns us as sinners. In the Sermon on the Mount, as in His whole ministry, Jesus revealed God's will for people. In what ways, if any, does the Sermon on the Mount condemn us? (See Rom. 3.19, 20.) How do you think a pastor could use the Sermon on the Mount to help people to see what they are really like, and to understand their true need?

3.21-31

God's Gift: Righteousness from God

OUTLINE

'I have said a lot about unrighteousness. Now I am going to speak about righteousness. Righteousness is God's gift to men. It comes to men because of what Jesus Christ did when He died, and it comes to anyone, Jew or Gentile, who has faith in Him—and there is no other way to get it. It changes a person's standing before God, because God sees such a person as righteous. Friendship and fellowship are established between him and God.'

INTRODUCTION

This short section of 11 verses is very important. In it Paul explained God's solution to man's problem.

1. *The Problem: God's wrath.* Paul had explained the bad news. We all go against God's will. We try to be our own gods, instead of letting God rule us. Most of the time we do not even listen to what He says to us. We rarely speak to Him except sometimes to call out for help. Yet in another way, we want Him to be our friend. But how can He be our friend when we go against Him in this way? How can He accept us? How can we be right with Him when we are unrighteous? This problem exists because of (a) man's sin, and (b) God's perfect justice. People who deny either of these do not see that there is a problem.

2. *The Solution: God's righteousness.* At this point, Paul turned from the bad news to the good news (3.21). He emphasized the contrast between the two in two ways:

(a) The words 'But now' introduce a completely new idea.

(b) The *Theme Signpost* of this section is 'the righteousness of God', in contrast to the theme of 1.18–3.20, which is 'the wrath of God'. The contrast between the two sections can be set out as overleaf.

The righteousness of God means both God's activity in saving men, and also His gift to them. Paul was here making seven main points concerning this righteousness:

1. It is God's gift to sinful men, by which He sets them right with Himself (vv. 22, 24).

2. Men receive this gift only through faith, not through any good works they may do (vv. 22, 28).

3. This gift abolishes the distinction between Jew and Gentile, because all alike have turned against God, and all alike can be accepted by faith only (vv. 22, 23, 27–30).

45

1.18–3.20	3.21–31
The Bad News: wrath against men	The Good News: righteousness for men
The wickedness of men	The righteousness of God
What men do	What God has done
Men's need	God's gift
In the past . . .	But now . . .

4. This gift is available to men because of the death of Christ, which Paul described as 'redemption' and 'expiation' (vv. 24, 25).

5. This teaching is found in the Old Testament, but is clearly revealed only in Christ (vv. 21, 25, 26).

6. In justifying sinful men in this way, God acts justly and righteously (vv. 25, 26).

7. This is God's way of upholding His righteous law which men had broken (v. 31).

INTERPRETATION AND NOTES

A. SOME FALSE SOLUTIONS TO MAN'S PROBLEM

1. Some people think there is no problem because God does not care: like a clockmaker, He has started the world going but is now no longer interested in it. Therefore, they say, the question of our relationship with Him is of no importance.

2. Some think there is no problem because God is always ready to overlook our sin: 'Forgiving is God's job.'

3. Some have thought that God's anger is so terrible that there is no escape at all: All wrong must be punished. See Note on *Wrath* (1. b), p. 221.

4. Some Jews made the mistake of thinking that, although it is difficult to keep God's law, it was always possible to offer Him a sacrifice instead. In this way sacrifice, they thought, enabled them to do as they liked.

5. Some Jews tried hard to keep every detail of God's law—and really thought they succeeded. They became very proud of this success (as they thought), and did not care about other people. Jesus often had to rebuke them.

6. Some Jews who tried equally hard to keep God's law were driven to despair as they realized their inability to do so. The harder they tried, the more they discovered evil in themselves. Paul was like this (see 7.7–13), and so are many people. For some examples, see p. 1.

7. Most people do not think very deeply about the problem at all.

'Let us hope for the best,' they think. 'Probably things will turn out all right in the end. Just now, anyway, God does not seem to be troubled about my sin.' But that is not what God says. The problem is a real one. He has solved it, and He has told us His solution.

8. One of the wisest men who ever lived, the Greek philosopher Socrates, admitted to his friend, Plato, that he could see no solution to the problem: 'Plato, Plato, I suppose that God can forgive deliberate sin; but I do not see how.'

B. PAUL'S TEACHING

Writers in the Bible used many different word-pictures to describe the one reality of God's salvation through Jesus Christ. Paul used at least three in this section. No one picture or illustration is sufficient. Therefore we should never think that one way of describing God's salvation is the only way, or even the best way. We need *all* the word-pictures that the Bible gives us. That is why we have them.

V. 21. But now: 'Now' is an important word in the New Testament. It is often used to emphasize the difference which Christ makes to men's lives when they come to believe in Him; and also the difference which His coming has made to the world. The Gospel is 'now manifested' in Jesus Christ in a way in which it had never been manifested before. See Special Note on p. 122.

The righteousness of God: See Additional Note, p. 215. This phrase contains three chief ideas in this section:

1. *God's saving action*, which is now manifested in Christ, puts right the wrong relationship between God and men which Paul had described in terms of God's wrath (v. 21).

2. *God's gift of righteousness* is offered to those who need it, i.e. all human beings (3.9, 20), and is given not to Jews only but to anyone who believes (v. 22). It means a right relationship with God, because it comes from His Son who had such a relationship.

3. *God's character* is shown to be righteous and just in the Gospel of Christ (vv. 25b, 26).

The righteousness of God, in all these senses, is fully revealed only in Jesus Christ (1.3, 17). Christ's work is the central and essential part of God's saving activity, and any true statement about salvation must say so.

Apart from the law: Here 'the law' has the third meaning (see Additional Note, p. 210). Knowing, or trying to obey, God's law can only result in failure, and so show up our wrong relationship with God (3.20). This is true whether we think of 'law' as the Ten Commandments, the Jewish rules, or the standards of right and wrong which people generally recognize. Thus the law cannot make us right with Him; we need faith in Jesus Christ.

'Righteousness is God's gift . . . it changes a person's standing before God . . . friendship and fellowship are established' (p. 45).

Edric Connor, the West Indian singer and actor, receives a citation naming him honorary life member of the Ghana Council for Cultural relations. What difference might this new standing make to him?

The law and the prophets: Here 'the law' has the second meaning. The Old Testament did not reveal the Gospel clearly, but did in many ways point forward to it. Paul wanted his Jewish readers to understand that the Gospel does not contradict, but fulfils their Scriptures. In chapter 4 he showed how. (See also p. 53.)

V. 22. Faith: See Additional Note, p. 206. According to chapter 4, Abraham's faith was his acceptance of God's promise to him; he said 'Yes' to God and 'No' to himself and his own ability (4.19, 21). But 'now', i.e. ever since the coming of Jesus, faith must be 'in Jesus Christ' (v. 22). By faith a person says 'Yes' to Christ and relies upon Him as the only one who can bring him a right relationship with God. In 1860 Charles Blondin four times walked across the Niagara Falls in North America on a rope stretched tightly from one side to the other. Once he pushed a wheelbarrow, once he carried a man on his back. Then he offered to carry across another man who was watching, but the man refused. 'Do you believe that I can do it? asked Blondin. 'Yes, I do,' replied the man, 'but I am not willing to try.' Faith in Christ means more than simply believing about Christ or accepting what He says. It means relying on Him and committing oneself to Him.

V. 23. The glory of God: See Additional Note, p. 208. 'No two people are alike,' we say; but when we think in terms of God's glory, all men are exactly alike, because all have fallen short of the way God meant them to live. If we admit this, we have taken the first step towards saying that all men are equal.

V. 24. Justified: See Additional Note, p. 210. This word describes God's action in setting a sinful person right with Him. It is similar to the action of a Judge who had to try the case of an old friend of his in the law-court. The Judge heard the facts of the case and saw that his friend was guilty. He declared him guilty and ordered him to pay a heavy fine, as the law required. Then the Judge took off his Judge's uniform, and went to stand beside his guilty friend. He took some money from his pocket and paid the fine on behalf of his friend. 'Now you are free,' he said. His friend was now right with the law; he was justified.

Grace: See Additional Note, p. 209. We get an idea of God's grace when we think of (a) how much God has done and still does for us; (b) how little we deserve it. Sometimes one person may show 'grace' to another person. For example, one day during the Boxer rebellion in China in 1900, some rebel soldiers came to a farm and murdered the farmer's wife and small son. The farmer narrowly escaped. Later the murderers were brought to trial and found guilty. The farmer, in accordance with the custom of that time, was asked to say how they should be punished. A friend said to him, 'I cannot advise you what to do. But I know what Jesus would do.' The farmer went into the court and said the murderers were to be set free. In this action the farmer showed grace to those who did not deserve it. But the word 'grace' is usually used only to describe what *God* does.

A gift: This word emphasizes the idea of grace: no contribution can be made by men. Justification is a work of God alone through Christ. An Archbishop once said: 'We contribute nothing to our own salvation except the sin from which we are saved.' The fact that our right relationship with God is a gift of His grace makes an important difference to the way we live:

1. We should not worry about our past failures, because God declares us righteous.

2. We can serve God confidently and without anxiety, because we know we are accepted by him. We need not be discouraged by fear of failure.

3. We have assurance for the future, because we know that our standing with God depends upon what He has done, and not upon what we shall do.

Redemption: See Additional Note, p. 214. In using this word here, Paul showed that it was not easy, but costly, for God to justify men. Through Christ, God paid a ransom-price in order to set men free from sin. The idea of a slave being set free through the payment of a ransom was familiar to Paul and his readers. For example, 200 years before Christ there lived a slave called Nicaea and her master, Sosibius. At the temple of the Greek god Apollo, there is an inscription (i.e. words carved on stone) which describes how Nicaea got her freedom: 'The god Apollo bought from Sosibius, for freedom, a female slave whose name is Nicaea, with a price of $3\frac{1}{2}$ silver coins. Sosibius has received the money. Nicaea has entrusted the purchase to Apollo, for freedom.' This means that a ceremony was held in which the god's priest paid over the money to Sosibius. From that moment Nicaea (a) was regarded as belonging to the god who had bought her; (b) could never again become anyone's slave.

In the same way, Christians have been redeemed by Christ and are regarded as belonging to Him. A story from the Congo/Zaire illustrates this: A hunter was out shooting one day, when he saw a lion who had attacked a man and was about to drag him away. The hunter shot the lion, took the man home, and nursed him back to health, until he was well enough to return to his home. A few months later the hunter, sitting at home, was surprised to see a little group of people approaching his house. There was a man, followed by women, children, two cows, and some chickens. The man came up to the hunter and knelt in front of him. It was the man whom he had rescued from the lion. He then stood up and said, 'It is the law of my tribe, sir, that when a man has been saved from a lion by someone else, he no longer belongs to himself. He belongs to the one who saved him. So here I am. All that I have belongs to you. My wives are your wives, my children are your children, my possessions are your possessions. I am your slave.'

V. 25. Expiation: Paul used here a special Greek word to explain how God, through Christ, dealt with the problem of men whom He loves and men's sin which He must condemn. Scholars have translated this word in two ways:

(a) Expiation: This refers to the removal of sin, and describes the way in which God takes away men's sin.

(b) Propitiation: This refers to the removal of wrath, and describes the way in which God puts away His wrath against sinners.

Scholars are not agreed about which is the better translation, but (b) seems to be suitable, because it deals with the problem of God's wrath against sin, which is the main problem described by Paul in 1.18—3.20. See Additional Note, Expiation, p. 204. Sinful men deserve to be condemned under God's wrath, but Christ bore this condemnation in their place, with the result that they are free from condemnation, free from wrath (see 8.1, 3). Two illustrations may help us to understand this idea:

1. Once when the army of Rome was being defeated by its enemies in the year 340 BC, one of its leaders, Decius Mus, offered himself as a propitiatory sacrifice to the gods. He died instead of his own army, and the army was saved. The Roman historian, Livy, wrote that it seemed as if Decius Mus had been sent by the gods themselves for this very purpose of bearing their anger.

2. During the Second World War some prisoners escaped from the German concentration camp at Buchenwald. The camp commander was so angry that he said that twelve of the prisoners who were left behind must die instead of the ones who escaped. One of those twelve prisoners was a young man with a family. A Roman Catholic priest stepped forward and offered to take the place of the young prisoner. His offer was accepted and, with the eleven other prisoners, he was shut in a small room without food or drink. All died after several days. In 1971 he was honoured by the Pope at a special ceremony in Rome, at which the man in whose place he had died was present.

But we must beware of thinking that any illustration can be an adequate picture of what Christ did for us. We must also beware of thinking in the wrong way about Christ's sacrifice. For example:

(a) It has sometimes been suggested that God was angry with men and wanted to punish them, but that Christ loves men and offered Himself to suffer the punishment instead. This teaching is not found in the Bible, and it overlooks the relationship between the Father and the Son. God *put forward* Christ (Rom. 3.25); God was *in* Christ (2 Cor. 5.19); the Father *sent* the Son (1 John 4.10). God Himself suffered at the cross for men's sin, because of His love for men. The pain of separation from God through sin was borne by God Himself (see John 10.30; Mark 15.33, 34).

(b) Some scholars have argued that one man cannot accept the judgement which another deserves. But there is a special unity between Christ and men—in particular between Him and those whom He redeemed, just as Decius Mus was part of the army for whom he was thought to have died, and the Catholic priest was one of the prisoners, like the one whose place he took. At a certain theological College all students have to spend part of their holidays doing manual work for the College. One of the students, who was about to be ordained, was engaged to one of the women students in the College. He wanted her to be present at his ordination, but her name had been written down for College work at that time. Her fiancé offered to do part of her work for her, so that she would be free on the date of his ordination. His offer was accepted, and his work counted as hers, because of their relationship with one another. Christ died instead of those who are one with Him.

In each of the two paragraphs (a) and (b) above we see Christ first as *God*, bringing God's love and grace to men in saving activity; and also as *Man*, suffering God's righteous judgement on human sin.

By His blood: These words mean 'by His sacrificial death'. See Additional Note, p. 203.

God's righteousness: This means the same as 'that he himself is righteous' (v. 26), and refers to God's own character (see p. 47, 3).

Passed over former sins: Throughout history, God had not judged sin as it deserved, although many times He declared that He would. He 'overlooked' the sins of the past. The same idea is found in Acts 17.30; 14.16; Romans 2.4. But how could a righteous God who had always promised to condemn sin overlook it? People might have thought: (a) He does not really mean what He says (i.e. He is not truthful), or (b) He does not really care about sin after all—He can easily forget it (i.e. He is not righteous). But the sacrificial death of Jesus shows that God *is* righteous, because in it He (a) dealt justly and righteously with sin (v. 26a), and (b) acted to save sinners (v. 26b). This was how God solved the problem described on p. 45.

Vv. 27–31 show how the Gospel takes away all distinction between men. Paul wanted both Jewish and Gentile Christians in Rome fully to understand that neither group had any advantage over the other in God's sight (see p. 3(e)). All alike were sinners; all alike were right with God only through faith (vv. 23, 27–30).

V. 28. Justified by faith: Luther translated this as '. . . justified by faith *alone* . . .' He was right to put in the word 'alone', because Paul was saying that human beings can do nothing at all to please God. We can only accept (i.e. have faith in) God's grace. Therefore theologians use the phrase 'by grace alone, through faith alone'. John Calvin wrote: 'Man is justified by faith alone, but the faith which justifies is never alone.' He meant that faith is always followed by good works in the life of the believer. Paul wrote about these good works in Romans 6.

V. 30. On the ground of means exactly the same as *because of*.

V. 31. We uphold the law: The Gospel fulfils the law in four ways:

1. It condemns sin (in Christ's death), as the law does.

2. It rewards good works (particularly those done for us by Christ), as the law does.

3. It enables people to do good works (through the power of Christ in them).

4. It fulfils the Jewish Scriptures. In chapter 4 Paul went on to show how it does so, using the example of Abraham.

STUDY SUGGESTIONS

WORD STUDY

1. In the following list, which words mean the same as 'forgive'? What do the others mean exactly?

   pardon   overlook   ignore   remit

2. In what way is the standing of a 'justified' person different from that of a 'forgiven' person?

REVIEW OF CONTENT

3. (a) In what way was the action of the Chinese farmer (described on p. 49 in the note on 'Grace') different from God's action as described in Rom. 3.21–26?

   (b) In what way was God's action different from the action of the Judge also described on p. 49?

4. What three chief ideas are contained in the phrase 'God's righteousness' as used in this section?

5. In what ways does the Gospel break down the barriers between men?

6. Abraham said ' "No" to himself and his own ability' (p. 49). What sort of 'ability' did the Jews rely on? What sorts of ability do men rely on today?

7. If we admit that all have fallen short of God's glory, 'we have taken the first step towards saying that all men are equal' (p. 49).

   (a) What is the second step?

   (b) In what sense are all men equal, and in what sense are they not equal? Illustrate your answer with examples.

8. Read the following verses. In which passage was Jesus thinking in

terms of: (i) redemption; (ii) the law-court; (iii) sacrifice; (iv) God's saving activity?

(a) Matt. 6.33   (b) Mark 10.45   (c) Mark 14.24   (d) Luke 18.14

9. Read again the description of the American farmer on p. 206.
(a) In what ways does the farmer exercise 'faith'?
(b) In what ways is his faith like the Christian's faith in Christ, and in what ways is it different?

10. In what three ways does the death of Christ show God's righteousness?

11. How is the problem of Socrates (p. 47) solved by the teaching of Rom. 3.25, 26?

BIBLE

12. What 'false solution' to man's problem were the writers in Amos 4.4, 5 and Micah 6.6–8 attacking?

13. 'The words "but now" introduce a completely new idea' (p. 45). What similar new idea does the word 'but' introduce in Ephesians 2.4 and 2.13?

14. (a) What do we learn from Exodus 21.29, 30 about the meaning of redemption?
(b) What special relationship between the redeemer and those who are redeemed is described in Isaiah 54.5?

15. Read Genesis 3. How does this chapter illustrate the statement that 'man, by turning against God, was "deprived of the divine splendour" ' (p. 208)?

16. 'There is a special unity between Christ and men' (p. 52).
(a) How is this unity shown in (i) Luke 22.37 and (ii) Heb. 2.11–17?
(b) With what group of persons is Jesus identified in each case?

17. Read 1 Cor. 6.19, 20; 7.23; Gal. 5.1. In what ways does the story of the man rescued from the lion (p. 50) illustrate our redemption by Christ? What truths about our redemption does it *fail* to illustrate? Do you think that the story of Nicaea illustrates the meaning of redemption more clearly? If so, in what ways?

APPLICATION, OPINION, AND RESEARCH

18. (a) Of the eight ways of looking at man's problem described on pp. 46, 47, which are those most usually followed today? What do you think most people believe about God's treatment of sin?
(b) What fact shows people both that God *does* care about sin, and also that it is not easy for Him to forgive?

19. Give some examples of the ways in which people separate themselves from each other. In what ways does the message of 3.21–26 'abolish' these distinctions?

20. (a) What would you reply to someone who asked, 'How can Christ's

death so long ago make any difference to people today? One might just as well expect animal sacrifice to be effective'? Cf. Heb. 10. 4–10; Rom. 5.19.)

(b) If you know of any group which offers animal sacrifices, try to find out what meaning and purpose they attach to the sacrifice.

(c) In what way, if at all, does the purpose of these sacrifices today differ from the purpose of the sacrifice described in the Old Testament? (See Heb. 9.9, 10; 10.1–3.)

4.1–25
God's Gift: The Witness of the Old Testament

OUTLINE

'If you want an actual example of a man who was justified by faith like this, there is none better than Abraham. "The Father of the Jews", he is called, but a better name would be "The Father of all Believers". He (and King David like him) accepted what God said—that is faith. As a result, God regarded Abraham as righteous, and he became famous as "God's friend". So you see how this good news, now clearly revealed through Christ, is no different from what we find in the most important parts of the Scriptures.'

INTRODUCTION

The Jews believed that in their Scriptures God had spoken. In Romans 3.10–19, Paul had used these Scriptures as supporting authority for his teaching that all men are sinners. Now in chapter 4 he used them to support his teaching that the only way to get right with God is by faith. In this chapter Paul was thinking especially of how a Jew would react to what he had said so far:

1. Any Jew would have been shocked to hear Paul saying that (a) Jews value circumcision too highly (2.25–29); (b) Jews value the law too highly (2.17–23); (c) Jews are no better than Gentiles (3.9–20); (d) God will accept Gentiles, as well as Jews, through faith only (3.27–30).

2. Any Jew would have said, 'This teaching of Paul is completely new! It is quite different from what God said to Abraham and the fathers of our people. It is therefore false. We must reject it.'

Paul's answer to these objections is found in two sentences in chapter 3 and all of chapter 4:

3.21: my teaching is the same as that found in the Scriptures;

3.31: my teaching is the only way of truly establishing and fulfilling God's law;

4: my teaching is confirmed by the example of Abraham himself, whom God justified on account of his faith.

The words 'the law and the prophets bear witness to it' (3.21) are a *Link Signpost* which prepare the reader for the theme of chapter 4. Paul had two reasons for choosing the example of Abraham as supporting authority for his teaching:

(a) Abraham was the founding father of the Jewish people, through whom all their blessings had come to them (Gen. 12.1–3).

(b) Abraham was regarded by the Jews as having fulfilled God's law. 'Abraham kept the law of the Most High, and was taken into covenant with Him' (Ecclus. 44.21).

This chapter has *five* clear sections, in each of which Paul showed that Abraham (and David) was justified by God through faith only:

1. The righteousness of Abraham came from his faith (vv. 1–5).
2. The righteousness of David did not come from his works (vv. 6–8).
3. The righteousness of Abraham did not come from his circumcision (vv. 9–12).
4. The righteousness of Abraham did not come from obeying the law (vv. 13–17).
5. The nature of Abraham's faith (vv. 18–25).

INTERPRETATION AND NOTES

It is not difficult to understand this chapter. A good way to work through it is to study each of the sections as a separate whole. The notes below will help you.

V. 1. Flesh: This word is used here in the same way as in 1.3.

Vv. 2, 3: The Jews thought that Abraham was the perfect example of a man who kept God's law. Paul said that Abraham was the example of a man who had faith. It was Abraham's trust in God, not any good works he could boast of, which God counted as 'righteousness'.

Vv. 4, 5: Paul was here contrasting two ways of approaching God. One way is to ask God to give us what we deserve (our 'wages'; v. 4). The other way is to accept the gift which God freely offers (v. 5). See Additional Note, Grace, 2, p. 209.

Vv. 6–8: Here Paul turned to the example of David, from Psalm 32. The Jews were as proud of King David as they were of Abraham. By showing that David, like Abraham, approached God in the *second* way, and was counted righteous by God apart from any good works he did, Paul proved that his teaching was fully supported by the Scriptures. In declaring that the man who trusts God is 'blessed', Paul meant that God is like a Judge who says that a prisoner is 'not guilty' (v. 8) of the crime of which he is accused. To say that he is 'not guilty' is the same as saying that he is innocent, i.e. righteous (v. 6) in the sight of the law of the land.

V. 9. The circumcised: Many Jews might have agreed with Paul up to this point. They might have said: 'We agree that we do not deserve to be accepted by God; we must have faith in Him to receive His righteousness, and this can even be true of Gentiles—but only for those who accept circumcision. Unless you are circumcised, you cannot be accepted by God.' Even many Jewish Christians thought this.

Vv. 10, 11a: Paul, however, reminded his readers that Abraham was counted righteous by God long before he was circumcised, i.e. *apart from* circumcision. The importance of circumcision lay in the fact that it was 'a sign' of Abraham's right relationship with God. See Additional Note, Circumcision, 6, p. 203. In this passage the word 'seal' has a similar meaning to the word 'sign'. When the President of a country puts his seal on a document, he is confirming it as an official statement of the Government of the country. He promises that the Government will fulfil whatever the statement says. Ordinary people today do not use seals, except to confirm a contract or other legal documents. They just write their signature, but it means the same thing. Through circumcision God assured Abraham that He would fulfil His promise.

Vv. 11b, 12. The father: In many countries a man may be called 'son of' his father more often than by his own personal name. A son is not only related to his father, he is also very often like him—and that is why the Jews boasted of being Abraham's children. He was not merely their ancestor; he was righteous—so were they; he belonged to God— so did they; he was circumcised—so were they. But Paul here reminded them that the most important thing about Abraham was not his circumcision, nor his obedience to God's law, but his *faith*. Therefore the true children of Abraham (i.e. those who are *really* like him) are those who have faith—with non-Jews (v. 11b) and Jews (v. 12) alike.

Abraham was a very suitable example for Paul to take. In some ways he is like a non-Jew, because he was justified by faith long before any thought of circumcision or the law. In other ways he is the first Jew, because they received circumcision and the promises through him.

Vv. 13–17: Again Paul considered the two ways of approaching God (see p. 56 and Additional Note, Grace, p. 209):

1. Grace (promise)—faith—gift (vv. 13, 16). There is no place here for the ideas of law or works or reward, because there is no thought of what a person may deserve. And there is no place for the idea of 'transgression' (v. 15b, see 5.13). Therefore those who, like Abraham, come to God in this way, can be sure (it is 'guaranteed', v. 16) that they will receive what God has promised. It depends not on what they do,

but on 'grace', i.e. God's free gift to all who will receive it. For this reason, Abraham is truly 'the father of us all' who believe. Because believers come not from one nation but from many, God's promise to Abraham in Genesis 17.5 is truly fulfilled through the Gospel.

2. Law—works—reward (vv. 14, 15). There is no place here for a promise, or for faith, or for a gift (v. 14). The person who comes to God in this way gets what he *deserves*—but what a transgressor of the law deserves is 'wrath' (v. 15).

These two ways of approaching God are rather like the two choices before a man when he goes back to stay in his home town. He can either go to a hotel, where the arrangement is contract—payment—food; or he can rely on his father's generosity and go to his house where he will be welcomed to meals freely.

Vv. 18–25: Before considering Paul's teaching on the nature of faith, let us first notice two *mistaken* ideas of what faith is:

(a) Some people (who may call themselves 'humanists' or 'rationalists' or 'communists') think that faith is trying to persuade oneself that something exists when it does not. God cannot be seen or heard—therefore, they say, He cannot exist. Faith, they think, goes against reason, and is therefore foolish.

(b) Others, including some Christians, praise faith, but describe it as 'a leap in the dark', i.e. one does not know what lies ahead. Such people hope that everything will turn out well in the end, but have no certainty that it will. They often say that they have 'faith', without saying what they have faith *in*. They try to go on 'in faith' without noticing the difficulties facing them.

Abraham's faith was not like this. Paul here made the following points about Abraham's faith:

1. There was, from one point of view, no hope that Abraham could have a son. He believed 'against hope' (v. 18).

2. He did not ignore the difficulties, but carefully 'considered' them (v. 19).

3. He also recognized that 'the promise of God' had been given a very long time before, and had not been fulfilled (v. 20).

4. He also considered what God, who had given the promise, was like (v. 21).

5. Therefore, because he carefully considered *all* the facts, he went on believing. It was *reasonable* to do so.

6. Abraham's faith brought three definite results:

(a) *Glory to God* (v. 20). Through his faith, Abraham bore witness to what God was like. This is the opposite of the actions described in 1.21, 23. We can never increase God's glory; we can only acknowledge the glory which He already has.

(b) *Faith* (v. 20). The only way to increase our faith is by believing.

As a boxer strengthens his muscles by using them, so our faith will only become stronger as we exercise it.

(c) *Righteousness* (v. 22). Abraham was right with God.

7. Abraham believed not in something vague or uncertain, but *in God*, who had revealed His purposes clearly and precisely, as follows:

(a) He would accept Abraham freely, apart from anything he might deserve (v. 5);

(b) He would enable Abraham and Sarah to have a child and many descendants (v. 17);

(c) He was able to do what He had promised (v. 21).

8. Abraham's example of faith is one which we should follow (vv. 24, 25). Once an old man was calling a little girl to come home. It was dark, and she could not see him, but she went, following the sound of his voice, until she felt his hand on her head. 'Now you know what faith is,' said the old man. 'When God tells you to go in the dark, go.' Abraham's faith was like this. So is ours, but it is not so dark for us as it was for Abraham, because we have the light of Jesus Christ.

V. 18. Hope: This word means 'faith looking forward to something in the future'. There is no suggestion of uncertainty. See p. 65.

V. 25: The words of this verse are a little unusual for Paul. Perhaps he used them because:

1. They may have been a well-known saying, or creed, used by the early Christians, perhaps based on Isaiah 53.6, 12.

2. They fit in very well with what Paul had been saying about Abraham's faith, i.e.:

(a) Abraham had failed to have a child, and so he had no hope for the future. He was 'as good as dead'. When Jesus was put to death, it seemed that His ministry had failed and that there was no hope (see Luke 24.21). But in fact He was dying 'for our trespasses' (see Isa. 53. 3–5).

(b) The birth of Isaac to Abraham and Sarah seemed like giving 'life to the dead'. In the same way the God in whom both Abraham and we believe raised Jesus to life. This means (i) that God accepted Jesus's work for us and we can be certain that Jesus really did take away our sin; (ii) that we are not simply forgiven, but also right with God—we share with Jesus His new life. Paul explained this idea in chapter 6.

SPECIAL NOTE C:
ABRAHAM AND THE WAY OF SALVATION

Abraham lived hundreds of years before Christ, yet he was accepted by God through faith. Is it, then, not necessary to believe in Christ in order to be saved? Can a man who has never heard of Christ be right with God, even though Jesus said, 'No one comes to the Father but by me.'? It is not easy to solve this problem, but note the following ideas:

1. Neither Abraham nor anyone else has ever been accepted by God on account of either their good works or their religion (3.20; 2.13).

2. God revealed Himself to Abraham in a special way; and Abraham trusted God as He had revealed Himself (see p. 59).

3. God has now revealed Himself to men through Jesus Christ (4.24), and this is the revelation which men must accept now, just as Abraham accepted the word he was given.

4. Romans 3.25b suggests that God was able to 'pass over' the sins of men before Christ because they were dealt with in the sacrifice of Christ. This idea is found in Hebrews 10.12, and elsewhere. If this is so, then Christ died for Abraham and David, as He did for us. Their forgiveness came through Him.

5. All New Testament writers said that faith in Christ is the only way in which a person can be right with God. Therefore Christians should be witnesses to Him, so that other people may come to share their faith.

6. It may, however, be possible that God has occasionally, in some places, revealed Himself in a special way apart from the name of Christ. There was a clan in West Africa whose chief had a dream in which he was told that white men would one day bring news of the true God. When missionaries arrived many years later, they found that the whole clan was ready to accept the Gospel immediately, though their chief had long since died. Can we not say that the chief was like Abraham, who lived before Christ and was justified by faith?

7. There are, however, not many stories like this one. For the most part, we can be sure that men need to hear about Jesus Christ before they can believe and be saved (Rom. 10.13, 14). As far as we know, there is no other way.

STUDY SUGGESTIONS

WORD STUDY

1. Romans 4.14 and 4.16 refer to 'adherents of the law'. Find out how this phrase is translated in any other English version, and any other language you know. What, if any, is the difference between the two verses.

REVIEW OF CONTENT

2. Which of the promises made by God to Abraham in Genesis 17 did Paul mention in Romans 4? (See question 10 on p. 43). Which of them apply also to Christians?

3. In what ways is the attitude of faith more reasonable than the materialistic view described on p. 58?

4. In what ways was the little girl's 'faith' in the story on p. 59 different from the 'leap in the dark' described on p. 58(b)?
5. In what ways is the faith of Christians *like* the faith of Abraham? In what ways is it *different*?
6. In the light of this chapter and the teaching of Jesus in John 8.56–58, how would you describe the relationship between Abraham and Jesus?

BIBLE

7. The Jews were proud of Abraham because (i) he was their father through whom all their blessings had come; (ii) he was thought to have fulfilled God's law. Which of these two reasons is mentioned in each of the following passages?
   (a) Isa. 51.1, 2 (b) Gen. 26.5 (c) John 8.33.
8. 'The Jews were as proud of King David as they were of Abraham.'
   (i) How is this seen in the Song of Zechariah in Luke 1.68–79?
   (ii) What was special about Abraham's and David's relationship with God, according to (a) Isa. 41.8 (b) 1 Sam. 13.14?
9. 'There were many Jewish Christians who thought that it was necessary to be circumcised in order to be accepted by God.' How are such Jewish Christians described in Acts 11.2, 3; 15.1, 5; Gal. 2.12–15? What exactly was their teaching?
10. 'A son is not only related to his father; he is also very often like him.' What use did Jesus, in His teaching, make of this common fact? (See John 5.19–27; 8.39–47; Mark 3.31–35. Compare Gen. 4.20, 21.)
11. How are the 'two ways of approaching God' (p. 57), illustrated by Jesus's parable in Matthew 20.1–16? Who received the wages they deserved, and who received a gift of grace? What word in Matthew 20.15 means the same as 'grace'?
12. 'There was . . . no hope' (p. 58). This is what Sarah thought (Gen. 18.12–14); also those described on p. 46 (3); and Jesus's disciples (Matt. 19.25, 26). What part does faith play in overcoming such difficulties? (Compare Luke 24.21 with Acts 5.30, 32.)
13. How accurate is the picture which Paul gives of Abraham's faith? What weaknesses did Abraham show, which were not mentioned by Paul? (See Gen. 16.1–3; 17.17–21.)

APPLICATION, OPINION, AND RESEARCH

14. One scholar has written, 'This chapter (Romans 4) has little interest and no importance for us.' But see vv. 23, 24; Gal. 3.6–9, 14, 29; Heb. 11.8–12, 17–19, and use a Concordance to find out what else the New Testament says about Abraham. What do you think is the value of the story of Abraham for us today?

15. What sign was given to Noah after the flood? In what ways was this sign like circumcision, and in what ways was it different?
16. Write down the following words in the order in which Abraham experienced them, according to Genesis and Romans 4:
    righteousness   grace   circumcision   faith
    What do we learn from this about God's activity?
17. Some people may say, 'I do not want any favours; I just want my rights. I have never done any harm to anyone; let God give me what I deserve.' For what reasons, do you think, do some people not want simply to receive God's gift, but choose instead to try to deserve His approval?
18. 'I have made you the father of many nations' (4.17). This promise has been fulfilled in the Christian Church. List the different nations (or tribes) from which you have Christian friends. How can Christians help to preserve their unity which crosses racial and national barriers? (See Acts 15.7–11.)
19. Read again p. 60, numbered para 6. Do you yourself think that the chief was justified by his faith, as Abraham was? Give reasons for your answer.

PART 3

'... SHALL LIVE'

5.1–11
Free From Wrath

OUTLINE

'What is the life of the man who is righteous by faith like? This life is first of all a life of peace: The "quarrel" between men and God is now over because God has given us a new relationship with Him. We now know that He loves us. If anyone doubts this, let him think of the death of God's Son. Jesus did not die as He did for good or worthy people—but for us who had turned against Him. That is what it cost Him to make us His friends. That—and that alone—is real love. But more is to come, because Christ is not dead but alive and will keep us in this right relationship with God for ever.'

INTRODUCTION

Having explained in chapters 1—4 *how* a person becomes right with God, Paul went on in chapters 5—8 to consider the second part of the verse from Habakkuk, i.e. to describe *the life* of the person who is right with God (see pp. 5, 15). Each of these four chapters shows that the Christian is free from some power which used to rule over him. Chapter 5 describes the first of these new 'freedoms': the Christian is 'free from wrath'.

In 5.1 there are two phrases which help us to follow Paul's thought:

1. *Therefore.* With this word Paul looked back to what he had already said. Thus the teaching in this chapter follows on from the teaching about justification in 3.21—4.25. The fact of being right with God ('since we are justified by faith') must make a difference to our lives. In chapter 5 Paul described what this difference is.

2. *Peace with God.* This is a *Theme Signpost* which points forward to what Paul was about to say, and gives us Paul's theme for this section.

Scholars have expressed this theme in three ways, i.e. as:

(a) *The fruit of justification.* Some scholars point out that Paul was here telling Christians about the results which come from being right with God.

(b) *Assurance of salvation.* Some scholars point out that Paul, who had been using some difficult language to explain justification, was now assuring his readers that God really does love them now and that they need never be afraid of losing His love. They have a peace which is sure.

(c) *The three 'tenses' of salvation.* Some scholars point out that in this section Paul spoke of the blessings which Christians have already received, those which they are experiencing now, and those which they will experience in the future, i.e.:

Past: We have been justified; Christ's work *for* us is finished; we have believed in Him; we are already right with God.

Present: We have peace and joy now, for Christ is continuously at work *in* us throughout our lives.

Future: We shall be saved, because Christ's work *in* us will be completed not in this life but afterwards in heaven.

INTERPRETATION AND NOTES

V. 1. We have peace with God: Some of the Greek texts have 'Let us have peace with God'. But the text followed by the RSV gives a better sense, because if God regards us as righteous, then there *is* peace between us and God. These words are another way of saying that we have a right relationship with God. Paul had described the wrong relationship as 'sin' on man's side, and as 'wrath' on God's side. Here he thought of it as 'war' or 'enmity'. This situation was the result of man's sin. But now that Christ has dealt with the problem of sin, the enmity is over. God and man are friends. This is a fact which we can be sure about because it depends not on ourselves, but on the work which Christ has done for us.

Through our Lord Jesus Christ: Paul repeated this phrase many times in chapters 5—8. There may have been two reasons for this:

1. The new life described in these chapters comes to us only through Christ. As He is at the centre of the Gospel (see p. 9), so He should be at the centre of our life and thinking.

2. The word 'God' is used in Romans more frequently than in any other book of the New Testament. But some of Paul's Gentile readers may have felt that God was remote and unreal, as some people do today. Others may have associated the word 'God' with wrong ideas (see 1.23). So Paul was trying to teach them to think about God in terms of Jesus Christ, whom they could more easily understand. For us, too, Christ is the only safe guide if we are to think rightly about God.

V. 2. This grace: The word 'grace' means God's undeserved love (see Additional Note, p. 209). Paul was describing our present 'standing' in God's sight—through Christ, we 'stand in' His love. Like righteousness, and like peace, this love is a present fact.

Our hope: What we possess now (God's grace) is the basis of our hope of receiving more (God's glory). A son who knows that his father loves him now is, for that reason, sure that his father will help him in the future. For the same reason Christians can *trust God for the future*. The word which writers in the Bible used for this idea is 'hope', but in using it they did not mean to suggest any doubt or uncertainty (as when we 'hope' that something might happen). On the contrary, they used it to express confidence in something which is certain. Hope is faith about the future. V. 2 shows us that God's blessings are of two sorts:

1. Those which we already possess: these strengthen our hope for the future.

2. Those to which we still look forward: these help us to rejoice now, without any anxiety, because God has promised them.

The glory of God: See Additional Note, p. 209. Jesus Christ came to live among men to enable them to 'share the glory of God' which they had lost. Christians share God's glory partly in this life, but they will not experience it fully until they are with Christ in heaven. Just as everyone feels happy, when he thinks of good things to come, so all Christians rejoice as they look forward to heaven. But unfortunately many of them do not rejoice in anything else! Paul went on to say that Christians can rejoice in other things as well.

Vv. 3–5a. We rejoice in our sufferings: This seems a very surprising thing to say. There are three different ways of facing suffering:

1. Most people complain about suffering.

2. Some people endure suffering bravely. This is sometimes called being 'stoical'. The Stoics were a group of Greek and Roman philosophers who refused to be affected either by joy or by sorrow, and many people admired them.

3. Christians, however, according to Paul, do not simply endure suffering; they can actually rejoice in it. Paul gave the reasons for this in vv. 3–5, where he said that suffering produces good fruit in our lives, as follows:

(a) **Endurance:** This word means that, in spite of sufferings, we go on without despairing. The idea occurs in 2.7. A good English translation is 'constancy'.

(b) **Character:** This word has the idea of testing something to see whether it is true, or genuine. If it passes the test, it is 'proved' or 'approved'. 'Character' here means 'approvedness'—but there is no suitable English translation of it. The idea occurs in James 1.3, 12 and 1 Peter 1.7.

(c) **Hope:** See above. As a result of these experiences, we get more confidence for the future. Having 'passed the test', we can be confident of coming successfully through further sufferings.

(d) **Does not disappoint us:** Paul meant that our hope is not in vain. We can be sure of final success, because all this work in our lives is being done by God Himself, through His Spirit. Although we alone could easily be defeated by our troubles, God cannot be defeated. Many people who are not Christians can derive benefits from sufferings, but only Christians can truly say 'hope does not disappoint us'—and in this respect they are different from everyone else in the world.

All these steps are very much like those which an athlete follows as he trains for an important race, and Paul often used the picture of the athlete as an illustration of the Christian life. (See 1 Cor. 9.25–27; 2 Tim. 2.3–5.)

It is usually difficult for a Christian who is suffering to see these steps actually working out in his own experiences. On the contrary, he often feels that he is going backwards, rather than onwards to victory. Indeed, there are few problems greater than that of suffering. (See Additional Note, Suffering, p. 220, and the Notes on pp. 110–114.)

We have seen here that suffering can always result in blessing for our own good. It helps us to know God better; it trains us for serving Him; it leads finally to glory. Paul wanted his readers to *believe* these things, and to rejoice at the way in which God can use even unpleasant things for our good and His glory, just as an athlete uses suffering and pain as a stepping-stone to victory.

Vv. 5–8: The athlete is confident in himself, but the Christian's confidence is in God. Therefore in vv. 5–8 Paul described what God has done for His people. He mentioned the work of God the Father, of God the Son, and of God the Holy Spirit, as follows:

1. **God's love:** This is the basis of everything which we as Christians receive from God. It is important to remember this fact, because unless we do, we shall get wrong ideas about Christ's death for us and about the Holy Spirit's work in us—all of which come from God's love. 'God's love' here means not our love for God, but His love for us and has almost the same meaning as 'grace'. The two chief ways in which we can see God's love are in Christ's death, and through the Holy Spirit.

2. **Christ died:** We can see God's love in many different ways, but when writers in the New Testament described it, they usually spoke of the death of His Son. See John 3.16; 1 John 4.10. Paul mentioned Christ's death in chapter 3; here he showed why it is so important for us. He said three things about Christ's death. Christ died:

(a) **while we were yet helpless:** Men were unable to solve the problem of evil in human life (see p. 41). They could not change their ways and would not return to God. All were defeated by the power of sin.

(b) **at the right time:** Christ's death was not an accident. It happened at a time chosen by God. This was a particularly suitable time because:

(i) It was a time of human need (see (a), above).

(ii) It was a time of opportunity. The world was at peace under

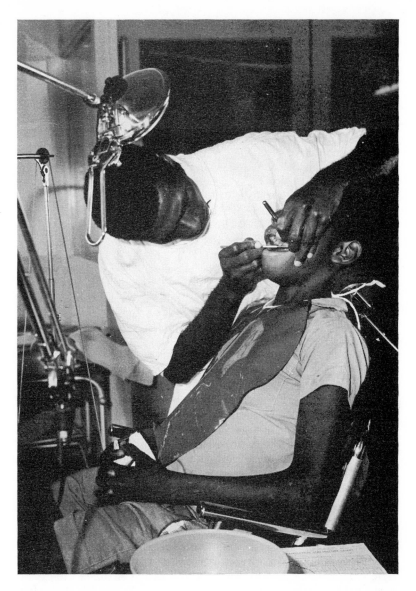

'Suffering can result in blessing . . . God can use even unpleasant things for our good' (p. 66).

Going to the dentist is often painful, but—like this patient in Port Moresby—we are confident that the dentist will help to prevent our getting toothache. What other sorts of pain do we sometimes go through, in confidence that good will result?

Roman rule; there were good roads linking all the main towns; one language was understood everywhere; people were becoming dissatisfied with the old religions and were looking for a new way of life which would satisfy their needs—if possible, they wanted a word from God Himself. Thus it was a good time to spread a new message. Origen, who lived at Alexandria in North Africa about AD 190, wrote, 'God had prepared the peoples for His teaching by causing them all to be united under the power of the one Roman Emperor.'

(iii) It was a time belonging to 'the last days' (see Special Note on p. 122). Paul taught that the 'new age' which the Jews expected at the 'Day of the Lord' had *now* come through Christ. Writers in the New Testament often called this new age 'the last days', because the Gospel brings to an end the old age of living in ignorance of God (see Gal. 4.4; Heb. 1.2; 9.26; 1 Peter 1.20). For Christians, Christ's coming was the most important time in the world's history. It was the right time, i.e. the time intended by God (see 1 Tim. 2.6; Tit. 1.3; Mark 1.15).

(c) **for the ungodly:** Paul used the following words to describe those whom Christ loved and died for: *ungodly, sinners, enemies.* Human beings do not often love those who are opposed to them. When we love people, we usually do so because there is something in them which attracts us and arouses our love, e.g. righteousness or goodness (v. 7). But God's love is different. Even a father who goes on loving a rebellious son is not an adequate illustration of God's love for us, because (a) the fact that the son is his own child arouses the father's love; (b) Paul never said that human beings are God's own children (although He created us); he taught that we *become* God's children *as a result of* His love for us, shown in Jesus Christ. God's love is therefore different from all kinds of human love. We have turned against Him, and there is nothing in us which can attract Him. But His love is like a spring of water; it flows from Him because this is His nature; He is love. This means that we shall never be able fully to understand God's love. But we can see it by looking at Christ's death on the cross. Because of His death, we need never doubt God's love for us, shown in Jesus Christ (see Additional Note, Sonship, p. 218).

3. **Through the Holy Spirit:** God's love has been *revealed* in the death of His Son *for* us, but we *experience* this love through the work of the Holy Spirit *in* us. Paul said a lot more about the Holy Spirit in chapter 8. Here he simply said that the Spirit lives in us and enables us to experience God's love in our hearts. 'Heart' is the word which Paul often used to describe a person's understanding and feelings, i.e. a person as he truly is.

It is not enough to know *about* God's love. A child who has been deprived of his parents is not helped by seeing how other parents love their children. He needs to experience love himself. For the Christian,

God's love is the most important fact in his life, more important than suffering, more important than comfort in this world. Therefore the Christian rejoices, not in his outward circumstances (which may change), but in God's unchanging love, revealed in the death of God's Son, which he experiences through the continuing work of God's Spirit within him.

Vv. 9–11: Having pointed out two important facts about God's love, i.e. *where* God's love has been most clearly seen, and the *character* of those whom God loves, Paul then went on to describe *how great* is God's love. He did this by means of a contrast between what God has already done and what He is going to do. Paul's aim was to help Christians to be sure that, if they belong to God now, they will be His for ever.

V. 9. Now: See Notes on 3.21, p. 47. In the death of Christ, God has *now* acted to save men from their wrong relationship with Him (described as 'wrath' in 1.18—3.20), and to set them right with Him (described as 'righteousness' in 3.21-31). If this is true, then we have no need to fear the future 'day of wrath' of God's final judgement.

V. 10: If God began to save us when we were rebels and enemies, we can be quite sure that He will complete the work now that we have been made His friends.

Also, if Christ was ready to die for us, He is certainly not going to abandon us now that He is living in heaven in power—especially since this new life of His is a life that we share with Him (see 5.17; 6.4).

V. 11: All this means that the Christian believer can be sure. He need have no doubts about the future. His salvation is certain. We need to understand this teaching, because otherwise we shall not truly rejoice in Christ, but we shall be defeated by troubles and doubts. We can sum up this teaching as follows:

To know what God *has* done for us makes us sure about what He *will* do for us.

To know what God *has* done and *will* do for us makes us rejoice *now*.

Vv. 10, 11. Reconciliation: The word 'reconcile' means to bring two people (or groups of people) into a state of peace. God reconciled us to Himself when He justified us through the death of Christ (5.1). A story which Jesus told can help us to understand this idea: A man is going to worship God, when he remembers that he has wronged his brother. Because of his wrong action, his brother 'has something against him'. He must go at once to say he is sorry and to try to put things right, so that his brother will forgive him. Then there will be peace. The man will be reconciled with his brother. (See Matt. 5.23, 24.)

In the same way, we have wronged God by our sin. God 'has something against' us. We need His forgiveness, so that there may be peace and reconciliation. But there is one big difference between the brother in the story and God. God does not wait for us to come to Him and say we are sorry. God has already acted. He has put away the enmity, through the death of Christ. All that remains for us to do is simply to receive His friendship, the reconciliation. The enmity was caused entirely by men; peace is achieved entirely by God (Eph. 2.14). See Additional Note, Reconciliation, p. 213.

STUDY SUGGESTIONS

WORD STUDY

1. The word 'hope' as used in the Bible does not have exactly the same meaning as the English word 'hope' as it is used nowadays. What is the difference? If you know another language, how would you translate the word 'hope' into that language, so as to bring out its true biblical meaning?

2. ' "Character" here means "approvedness" ' (p. 65). Do you know of a word in any language which means the same as 'approvedness' or 'triedness' or 'testedness'? None of these are good English words. The word 'character' is a good word, but not a clear translation of what Paul meant. Perhaps you know a language which can provide a better translation than English can.

REVIEW OF CONTENT

3. What is the connection between chapter 5 and chapters 1—4?

4. (a) What does this section tell Christians about their new relationship with God?
(b) What is the practical effect on their lives of this new relationship?

5. Write three short sentences to show how God's love for human beings involves the work of (a) the Father; (b) the Son; (c) the Holy Spirit.

6. Make two lists of the blessings which Paul mentioned in 5.1–11; first, those blessings which we experience now, in this life; second, those which we look forward to experiencing afterwards. (Some may occur in both lists.)

7. Give three reasons why the first century AD was a specially suitable time for God to send a new message to mankind.

8. What two reasons did Paul give in v. 10 for his certainty that God would complete the work of salvation which He had already begun?

9. Some people have said that, because of all the misery in the world, they cannot believe in a God who loves men.
(a) How can Paul's teaching in this section help us to answer this?
(b) What chief point would you emphasize in trying to show a person that God truly loves us?

10. Many Christians seem to have no joy in their lives. There can be many reasons for this. What reason does this chapter suggest?

BIBLE

11. The way is open for men to approach God (Rom. 5.2). This is one of the chief ideas of the letter to the Hebrews (see 4.14–16; 7.25; 10.19–22). Of what important Christian activity is this doctrine the basis?

12. 'Now that Christ has dealt with the problem of sin, the enmity is over' (p. 64.) Why does Christ's work result in peace, according to 2 Cor. 5.19? In that verse, which phrase reminds you of Rom. 4.8 and which phrase reminds you of Rom. 5.1b?

13. Which of the following verses describe: (i) sharing God's glory again; (ii) becoming like God again; (iii) the Christian's *present* experience; (iv) his *future* experience?
(a) 1 John 3.2b   (b) 2 Cor. 3.18   (c) Eph. 4.24   (d) Rom. 8.18
(e) Rom. 8.29   (f) John 17.22   (g) John 17.24

14. Romans 5.6, 8, and 10 emphasize (i) the greatness of God's love to us; (ii) the character of those whom God loved; (iii) the greatness of Christ's sufferings for us.
Which of the following verses does the same?
(a) Rom. 8.32   (b) 1 Pet. 2.24   (c) 1 Pet. 3.18

15. Through God's power, evil and suffering have often been used to bring great good to many people. Examples of this are found in Gen. 45.5, 8 and Acts 2.23, 24.
(a) In what way do these two passages show God turning men's evil intentions into good?
(b) Give an example from everyday life of suffering being the means of God's blessing coming to a person.

APPLICATION AND OPINION

16. In what sense, if any, can God be said to be 'against' men? What would you say to a person who said, 'I cannot believe in the Christian faith because it speaks of God being against men'?

17. A Christian living in Africa wrote, 'Life is troublesome and miserable now, but I am going to heaven where everything will be all right.' Do you think this is the right way for a Christian to think? How does the teaching of this section suggest a better way of looking at things?

18. 'The blood of the martyrs is the seed of the Church.' How does Romans 5.1–11 (especially vv. 1–5) help us to understand why the more the Church is persecuted the more it grows?

19. In what ways do you think a Christian's attitude to suffering should differ from that of a non-Christian?

20. Christ died for those who were both helpless and His enemies. Can you think of any similar act of love (in history or in your experience)

which can help us to understand God's love? In what ways is the act you have chosen like God's love, and in what ways is it different?

21. Someone said, 'I think men should follow the practical teaching of Christianity and the example of Jesus, but Christians should stop emphasizing unimportant things like the death of Jesus.' How could Rom. 5.5–8 help you to answer such a person?

5.12–21
The Two Families

OUTLINE

'The change in our lives is a real one. For we have become members of a new family, which has a completely different kind of life. We were in the family of the first man, Adam. We all know how he failed. We share his failure—and its consequences. But Christ came to cancel Adam's failure and to start a new family. Unlike Adam, Christ obeyed God. Just as we shared in Adam's sin, so now we have been given a free share in Christ's obedience. That means friendship with God, and true life.'

INTRODUCTION

In this short section Paul was not describing any particular freedom which Christians have (as he was in the rest of chapters 5—8). He was explaining how *one man* can make such an immense difference to the whole human race. There is a real connection between Christ and mankind, which means that Christ really does bring to an end people's wrong relationship with God, and brings them the new life described in 3.21—5.11. The word 'therefore' (v. 12) links this section with all that has gone before, and shows that its teaching is a very important part of Paul's explanation of the Gospel. It is also the basis of Paul's thought about being 'in Christ', one of his favourite phrases (see Special Note, p. 78).

The theme of these verses is very simple. It is a comparison between Adam and Christ; between Adam's work and Christ's work; between the effects of Adam's work and the effects of Christ's work. Although the teaching is simple (especially in vv. 18, 19, which guide us to the true meaning), many Christians, especially in Western countries, have found it difficult to understand. They tend to think of the human race as a collection of separate individuals who have little relation to one another.

'We have become members of a new family which has a completely different kind of life' (p. 72).

An immigrant worker in France attends a literacy class. To share fully in the life of his new country he needs the skills of reading and writing. What skills, if any, do Christians need, to share fully in the new life which Christ offers?

Jews did not think in this way, nor did Paul. Paul taught that all human beings belong to one another because all are descended from the first man. When Adam rebelled against God, his rebellion was ours; and the consequences of his rebellion affect us too. But now Jesus, unlike Adam, has obeyed God perfectly. If we are related to Him, then His obedience becomes ours.

'In Adam' we sin, we are guilty before God, we die.

'In Christ' we are obedient, we are righteous, we live—in the way God meant us to.

INTERPRETATION AND NOTES

Many scholars have found Paul's thought in v. 12 difficult to understand. Paul was writing about the first man, sin, death, all men. Before we go on to consider what Paul meant, it will be helpful to consider some examples of what other peoples have thought about these subjects:

A. AFRICAN TRADITIONAL THOUGHT

1. *The first man:* Most tribal groups tell their own stories about the first man who lived on earth. For example the Baganda call him 'Kintu'; they say that he was created by God and received life from God. The Yoruba say he gave men their laws and family customs.

2. *All men:* Men receive life from the first man, through their ancestors. Therefore all who belong to the community, both dead and living, belong to one another. People must respect the community and preserve its customs, which are, like life itself, handed down from the first man. Those who act differently, or try to change things, are disowned by the community. One person's action can affect the whole community.

3. *Sin:* Some tribes believe that human beings in some way offended God, and that this has spoilt their relationship with Him (see p. 25). But the offences which people commit against one another—and so against the community as a whole—are normally considered the more serious.

4. *Death:* Men were not originally intended to die. Death is unnatural. The Lamba of Zambia say that God gave His messengers some little bundles to take to the chief of men, who had asked for some seeds to sow. God told them to be sure not to untie one particular bundle, but they were so curious that they did so. Out of the bundle came death, which then spread into the world.

B. JEWISH THOUGHT

1. *The first man:* Adam possessed a glory which came from God Himself (Luke 3.38).

2. *Sin:* Adam's rebellion brought general disorder to the world, which God had created for the sake of men. (See 8.19 and Notes on pp. 111–114).

3. *Death:* Death entered the world as a result of the first man's rebellion.

4. *All men:* Adam represents the real unity of mankind. All Adam's descendants share the guilt of Adam's rebellion. They therefore have to live with the consequences of that rebellion, the chief of which is death.

5. *The new creation:* In addition, the Jews looked forward to a new age when the Messiah would come to remake the world as God had intended it to be. He would cancel the results of Adam's sin.

Much of this teaching can be found in the Apocrypha, e.g. Wisdom 2.23, 24; Ecclesiasticus 25.24; 2 Esdras 3.7, 21, 22; 4.30; 7.11, 29-31, 48 (118); 8.44. These Jewish ideas are very similar to the traditional thought of Africa. They are the background of Paul's teaching in vv. 12-14, which may be summed up as follows:

Vv. 12–14:

1. Adam received God's command, broke it, and died.

2. At that time death entered the world, and reigned not only over Adam but over all.

3. The people who lived between Adam and Moses could not be counted as sinners, because they had not received any particular command, or law, from God, as Adam had. Yet they died. Even young children died. All men suffered the penalty of sin, which is death. Why? They died because they were all involved in the sin of their ancestor, Adam. '*All men sinned*' in Adam—therefore all men die.

Paul meant that Adam is the 'head' of the human race, and therefore what Adam did affects us all. In Northern Ireland the terrorists are only a few, but the whole territory has been affected by them. The pattern of life of the whole population has been changed for several years. Just as the peace-loving people of Ireland have not been able to prevent the terror which surrounds them, so we can do nothing about changing our present state. Notice what Paul has said so far about man's sin:

(a) *All men sinned*, when Adam did . . . *in Adam* (5.12);

(b) We are all *under the power of sin*, inherited *from Adam* (3.9);

(c) We *have all sinned* personally . . . *like Adam* (3.23).

The situation is hopeless. There is no escape. Sin reigns. In 5.14 Paul said that death, too, is like a king over us. This is true in two ways:

(i) Man's life is *always* followed by death.

(ii) Men have lost their life of fellowship with God. The word 'death' indicates a wrong relationship with God (see Additional Note, Life, p. 211). Unless we are set right with God, this wrong relationship will last for ever—this state is called 'the second death', in the Book of Revelation.

Vv. 15–21: But there is hope in **the one who was to come** (v. 14b). Paul did not want to discuss at length the question of Adam. He wanted to write about Christ. By describing Adam as 'a type', Paul showed that Christ is far greater and more important than Adam. In these verses Paul emphasized that Christ:

1. is the True Man, who lived as God intended man should live;
2. rescues us from the ruin into which Adam led us.

Although there is no hope at all, from the human point of view, God has sent a Second Man to be obedient where the First Man was disobedient (see Additional Note, Righteousness (5), p. 216). When Paul started to write v. 12, he was thinking of how Christ's work is *like* Adam's. But when he got to v. 15, he said that in fact what Christ did is far greater than what Adam did (vv. 15–17).

In vv. 18, 19 Paul showed how Adam and Christ are *alike*. These two verses are easy to understand and are a guide to the meaning of the whole section. They show that there are two great families of men— Adam's family and Christ's family. We are all in Adam's family by nature; we share his guilt and his condemnation by God. But Christ's new family is one of grace, and those who are in it share Christ's obedience and have a new standing with God.

At this point (vv. 20, 21) it was necessary for Paul to say something about the law on which most Jews relied, because any Jewish reader would have made the following objection to his teaching: 'In speaking about Adam and Christ, Paul seems to have forgotten the most important person of all, Moses, who brought God's law in order to lead us Jews to God.' But Paul replied that the law could not itself make people good, it could only show up how bad they were. The law had two effects:

1. It pointed out to men what actions were sinful (see Additional Note, Law (3), p. 210).

2. It tempted men to disobey, and made their disobedience all the worse, when they did wrong in spite of having the law to show them what was right (see also pp. 84, 94).

But however many commands God gives, and however much people sin against them, Christ's work is greater than all. By using the words 'came in' Paul meant that the law is not as important as the Jews thought it was. The *law* always leads to *sin*, which leads to *death* (i.e. a wrong relationship with God, or wrath). *Grace* brings *righteousness*, which leads to *life* (i.e. fellowship with God, or peace).

THREE QUESTIONS

1. *Was Adam a real person, just as Christ was?*

(a) Adam does not belong to history in the same way as Jesus of

Nazareth, for we cannot make a historical study of the times when Adam lived.

(b) Human beings, as they exist today, are quite different from animals in many different ways. Scientists are continually discovering more about the ways in which both men and animals have developed since prehistoric times. Many tribes have traditional beliefs about a first man. But we cannot say when the 'first man' came into existence. The name 'Adam' simply means 'man', and the teaching about God and man in the Book of Genesis is equally true, whether we use it to mean one single person or to mean 'the first human beings'.

(c) Whoever the 'first man' was, he certainly could not write about his experiences, and traditions handed down from so long ago can hardly be reliable. But Paul believed that through the writers of Genesis God had told men all they needed to know about these early beginnings.

(d) These stories tell us about man in his relationship with God. We are not in a position either to prove that they are true, or to disprove them (as long as we do not try to use them as a science or history textbook). Our own experience of life, however, does show us that human beings are indeed as the stories describe them.

(e) As man had a beginning, so sin had a beginning. In this sense the first sin must be a historical fact which has affected all men, just as Christ's life and death is a historical fact affecting all men. Therefore many scholars have wanted to describe the stories about Adam as 'pre-history' or 'super-history'.

2. *Did death not exist even before Adam sinned?*
It may be impossible to answer this question, but the following points show what some people have thought about it:

(a) Death is an inescapable fact in the world as we know it.

(b) The traditions of most tribes teach that death is *unnatural* (p. 74). This is probably what the writer of Genesis meant to teach.

(c) Many Jews at the time of Paul taught that if Adam had not sinned, then God would have rewarded him by allowing him to live for ever. The presence of the tree of Life in the garden may suggest this (see Gen. 3.24; Rev. 2.7; 22.14).

(d) What makes death frightening is the fact that human beings usually regard it as unnatural and mysterious, and sometimes as a sign of God's displeasure at man's sin. There may once have been a time when people regarded death simply as a physical event, and did not associate it with any of these rather fearful ideas.

3. *Is it right that individual people should suffer for someone else's wrongdoing?*

(a) This idea is accepted by those who live in tribal societies (p. 25). Perhaps the social pattern of life of such people is more like the way

God intended men to live than the more individualistic pattern of modern urban society.

(b) This individual suffering is in fact a common human experience. Thousands of children in the world starve and even die because their fathers spend money on beer or gambling, instead of on good food for the family.

(c) We should not complain that God deals with men under two 'heads' or 'representatives', for two reasons:

First, no one can say, 'I do not deserve to suffer for Adam's sin', because no one is different from Adam. We are all, in any case, guilty because of our own sin also.

Secondly, God deals with us in exactly the same way when He sets us right with Him. We receive the reward of someone else's obedience, i.e. Christ's. God could have left each person completely to himself; but in that case none of us could be confident of ever being right with Him. It is because of His grace and love for us that he deals with us through two 'representatives'. In this way, anyone can be right with God through Christ, however bad a start in life he may have inherited from his family or circumstances. There is no difference between men, in God's sight.

SPECIAL NOTE D:
IN ADAM—IN CHRIST

In many tribal traditions the first man is believed to be the founding father of the tribe. A man's unity is with his tribe, or family.

The Jews also thought mainly of ther own national unity. Therefore their founding father, Abraham, and their law-giver, Moses, were more important to them than Adam (see Rom. 2 and 4). But they, unlike most peoples, had a definite hope to which they looked forward. This hope was for all who, through circumcision, were the children of Abraham.

Paul did not think chiefly in terms of tribal or national or religious groups. He thought in terms of the whole human race who share a unity which comes from Adam. In Romans 5.12–21, therefore, he emphasized the same point as he did in chapter 3—in God's sight there is no difference between men. All are '*in Adam*' (see p. 3 (e)).

Therefore Christ was, for Paul, not simply Son of David, or a prophet like Moses, or a descendant of Abraham. He *was* all these, i.e. He fulfilled the hopes of the writers of the Old Testament in that He is the expected Davidic King, the Messiah (see Notes, pp. 9, 10). He fulfilled the law given by Moses (see Notes, p. 142). He is the seed of Abraham, in whom we, like Abraham, must believe. But for Paul Christ was primarily the Second (or 'last'—1 Cor. 15.45) Adam. Paul saw that Christ's work was not to establish the Jewish nation or the religion of Israel, but to bring about a *new creation*, and to set up a new family which will include *all mankind*. 'Therefore, if anyone is *in Christ*, he is a new creation' (2 Cor. 5.17). We have here the clue to what Paul meant by 'in Christ':

(a) All people are 'in Adam', because he is their 'head' and they are in his 'family'. What was true of him is true of them (chapter 5).

(b) Through faith, and in baptism, people become 'in Christ'. He is their 'head' and they belong to His new 'family'. What is true of Him is true of them (chapters 5 and 6).

(c) All people can have a living fellowship with Him (chapter 8).

If this short section only of Paul's writings had been recorded, we might perhaps think that Paul believed that in the end *everyone* will be in Christ and right with God (see v. 18). But his constant emphasis on the need to have faith shows that this was not his teaching. However, by writing 'all men' in v. 18b, he *did* teach that:

1. *All* who are in Christ are right with God;

2. *All sorts* of men are in Christ, without any human distinctions.

STUDY SUGGESTIONS

REVIEW OF CONTENT

1. What do people receive from their connection (a) with Adam, by nature; (b) with Christ, through faith in Him? Use words which occur in 5.12–21 and list your answers in two columns, (a) and (b), as pairs of opposites.

2. How is it that one man, Jesus, can be of such importance for all men?

3. What relationship do all human beings have with one another?

4. (a) What are the differences and similarities between what Adam did and what Jesus did?
   (b) How did Jesus cancel out the failure of Adam and ourselves?

BIBLE

5. Who shared the guilt of Achan's sin as described in Joshua 7? Who sinned? Who suffered? Who did God say had sinned?

6. The Jews of Paul's time held certain beliefs about (i) the first man, (ii) sin, (iii) death, (iv) all men, (v) the new creation (see pp. 74, 75). Which of these Jewish beliefs is mentioned in each of the following five groups of verses?
   (a) Gen. 2.17; 5.5, 8, 11   (b) Gen. 3.17–19; Rom. 8.20–22
   (c) Gen. 5.1; Psalm 8.5; Luke 3.38 (d) Gen. 5.3; 1 Cor. 15.22a
   (e) Isa. 11.6–9; 2 Pet. 3.13

7. 'Death spread to all men' (Rom. 5.12). In what two ways does

death rule over men? How are these two ways described in (a) Gen.
3.23, 24; (b) Psalm 90.9, 10? Which of these two ways did writers
in the Bible regard as being the more serious? See Rev. 21.8 and
20.6.

8. Which of the following passages emphasize that Israel is God's
chosen people, and which show that all men have a unity which
comes from God the Creator?
(a) Matt. 1.1, 2, 16 (b) Luke 3.23, 38 (c) John 8.33 (d) Acts
17.26

9. In what ways are people 'one with' Jesus according to His teaching
in the following passages? (a) Matt. 18.20 (b) 25.40, 45 (c) John
15.4, 5

APPLICATION, OPINION, AND RESEARCH

10. '(Men) will . . . reign in life' (Rom. 5.17).
(a) In what ways do you think that God originally intended men
to 'reign'? (See Gen. 1.28; 2.19, 20; Psalm 8.6–8.)
(b) In what ways does it seem to you that men have lost their power
to reign? Give examples from everyday life.

11. What, if any, traditional beliefs do you know of on the subject of:
(a) the first man (b) sin (c) death (d) all men (see p. 74).

12. Give some present-day examples of how a group of people was
involved in the consequences of someone else's action—either
good or bad.

13. A Jewish tailor in east London shouted to two Christians who were
passing his shop, 'You worship the same God as we do. Let's join
together; then we can do some good in the world. Just forget about
your Jesus Christ. He is the cause of all the trouble.' What reply
would you give to this man?

14. 'Westerners tend to think of the human race as a collection of
separate individuals . . . Paul taught that all human beings belong
to one another' (p. 72, 74).
(a) Give examples from the world today to support the first part of
that statement.
(b) What is the understanding of your own people on the subject?
(c) In what ways, if any, do you think people's understanding on
this subject affects (i) their relationship with other human beings,
(ii) their relationship with God?

6.1–23
Free From Sin

OUTLINE

'Some people misunderstand this good news about a new life. They say that if God forgives us freely, then we can live as we like. But they do not know what it means to be "in Christ". It means that what happened to Christ has happened also to us. He died on the cross—we also died, we were buried, we have been raised with Him to a new kind of life, as our baptism shows us. We are not what we were. Now we belong to God, not to sin. Sin, which used to control us without our realizing it, has been conquered. Christians need to know this and to fight against anything of sin which remains in them.'

INTRODUCTION

This chapter is connected with the previous section in three ways, as follows:

1. The question in 6.1 arises from the teaching in 5.20b: 'if God gives His grace to sinners (5.20), should we not sin more, so as to gain more grace?' In chapter 6 Paul corrected this misunderstanding of his teaching (which he had already briefly mentioned in 3.8). Thus 5.20b is a *Link Signpost* pointing forward to chapter 6.

2. 5.12–21 gave the basis of Paul's teaching about being 'in Christ'. This teaching is more fully explained in chapter 6. If we had not read chapter 5, we should find chapter 6 difficult to understand.

3. In 5.15–19, we saw that Christ set up a new family. Those who are in His family are 'a new creation' (see p. 79). The old state, 'in Adam', is finished. In chapter 6 Paul described this fact by saying, 'our old self was crucified', and 'we have died'. But he also said that we share the life of the risen Christ (v. 4), and are 'alive to God' (v. 11). As we shared sin and condemnation with Adam, so now we share death and new life with Christ.

The words 'died to sin' are Paul's *Theme Signpost* for chapter 6. They show that Paul was going to explain the second freedom which a Christian has, i.e. freedom from sin. This is a very important subject for anyone who want to live as a Christian, but many Christians have found it difficult to understand. The chief divisions of this chapter are as follows:

V. 1: Paul began by asking a question.

Vv. 2–10: He then answered the question by describing what has happened to every Christian. In these verses Paul was not saying what

Christians *should* be like; he was describing what Christians *are* like.

V. 11: Our first duty is to understand these facts about ourselves in Christ.

Vv. 12–14: Our second duty is to live the kind of life which is suitable for the kind of people we now are.

Vv. 15–23: This can be described in one way as a life of freedom, and in another way as a life of slavery.

INTERPRETATION AND NOTES

The question arises from what Paul said in 5.20b. Perhaps Paul had been asked this question many times. There were three groups of people who might have asked it: each group having a different idea of what sin is.

(a) Christians, who thought that they were now free to live as they liked, because their right relationship with God was a free gift which they could neither gain nor lose by anything which they did.

(b) A few people who actually thought it was good to sin, because then they could repent often, and so receive more of God's grace.

(c) Paul's opponents, who said that Paul's teaching must be wrong, because it offered freely what people ought to earn through keeping the law. They thought that Paul's teaching took away any reason for obeying God's law.

The answer which Paul gave is an explanation of his teaching about being in Christ. This explanation has four parts:

1. (V. 2): A one-sentence answer: *we died to sin.* Our bodies did not die, but we died as far as sin is concerned. (Remember that 'sin' means going against God.) Our old relationship with sin came to an end. If a man dies, he can no longer continue to have his old relationship with those who are left alive—this is why death causes so much grief. We who died cannot continue in the old relationship which we had with sin. 'How can we?' asked Paul. He meant that, because the old life has come to an end, it is unthinkable for us to go on 'against God'.

2. (Vv. 3–5): *How we died:* by being united to Christ in baptism. Paul meant that our baptism was (a) the *time* of our death, and (b) the *sign* of our death. When we shared Christ's death and resurrection in our baptism, and through faith, then our old life came to an end. See Additional Note, Baptism, p. 202.

V. 4. Glory: This word may mean the same as 'power' here, but by using this 'eschatological' word, Paul was saying that in Christ the new age has come (see p. 122).

V. 5. Shall be united: Paul was still speaking of the new life which we have *now* in union with Christ. He used the future tense in order to show that this new life is a sure consequence, which always results from our dying with Christ.

3. (Vv. 6–8a, 10a). *The meaning of dying with Christ.* Scholars have given different interpretations of these verses. They are not easy to understand, but the explanation given below emphasizes the main points which Paul made. There is room for differences of opinion on some of the smaller points of detail.

V. 6: Paul said there are three distinct stages in our victory over sin. Stage 1 results in stage 2, and stage 2 results in stage 3, as follows:

Stage 1: **Our old self was crucified with Him.** 'Our old self' is what we were in the past. This was described in various ways in the preceding chapters, e.g.:

We *were* under wrath; in a wrong relationship with God; His enemies; in Adam; guilty; condemned; ruled by death.

But if we belong to Christ, this 'old self' is dead; it has come to an end. This, too, was described by Paul in the preceding chapters:

We *are* at peace with God; in a right relationship with Him; His friends; in Christ; righteous; justified; alive.

Through our union with Christ, therefore, 'our old self' no longer exists. We are not (and never can be again) what we were. We died; we were buried. See Special Note, p. 89.

Stage 2: **So that the sinful body might be destroyed.** This is the result of stage 1. 'The sinful body' is the sinful nature which lives in our bodies and uses them. It is the same as 'the power of sin' (see p. 218, 2), and is like a king, ruling over all men. Paul probably thought of this power of sin as one of the results of our guilt in Adam, so that the way to destroy it is by removing that guilt and setting us right with God (see stage 3).

Stage 3: **and we might no longer be enslaved to sin.** This is the result of stage 2. If the power of sin is destroyed, then we shall no longer be ruled by it. Our lives will not be dominated by sin (see v. 14).

This verse is difficult, but important. We often think of sin as wrong actions, but it is far more than that. Wrong actions come from sin's power which rules us, and sin's power rules us because we are guilty before God. There are many examples from daily life which show that this is true:

(a) A thief who has killed someone will often be ready to kill others, because he knows that he is guilty in any case.

(b) If you keep telling a child that he is a certain kind of person—e.g. shy, or clever at handwork—then he will probably grow up to be that kind of person.

(c) John Bunyan wrote that he felt on one occasion, before he came to trust in Christ, that he was guilty and condemned by God; therefore he 'decided to go on in sin . . . for if I must be condemned, I would as soon be condemned for many sins as be condemned for a few.'

(d) The same idea is found in Romans 7.8, 9 (see also 1 Cor. 15.56).

The law shows us that we have done wrong, but in doing so it actually stirs us up to more wrong-doing. A man who knows he is guilty will go on doing wrong. It has been written that 'sin cannot be conquered in the life until it is first pardoned in the conscience'. Paul knew that the first step in conquering sin is for us to accept God's forgiveness, and to realize that we are right with Him, and 'not guilty' (see v. 11). The three stages of v. 6 can therefore be set out as follows:

	1. Our status	2. Our state	3. Our actions
In the past	we were guilty in Adam	under sin's power	we sinned
But now	we are crucified	sin's power destroyed	slavery to sin ended

V. 7: Paul was using here the language of the law-court. If a man is found guilty of theft in a court of law, he can become a free man again only by paying his fine, or by serving his sentence in gaol. But we are guilty of breaking God's law, which says, 'the soul that sins shall die' (see 6.23). The only way to become free is by dying. That is exactly what has happened to us in Christ. We have been united with Him in His death. He did not only die instead of us as our substitute—he died also as our representative. His death is ours also. Therefore if a Christian should be accused (by another person or by his own conscience) of being a sinner, he can answer, 'Yes, I am, but I have paid the penalty of sin, because I have died, together with Christ. I am now right with God.' Just as no British colonial officer can any longer give orders to a Nigerian citizen, because the colony of Nigeria no longer exists, so sin can no longer have any claim on us, because our old self has died, and we are free from sin.

What is the meaning of 'to die to sin' (vv. 2, 10, 11)?

(a) It cannot mean that we are set free from the influence of sin, for we are not.

(b) It cannot mean that we are set free from actually sinning, for we are not.

(c) It must mean that we are free from the guilt, and from the penalty of sin which is separation from God, even though we still suffer many of its consequences in this life. Christ 'died to sin' in the sense that He bore human sin and its severest consequences on the cross—and we share in His death. This fits in with what we have said about being 'not guilty' and right with God.

4. (Vv. 8b–10) *The meaning of being risen with Christ.* As we have seen we can only be set free from sin by dying. But if we die, we are in no position to enjoy our freedom. Yet Christ did not only die; He rose. As we shared His death, so we share His new life. Guilt, wrath,

and enmity are finished; we now 'live to God', i.e. we have fellowship and a right relationship with Him. In the past our life was 'against God'; now it is for Him. We have not achieved this ourselves; it all comes from what Christ has achieved and from our union with Him.

In his letters, Paul considered our union with Christ from three different points of view:

(a) In our own experience, we were united with Christ at the time when we believed in Him and were baptized (Rom. 6.4; Col. 2.12).

(b) When Christ died on the cross, and rose again, all those who belong to Him (i.e. His new family) were, in a sense, there with Him (Rom. 6.6; Gal. 6.14).

(c) In the Father's purpose and plan, we were united with Christ before the world was created (Eph. 1.4). Paul did not mention this idea in chapter 6, but see 8.29.

V. 8. We shall live with him. See v. 5b. We truly live with Christ *now*; we shall experience this life in an even fuller way when out bodies are raised from the dead.

Our first duty is to understand what has happened to us. 'Consider' (v. 11) means the same as 'reckon' (4.3). If we consider our weaknesses, our failures, and our feelings, we might think that we are no different from what we were. Certainly it does not *seem* as if we are dead and risen! But Paul wanted his readers to consider Christ, rather than themselves, and to *realize* that in Christ our condition is indeed different. Paul meant, 'First of all *understand* this fact.'

In all his letters, Paul emphasized the importance of the mind, or the understanding:

(a) Men's *thinking* went wrong when they turned against God (Rom. 1.21, 22).

(b) Men come to have faith in Christ through *thinking* about Him (Rom. 6.17).

(c) When men become Christians, their *minds* are renewed (Rom. 12.2).

(d) Christians' first duty is to *understand* what they are in Christ (Rom. 6.11).

In writing like this, Paul was not referring to clever or scholarly people. There were very few such people in the Churches to which Paul wrote. Paul wanted *all* Christians to use their minds, because what we *feel* like is less important than what we are. Therefore the chief parts of Paul's letters consist of explanations of what Christians are. If we are defeated by sin in our lives, one of the chief reasons may be that we have never really understood what it means to have died and to have a new life together with Christ. If this is so, Paul's writings can help us.

Our second duty is to make sure that our behaviour matches our new life. Paul's teaching is always followed by a command. When we have understood what we are, we must then live like it. In vv. 12–14, Paul was saying, '*Be what you are!*' Tanzanians are now free from foreign rule; therefore 'Uhuru' (freedom) is the first word of the country's motto. But President Nyerere has added another word to it—'Work'. Freedom is the basis of Tanzania's new life, but the only way to maintain the new life is if everybody works. The nation's leaders tell the people that much of the work that was done in the past benefited foreigners, but that now they have freedom, they must work in a different way—for their new country: Freedom and Work.

Now that we belong to God, we must serve Him. In the past our bodies were under sin's control (see p. 83); now, in Christ, the rule of sin is over and we live to God. We should make sure that our 'members' (i.e. every part of us) behave accordingly. Two illustrations can help us to understand Paul's meaning:

(a) A mother may say to her son, if she sees him behaving childishly, 'Don't be a baby; be your age.' She means, 'You are not a baby; do not behave like one; let your behaviour match the age you really are.'

(b) A young woman was married, but continued to spend much time at her father's house. Her friends told her, 'Now you are married; you are different; therefore you must live a different kind of life—with your husband, as a married woman.'

V. 14. Sin will have no dominion: This is a promise that sin will not rule over us like a king. There is no promise here that we shall not be tempted, or that we shall never sin. But now, through Christ, God, not sin, is our king. Paul showed in chapters 7 and 8 how this works out in our experience.

Not under law but under grace. See Additional Note, Grace (2), p. 209. Paul went on to explain our relationship to the law at greater length in chapter 7.

Freedom and Slavery. Paul began this section with another question. This question is similar to the one in v. 1, but it emphasizes the law: 'If we are free from God's law, does this not mean that we are free to sin?' Paul answered his question as follows:

(a) Complete freedom is an impossibility (v. 16). Tanzanians are now free—but they are not free to behave as they like. Their freedom means freedom from foreign rulers.

(b) Christians are like slaves whom Christ has set free. Because they have agreed to be bought by Him and to belong to Him, they are free from the service of their old master, sin. To serve Christ is to serve righteousness (vv. 17, 18).

(c) This comparison with slavery is not an exact or scientific description; it is a word-picture drawn from human life (v. 19a).

(d) Paul summed up his teaching in v. 19b. He had shown how sin increases in the world (ch. 1), but the Christian should increase in

' "Sin will have no dominion over you"—this is a promise that sin will not rule over us like a king' (Rom. 6.14 and p. 86).

When Botswana secured its independence the Union Jack was lowered to show that the British protectorate government no longer ruled there. In what ways is a Christian's 'independence' from sin like, and unlike, a country's independence from colonial or other alien rulers?

righteousness. The word 'sanctification' here is the opposite of iniquity and means a life pleasing to God.

(e) In vv. 20–23 Paul described in detail the contrast between the old and the new slavery. In each kind of slavery there is (a) a master, (b) a freedom, (c) a return (i.e. the immediate result, or profit, which the slave gets), and (d) an end (i.e. the final result).

V. 17: Although the way in which a person comes to faith in Christ will always be a mystery, this verse can help us to understand something of how it happens, and so help us to fulfil our task of presenting the Gospel to men. Paul mentioned four stages in the experience of becoming a Christian:

1. You were slaves of sin.

2. You were handed over ('committed') to the teaching.

3. You heard and understood the teaching ('standard' means 'pattern' or 'form').

4. You obeyed the teaching from the heart.

The order in which these stages take place is important and teaches us the following lessons:

(a) A person cannot 'decide' to believe on his own. He does so only if God works in him first and 'commits' him to the teaching of the Gospel, which has power to draw out his faith (1.16).

(b) Teaching should be given before anyone decides to become a Christian. It is not right to appeal to people to 'decide for Christ', unless we have first explained Christ to them in a way they can understand.

(c) To have strong feelings ('from the *heart*') about Christ will very likely form part of a person's experience of conversion. But this is not in itself conversion. We are called not to feel, but to respond in obedience to the Gospel. This is an act of our will. Without it there can be no conversion. See Additional Note, Obedience, p. 213.

SPECIAL NOTE E:
THE OLD MAN AND THE NEW MAN:
NEW TESTAMENT TEACHING

This was one of Paul's favourite themes, and nearly all the New Testament writers dealt with the subject, although they describe it in various ways, e.g. as opposite.

In Ephesians 4.22, 24 the context shows that Paul was not telling his Christian readers to do something; he was describing the truth which they were taught when they became Christians, i.e. they put off the old nature and put on the new nature. The words in 2 Timothy 2.11 are probably not Paul's own, but come from an early Christian 'confession', or statement of belief. Thus we see that Paul's teaching was the same as that of other Christian leaders in New Testament times. This teaching probably originated in the sayings of Jesus Himself about becoming His disciple. To 'take up the cross' meant to be like a man

Gal. 2.20	I have been crucified with Christ.	Christ lives in me.
Gal. 5.24	We have crucified the flesh.	We live by the Spirit.
Gal. 6.14,15	I have been crucified to the world.	A new creation.
2 Cor. 5.14,15	All have died.	Those who live, live for him.
2 Cor. 5.17	The old has passed away.	A new creation in Christ. Behold the new has come.
Col. 2.12	You were buried with him in baptism.	You were raised with him through faith.
Col. 3.1,3		You have been raised with Christ.
Col. 3.9,10	You have put off the old nature.	You have put on the new nature.
Eph. 4.22,24	(that you) put off your old nature.	And put on the new nature.
2 Tim. 2.11	If we have died with him.	We shall also live with him.
1 Pet. 2.24	That we might die to sin.	And live to righteousness.
Mark 8.34	Let him deny himself and take up his cross.	And follow me.
Luke 14.27	Whoever does not bear his own cross.	And come after me.

condemned to death. A man who was seen carrying a cross through the streets was regarded as already dead. The same idea is present in the words 'deny himself'. It means to refuse or to say 'No' to ourselves and our old life. On the other hand, to 'follow' or 'come after' Jesus means to say 'Yes' to Him, and to live for Him and with Him. Jesus was saying that discipleship means the end of the old life and the beginning of a new one with Him. Paul's teaching is the same.

STUDY SUGGESTIONS

WORD STUDY

1. Which two of the following phrases mean nearly the same as 'consider yourselves' (6.11)?
    (a) think that you are (b) reckon yourselves (c) show that you are (d) pretend to be (e) realize that you are

REVIEW OF CONTENT

2. Do you think that the 'some people' of whom Paul spoke in 3.8 were right in their accusation against him? Do you think chapter 6 is a complete answer to the accusation they made?
3. (a) What does it mean to be 'in Christ'?

(b) What difference does being 'in Christ' make to the way people behave?

4. (a) What is the Christian's relationship with sin?

(b) What should a Christian do to gain victory over sin?

5. Which of the following is the best explanation of being 'dead to sin'? Give reasons for your answer.

(a) Sin holds no attraction for us.

(b) Although we are tempted, we do not now sin.

(c) We are no longer in a position of being guilty sinners.

6. Why was Paul careful not to baptize his converts himself? (See 1 Cor. 1.13, 15.) What light does this throw on the meaning and importance of Christian baptism? (See also 1 Cor. 10.2.)

7. 'You were slaves of sin' (6.17). In what ways is this true of a man before he becomes a Christian? (See Luke 16.13; John 8.34.)

8. 'Complete freedom is an impossibility' (p. 86). In what ways is the Christian free? List some of the things which limit our freedom. See Matthew 12.43.

BIBLE

9. Three different ideas about sin, all of them false, are mentioned on p. 82. Which of these ideas is referred to in each of the following:

(a) Rom. 3.8a   (b) Rom. 3.31a   (c) 1 Pet. 2.16

10. The death, burial, resurrection, ascension, and glory of Jesus are mentioned on p. 202, Baptism (4). Which of these experiences do we share with Him, according to each of the following?

(a) 2 Tim. 2.11   (b) Col. 2.12   (c) Eph. 2.6   (d) Rom. 8.30

11. 'Paul emphasized the importance of the mind' (p. 85). What four different points about men's minds (i.e. their 'hearts', or understanding) are made in the following verses?

(a) Acts 16.14;   (b) 2 Cor. 4.4;   (c) Eph. 1.18,19;   (d) Col. 3.10

12. List some of the ways in which a Christian can 'increase in righteousness', according to 2 Cor. 3.16–18; Eph. 4.11–16; and Phil. 3.12–16.

13. According to 6.17 a person (a) only believes if God works in him first; (b) needs to receive teaching before trusting in Christ; (c) is converted when he responds in obedience to the Gospel (p. 88). What practical differences will these facts make to the way in which we present the Gospel to others?

The following passages may help you to answer: (a) 2 Tim. 2.25; 2 Thess. 3.1. (b) Acts 17.2, 3, 17; 18.4, 11. (c) 2 Cor. 4.2, 5; Col. 4.3, 4.

14. 'Baptism *alone* . . . cannot unite a person to Jesus.' 'If baptism is unobtainable . . . a man who has faith in Christ is truly united with Him.' How are these two statements supported by (a) the story of

Simon Magus (Acts 8.13, 21, 23); (b) Jesus's last commission (Matt. 28.19); (c) the penitent thief (Luke 23.43)?

15. What light do the following verses throw on the connection between faith and baptism? Acts 2.38, 41; 16.31, 33; 22.16; Gal. 3.26, 27; Col. 2.12

APPLICATION, OPINION, AND RESEARCH

16. In 6.23 why do you think Paul did not say 'the wages of God is eternal life'?
17. 'Do you know . . .?' (6.3); 'We know . . .' (6.6). Paul expected his readers to be familiar with this teaching about having died and risen with Christ. Are Christians today familiar with it? Ask some of them, and find out. Is this teaching often given in your Church? Do you think people understand it? What difference, if any, do you think it might make to the life of the Church if this teaching were emphasized more?
18. How long has your country had political independence? In what ways, if any, can this independence be used as an illustration of our freedom in Christ?
19. What would you reply to someone who said: (a)'It is too difficult to be a Christian, because you have to spend all your time fighting against sin. I should very soon be defeated and discouraged. Christianity makes too many demands on you'? (b) 'Being a Christian is too easy, you just let God do everything. Even if you sin, He forgives you. I want a religion which is more of a challenge'?

7.1-25
Free from Law

OUTLINE

'We have died not only to sin but also to the law. This means that we no longer try to get right with God through obeying His law, because we are already right with Him through Jesus Christ. But I do not mean to say that the law is bad in any way—only that it never helped me to conquer sin. It only exposed the evil in my life, condemned it, and even increased it! Even now I know that evil is still present in me. But, because I love God's law, I hate evil and fight against it all the time—thanks to Jesus Christ, to whom I really belong! And He will deliver me from it completely in the end.'

INTRODUCTION

This chapter is closely connected with chapter 6, for it explains the words 'you are not under law' (6.14). 6.14 is thus a *Link Signpost* pointing forward to the theme of chapter 7. Paul began chapter 7 with an illustration from human law (vv. 1–3), then at once set up his *Theme Signpost* in v. 4—'died to the law'. God's law condemns us because we have broken it, but now that we belong to Christ we are right with God apart from the law. We are therefore free from its condemnation, i.e. 'not under law'.

This teaching is not difficult to understand, but it does raise one problem. If Christ sets us free from the law, it seems as if the law is evil, like sin, or as if it is the result of evil, like wrath or death. Therefore Paul added two paragraphs to show that the law is good:

1. In vv. 7–13 he showed, from his own experience of trying to keep God's law, that it is not the law which is evil, but our sin.

2. In vv. 14–25 he used vivid language to show that God's law still affects him. Although he is free from it as a way of earning God's approval, it is still an important part of his life. It is, in fact, more important to him than it was before he became a Christian, because he now loves it and *wants* to keep it. But he often fails to do so. This is the 'warfare' of the Christian life. It shows that Christians acknowledge the law to be good.

INTERPRETATION

Throughout the history of the world, men of all religions have tried to earn God's approval by doing things which they think will please Him. For example:

1. Martin Luther, when he visited Rome in 1510 several years before he saw the meaning of the Gospel, crawled up the Holy Staircase on his hands and knees, kissing the steps and saying the Lord's Prayer on each step as he climbed. He had been told that such an action would please God and earn a special blessing from Him.

2. Buddhist monks used to travel along the road to their holy city, Lhasa, in Tibet, by means of stretching themselves out in the dust, then getting up and placing their toes in the marks made by their fingers and stretching themselves out again. This laborious method of travel would, they believed, gain for them God's favour.

In a similar way, writers in the Old Testament sometimes suggested that a person could earn God's approval by keeping God's law, but that disobedience would bring punishment and death. Most Jews therefore accepted God's law as the 'way of life' or, if they failed to keep it, as the 'way of death'. Those who think of the law in this way are 'under the law'. Their lives are controlled by its commands, and they fear the punishment which it threatens.

In Romans 7 we find Paul's chief teaching about the law:

AN ILLUSTRATION (VV. I-3)

Paul said that death sets a person free from the law. This can clearly be seen in the case of the law of marriage, well known to both Jews and Gentiles living at Rome. A wife whose husband dies is free from the law which bound her to him; she is free to start a new life with another man. In the same way, Christians are now free from the law; they are free for eternal life with Christ.

THE TEACHING (VV. 4-6)

Jews, and many others, are 'under the law', i.e. they try to gain God's approval by obeying His law. But in fact the law only shows up wrong-doing and punishes it with death. The *law* leads to *sin*, which leads to *death* (v. 5; see also p. 76). But we who belong to Christ have *already* died—with Him; and because He rose from the dead, we share His new life and live for God (v. 4; see also pp. 84, 85). Therefore obeying the law is no longer, for us, the way to God, or the 'way of life'. We have become right with God and we have new life, not through the law but as a gift through Christ.

The law is no longer our master, because

(a) we do not have to obey it in order to live;

(b) we can never be condemned by it, because our righteousness now comes from Christ, not from our own obedience.

We *do* obey the law, or try to (v. 6), but we now do so not in order to *gain* life, but *as a result of* the new life which God has already given us through Christ. In this new life we are led by Christ's Spirit (mentioned in v. 6, but not explained until chapter 8). His Spirit, not the law, enables us to conquer evil in our lives.

AN OBJECTION CONSIDERED (VV. 7-25)

Up to v. 6, Paul had spoken about dying to the law in the same way as he had spoken about dying to sin. He had made the law sound like an enemy, and like something evil. But it is not. God's law is good. In vv. 7-25 Paul demonstrated this by showing, from his own experience, the effects of God's law in people's lives:

1. (vv. 7-13): *Before Paul became a Christian*, he experienced the law in three ways:

(a) It showed him that many of his thoughts and deeds were wrong (vv. 7, 9). Before Paul began to think seriously about God's will for man's life, he thought that he was 'alive', i.e. right with God (see

'The law only shows up wrong-doing and punishes it' (p. 93).

Radar speed-checks in Los Angeles, USA, show when motorists are breaking the limit. Good drivers adapt their speed to traffic conditions, but how many could truthfully say that they *never* disobey the speed regulations?

Additional Note, Life, p. 211). The law showed him that he was in fact sinful and spiritually dead. The law is like the sun which shines in through the windows of a house and reveals the insects and the dirt. At night, by the light of an oil lamp, the house seemed to be quite clean. The sun does not bring the dirt, it only reveals it. The law is also like a plumb-line, which shows the mason that the wall which seemed to be quite straight is really crooked.

(b) The law also increased Paul's sinful desires (vv. 8, 9, 11; see also 5.20; 7.5). When people learn that they are forbidden to do something, they often want to do that very thing. Two boys went to the house of their schoolmaster one night when he was asleep and stole the beer which he kept in his cupboard. They did not like the beer, but they took it because they were forbidden to do so. See also the story on p. 74, para. 4.

(c) The law condemned Paul for his sin (vv. 10, 11b). The law says that those who go against God deserve to die (1.32). Therefore when Paul began to think about God's law in this way, he realized that: (i) He was already condemned by that law and was therefore 'dead', i.e. in a wrong relationship with God. As a Jew he had been given the law, so he could not plead ignorance as an excuse for wrong-doing. (ii) He would be condemned by that law on the day of judgement.

In this passage Paul probably had the following ideas in his mind:

(a) His own experience. He did not say *when* he began to realize that he was a sinner. Perhaps it was at the age of thirteen, when every Jewish boy became a 'Son of the Commandment' and was expected to keep the law. Paul named the Tenth Commandment as the one which convinced him of his sinfulness, perhaps because that commandment is not about wrong deeds but about wrong desires.

(b) The experience of all men. Most people at some time in their lives become conscious of the evil which is within them. A person may go on happily for many years, until he begins to realize that things in his life which he thought were right are really wrong. Sin was in his life all the time, but he sees it clearly only when he begins to think how God wants him to live. See vv. 7, 13, and the examples on pp. 1, 2.

(c) The story of Adam. See question 11 on p. 101.

In this passage, Paul used the *past* tense, and seems to have been speaking of a past experience. He was remembering how he felt before he became a Christian. But in v. 14 he began to use the *present* tense.

2. (Vv. 14–25): *In Paul's Christian life*, the law of God still had a part to play. In these verses, Paul was still saying that evil is in men, not in God's law, and he proved this from his own daily experience. His life was like a battle-field where two forces are at war. He described them as follows:

The Forces of Good	The Forces of Evil
The law (spiritual)	Paul's sinful self
Paul wants to do good	Paul often does evil
Paul hates evil	Sin in Paul does evil
The real Paul loves God's law	Sin in Paul's body defeats him
Paul's mind is on the side of goodness	Paul's body sins

Paul was here describing himself as a man who is a servant of God but who is often defeated in his desire to please God. He has good aims but he cannot achieve them. His mind is on God's side, but his body is weak and defeated. Paul's mind is therefore a strong witness to the fact that God's law is good. (See pp. 98–99 for a discussion of the relationship between mind, body, etc.)

A QUESTION

Most people who read these verses ask, 'Was Paul here describing himself as a Christian, or as he was before his conversion?' This question is, in one sense, unimportant. These verses are not a main part of Paul's teaching. He was only discussing the secondary question of the goodness of the law. Therefore the answer we give to the question does not affect the way in which we understand his teaching. But, in another sense, the question is very important because these verses are a vivid description of how Paul himself thought and felt, and so the reader cannot help asking himself, 'Do I ever feel like this? Is it good to feel like this, or is it a sign that something is wrong with me? How should a Christian feel about these things?' Therefore we must try to answer the question. Here are four possible answers:

1. Perhaps Paul was describing the state of a person who is without Christ and in a wrong relationship with God. This answer seems unlikely to be correct, because Paul's usual teaching was that such men go *against* God. They do not 'delight in the law of God' (7.22), nor do they 'will what is right' (7.18), nor do they 'serve the law of God with their mind' (7.25); on the contrary, they 'cannot submit to God's law' (8.7). In Paul's descriptions of himself before his conversion, there is no sign of the 'conflict' which is evident in these verses.

2. Perhaps Paul was describing the state of a man who has not yet become a Christian, but has already recognized the evil in his life, and has begun to hate it. Although it is true that such a man is aware of conflict in his life, this is probably not the correct answer, for two reasons:

(a) The words 'no longer' (vv. 17, 20) show that a change has taken place in this man. In the past *he* sinned, for it was his nature to do so. But now his old self has been crucified, and now if he sins, 'it is no longer' *he* (i.e. 'his inmost self', v. 22) that sins, but the remains of sin which are still in him. Sin is now against his nature because he is a new man. This, therefore, is probably a description of a Christian person.

(b) In v. 14 Paul began to use the present tense. Therefore he was probably describing himself as a Christian.

3. Perhaps Paul was describing the state of a Christian as he is in his worst moments, i.e. when he forgets that he belongs to Christ, has Christ's Spirit, and is a child of God. This answer may be correct, but many of the phrases seem to describe not a Christian's worst moments, but his best moments, e.g.: 'I do not want the evil . . . I want to do what is right . . . I delight in the law of God . . . Thanks be to God . . . I serve the law of God with my mind' (vv. 19, 21, 22, 25).

Therefore, perhaps, none of these three answers is the best one.

4. Paul was describing the normal Christian life (although he was not giving the *whole* truth about it, e.g. he did not mention the Spirit; and he was describing more how a Christian feels and thinks than what he *is* actually like). The following ideas can help us to see this:

(a) The man described in 7.14–25 is just like the Christian described in chapter 8: In his mind he is firmly on the side of the law, which is spiritual (7.14, 25; 8.5). He groans as he longs for his salvation to be complete (7.24; 8.23). He praises God for the hope of this salvation (7.25a; 8.25).

(b) Every true Christian ought to feel like this: He wants, more than anything else, to please God; he hates every kind of evil which remains in his life; he fights against evil and is sorry that he is so often defeated by it; he is so conscious of his failure that he is sometimes near to despair; he rejoices that this conflict will not go on for ever; he knows that Christ will deliver him from evil, sin, and weakness.

(c) The reason for this state of conflict is that a Christian belongs to two worlds (or, two ages) at the same time. He belongs to *this world* where evil, suffering, and death are present, even in his own life—he is *not yet* saved from these things. On the other hand, he belongs to the *new world* where Christ is King—he *already* has righteousness, life, and peace; he is a new man. This is why Paul wrote, 'I do not understand my own actions'; this is why there is this conflict in the life of every Christian. The new and the old fight against one another, and this fact should not surprise us. See Special Note, p. 123. In Galatians 5.17 Paul described this same conflict as follows:

'The flesh (which belongs to the old age) and the Spirit (who belongs to the new age) are opposed to each other, to prevent you from doing what you would (the present conflict of the Christian life).'

Those who belong only to the old age do not experience this conflict;

and we shall not experience it in the age to come. But Christians should expect to experience this conflict now, as Paul did, because they live in both ages. They belong to God, but around them and in them are things which hinder them from serving Him as they want to.

NOTES

Vv. 2, 3: Some scholars have said that Paul's illustration here is a poor one, because in the illustration the husband (who is compared with the law) dies, but in the teaching (v. 4) the Christian (who is compared with the wife) dies. But Paul did not actually compare the husband with the law or the wife with the Christian. He only said that death sets a person free from the law—and his illustration clearly shows this.

V. 4. The body of Christ: Because we have been united with Christ in baptism and through faith, we have died through the death of His body. Because He has also risen, we belong to Him and His new family.

V. 5. Living in the flesh: These words refer to the old life which we lived before we were united with Christ. See Additional Note, Flesh, p. 208.

V. 6. That which holds us captive . . . the old written code: These words describe our former relationship with the law. The law is a terrifying master because:

1. It tells us to do what we cannot succeed in doing (Lev. 18.5).

2. It threatens us with punishment when we do not do it (Deut. 27.26). When our relationship to the law is merely one of obedience or disobedience to a set of rules we can only 'bear fruit for death'.

V. 14. The law is spiritual: Paul meant that the law comes from God and shows us how we can enjoy the full life He wants us to live. It describes the sort of fruit, 'holy and just and good', that we may bear for God in the new life of the Spirit (see vv. 6 and 12).

I am carnal, sold under sin. Paul found that he could not fulfil the 'spiritual' law, because he was a man of flesh ('carnal'), i.e. with a tendency to go against God. He was like a slave, with sin as his master. This is not the whole truth about Paul as a Christian; but he was here describing *how he felt*. He was not using the careful theological language of chapters 6 and 8.

Vv. 17–20. It is no longer I that do it . . . nothing good dwells within me, that is, in my flesh: Most people have no difficulty in thinking of themselves as consisting of two, or even more, parts; and frequently do so. The Greek philosophers found it useful to think of man as consisting of two parts, as follows:

1. A 'higher' part which they called the 'soul' or, sometimes, 'mind'.

2. A 'lower' part which they called the 'body'.

Paul also thought of man as consisting of two parts, but not in the same way as the Greeks. In these verses he was describing himself as a

Christian man, in whom he saw a 'higher' and a 'lower' part, as follows:

1. He called the higher part 'my inmost self' (v. 22), or the 'I' which wants to do good (vv. 17, 20), or 'my mind' (vv. 23, 25), renewed by Christ. These terms refer to the new man in Christ described in 6.4–14 (see p. 89).

2. He called the lower part 'the flesh' (v. 25), or 'sin which dwells within me' (vv. 17–20). This lower part appeared to Paul to be connected with his body (or, his 'members'), and sometimes even to dominate it.

However, though Paul found it useful, when describing what a Christian is like, to think in terms of these two parts, he recognized at the same time that a human being is a unity. He knew that 'I' am always responsible for my sin, yet the same 'I' may truly love God and hate my own sin (compare v. 14 with v. 17). He was not saying, as some Greek philosophers did, that what the body does is bad, and only the things of the mind are good. We serve God with our bodies as well as with our minds. (See 1 Cor. 6.15.)

Vv. 23–25. Law: See Additional Note, Law, p. 210. This word occurs five times in these verses, not always with the same meaning. Paul's meaning was as follows:

In v. 21 he meant 'a principle', i.e. an invariable rule, that *whenever* he wanted to do good, he was tempted to do evil. Because this always happened, he called it a 'law' of his experience.

In v. 22 he meant God's will which he wanted to obey (see also v. 25).

In v. 23 he meant 'principle' on all three occasions when he used the word. He was saying that he could see three principles which operate in his life:

(a) sin, which is always with him, is connected with his body, and draws him away from doing God's will (see also v. 25);

(b) his mind, i.e. he is right with God, loves God, and wants to live for God;

(c) the conflict between (a) and (b) which is always present in his life. This is the Christian life as we live it in this world.

V. 24. Wretched man: From one point of view, the Christian is a wretched man. He is weak, and never fully succeeds in practising what he preaches. Many people despise him for this reason. He even despises himself. But one day he will be victorious, when Jesus Christ will finally release him from everything that draws him away from God. But even now he knows what it is to be victorious through Christ's work in him—though this victory is only partial in this life. In the next chapter Paul went on to speak more about the victories in his life than the defeats, though, as we shall see, the conflict is still clearly present.

99

STUDY SUGGESTIONS

WORD STUDY

1. (i) In what two senses did Paul use the word 'flesh' in Romans?
   (ii) In which of these two senses is it used in each of the following?
      (a) Gal. 1.16   (b) 2.20   (c) 5.16   (d) 6.8
2. The word 'law' in 7.14–25 can mean either 'a principle' or 'God's revealed will'.
   (a) Write a sentence using the word in both senses, to make the meaning clear.
   (b) If you know a language other than English, do the same using two or more different words to translate 'law' which will make the two meanings clear.

REVIEW OF CONTENT

3. What is meant by the phrase 'under the law'? Give examples to support your answer.
4. Paul had a special reason for writing vv. 7–25. What is the one point which he was trying to make in these verses?
5. Someone said, 'What people need to know most is how God wants them to live. If they took more notice of God's rules they would be far better.' What is your opinion? What did Paul say about the effect of 'God's rules' upon men?
6. Why do Christians so often fail to do what they know to be right, and so often do what they know to be wrong?
7. In 5.1 Paul said 'we have peace', but in 7.23 he spoke of 'war'. How can both 'peace' and 'war' be true of the Christian at the same time? (See Matt. 10.34.)

BIBLE

8. 'Most Jews accepted God's law as the "way to life"' (p. 92).
   (a) How was this seen in their behaviour? (See Luke 11.42; 18.9–12; John 7.22, 23.)
   (b) How do these same passages show that the 'way to life' became for them the 'way to death'?
9. (i) In what way, if any, did Jesus reduce the demands of the law, in order to make it easier to keep? (See Matt. 5.17–20, 22, 28, 39–44, 48.)
   (ii) What two things did Jesus do to stop the law from terrifying people in the two ways described on p. 98? (See (a) Gal. 3.12 and Heb. 4.15; (b) Gal. 3.10; 3.13.)
10. 'Paul had spoken about "dying to the law" in the same way in which he had spoken about "dying to sin"' (p. 93). Which

expressions in chapter 6 (about sin) correspond to the following expressions in chapter 7?

(a) 'How we are discharged (i.e. set free) from the law' (v. 6).

(b) 'Dead to that which held us captive' (v. 6).

(c) 'You have died to the law so that you may belong to another . . . bear fruit for God' (v. 4).

11. In what ways was Paul's experience, as described in 7.7–13, similar to the experience of Adam and Eve in Genesis 2 and 3? Notice especially the following words in Romans 7:

Opportunity in the commandment   covetousness   I died   deceived me

12. In the following passages describing a Christian's life which are the words and phrases which refer to conflict?

Luke 12.49–53   1 Cor. 9.24–27   Eph. 6.10–17.

APPLICATION AND OPINION

13. Give examples to show that a command *not* to do something sometimes leads people to do that very thing.

14. Why do you think Paul quoted the Tenth Commandment in v. 7? In your own experience, what especially helped you to recognize the fact of sin in your life?

15. What would you reply to people who said: (a) 'I feel so depressed by my failure to do God's will in my life that I even hate myself at times. Surely a true Christian should not feel like this? Perhaps it shows that I am not a true Christian.'? (b) 'It is wonderful to be a Christian; I have victory over sin every day, and the devil is completely defeated. It is like living in heaven, and nothing ever spoils my happiness.'?

16. Give examples of things which people do today, hoping to gain God's favour. Do you think they *can* gain God's favour in that way?

8.1–17
Free from Death (1)

OUTLINE

'In Christ therefore we are free from our old masters. We can be sure of this from the fact that Christ's Spirit lives within us. It is He who causes us to love God and to hate sin. It is He who gives us true life now, which we shall experience more fully when He raises our bodies from the dead. It is He who assures us that we are God's sons.'

101

INTRODUCTION

In 7.6 Paul mentioned 'the new life of the Spirit' (see p. 93). This was his *Link Signpost*, pointing forward to the theme of chapter 8. Up to chapter 8, he mentioned the Spirit only three times, but never explained its meaning. In chapter 8, he used the word 'Spirit' twenty times, and its meaning becomes clear. It is impossible to describe the life of a Christian properly, without speaking about the Spirit of Christ. This chapter could, therefore, be given the title 'Life in the Spirit'.

Thus Paul's *Theme Signpost* for chapter 8 is 'the Spirit of life in Christ Jesus' (v. 2). The whole chapter describes the new life of the man who is in Christ. This life is under the control of Christ's Spirit. Paul described the work of the Spirit in five paragraphs:

1. The Spirit, not the flesh, controls the Christian (vv. 5–8).

2. The Spirit is the Christian's source of life (vv. 9–11).

3. The Spirit assures Christians that they are God's children (vv. 12–17).

4. The Spirit encourages Christians in suffering by giving them hope (vv. 18–25).

5. The Spirit helps Christians to pray in the right way (vv. 26, 27).

INTERPRETATION AND NOTES

THE STATE OF A MAN IN CHRIST (VV. 1–4)

The word 'therefore' shows that these verses are chiefly a summary of what the Christian has become, as a result of having died to the law (7.6). We have seen what Paul had to say on this subject in earlier chapters. If readers wish to refresh their memories about it, the study questions indicated below will help them to do this.

Vv. 1, 2. Now: See study question 13, p. 54 (see also Notes on 3.21, p. 47). See study questions 2–5, p. 108.

Vv. 3, 4: Here Paul explained how God set us free from the law of sin and death. This too Paul had mentioned earlier, and the study questions indicated will remind us of his teaching about it. There are three steps in his explanation:

1. *What the law could not do:* see study question 6, p. 108.

2. *What 'God has done':* We might expect to read at this point that God set us free by not condemning our sin. But in fact Paul said the opposite—God set us free by 'condemning sin in the flesh'. Paul distinguished three stages in what God did:

(a) **Sending His own Son in the likeness of sinful flesh:** Paul chose his words carefully here (see study question 7 on p. 108).

For sin: Perhaps these words mean 'to deal with the problem of sin'.

Perhaps they mean 'to be a sin-offering', i.e. as a sacrifice to bear men's sin.

(b) **He condemned sin in the flesh:** Sinful men deserve to be condemned. Though Christ was truly man He was not sinful. Yet He bore the condemnation of men's sin at the cross (see pp. 51, 84). Therefore God did condemn our sin in Christ's flesh (or, body).

(c) **In order that the just requirement of the law might be fulfilled in us:** Some scholars think that these words refer to the new way in which a Christian lives ('we serve . . . in the new life of the Spirit', 7.6), and this interpretation may be correct. However, Paul had already taught that no Christian ever fulfils what God's law requires; that Jesus alone did so; and that those who are united with Him share His righteousness. His obedience is ours (5.19; 6.4–11). Therefore Paul was probably thinking here not of how Christians live day by day, but of the fact that God counts us righteous in His Son. In this way the Gospel 'upholds the law' (see note on 3.31 (2), p. 53).

3. *For whom God did it:* These things are true of those 'who walk not according to the flesh but according to the Spirit'. They walk (i.e. live) in this way *as a result of* what God has done for them, not *in order that* He may do it. These words introduce a new idea which prepares us for the teaching about the Spirit in the rest of this chapter. For a full explanation of this new idea, see Additional Notes, Flesh, p. 208; Spirit, p. 219.

THE SPIRIT AND THE FLESH (VV. 5–8)

In these verses Paul showed the difference between those who belong to Christ and those who do not. As we have seen, he was using the words 'Spirit' and 'flesh' to describe these two conditions.

V. 5: The Greek word translated 'live' in this verse really means 'are'. Paul was here saying that you can tell what people are really like by what they think about ('set their minds'), and by the way they behave ('who walk . . .', v. 4b). The person who directs his thoughts to the things of God and behaves as a new man, does so because he belongs to God's new age and has the Spirit, who is the chief blessing of the new age. Those who think and behave as if there were no God, do so because they are 'according to the flesh', i.e. they are 'unspiritual' (Jerusalem Bible); they have not experienced God's new age. In this way Paul described the difference between a person who belongs to Christ and one who does not.

Vv. 6–8: For explanations of the following words, see the pages indicated: Life, p. 19: Death, p. 75; Peace, Hostile (i.e. at enmity), pp. 64, 69, 70. Paul used all these words in explaining the contrast between the life of the old age (in the flesh) and the life of the new age (in the Spirit). See Special Note, pp. 122–123.

V. 8. Cannot please God: Paul had already shown that people who have no knowledge of God's revealed law or of Christ can—and often do—do good (2.14, 15). But here he clearly stated that such people 'cannot please God'. These two statements may seem at first to contradict each other, but Paul's meaning was probably as follows:

1. It was God's will for men that they should not merely perform correct actions, but also perform them in the right way, i.e. out of their love for God and their desire to glorify Him (see 1.21). Jesus's own interpretation of the law (Mark 12.30, 31) shows that this was God's intention.

2. Thus men cannot possibly please God merely by good actions. People frequently do good for wrong motives, e.g. to get God's reward, or, as one scholar has written, to 'gain control over God by paying Him His fee'. St Bernard of Clairvaux was conscious of such wrong motives when he wrote, 'So far from being able to answer for my sins, I cannot even answer for my righteousness!' Actions which may appear outwardly good may not be good at all in the sight of God who knows men's thoughts.

3. When Biafra revolted against the Federal Government of Nigeria, Colonel Ojukwu, Biafra's leader, organized education, medical care, and social services for the people of Biafra. These were good actions, but Ojukwu did not win the approval of the Federal Government for them because he was a rebel against its authority. In the same way, men's outwardly good actions 'cannot please God' as long as men are 'in the flesh', i.e. reject God's rule and authority over them.

THE SPIRIT OF LIFE (VV. 9–11)

Vv. 9, 10a: In these verses Paul used different phrases to describe the one reality of the new life of the Spirit, as follows:

1. To be 'in the Spirit', and to have 'the Spirit in you' (v. 9a).

2. To 'have the Spirit of Christ', and to have 'Christ in you' (vv. 9b, 10a).

3. 'The Spirit', 'the Spirit of God', and 'the Spirit of Christ' (v. 9).

The Church today needs this teaching, because many Christians are uncertain about the relationship between Christ and His Spirit and the Christian believer. Paul's teaching here shows that:

(a) Everyone who has Christ has Christ's Spirit. Therefore receiving the Spirit cannot be a second step in the Christian life which we take *after* receiving Christ.

(b) To become 'in Christ' in baptism, through faith, is to be in the Spirit. Therefore baptism cannot be the sacrament of the forgiveness of our sins only, or of our union with Christ only; it must also be the sacrament of our new life in the Spirit (see 7.6).

(c) A man cannot be 'spiritual', in the New Testament sense of that word, unless he loves and honours Christ, because the Spirit is the Spirit of Christ.

Vv. 10, 11: Paul described the two ways in which the Spirit gives life: (a) He *gives* us life *now* (v. 10); (b) He *will* give us life *in the future* (v. 11). In each verse Paul said something about the body, and something about the Spirit, as follows:

1. **Your bodies** (v. 10) do not in any way change when you become a Christian. You can expect them to fall sick, to be weak, to get old, to die, even to sin, just like everyone else's bodies. This is because, in the body, Christians still live in the old age and still suffer from many of the consequences of human sin.

But *in the future* 'your mortal bodies' (v. 11) will share in the life of the new age, free from death, sin, weakness, and sickness. You can be sure of this because (a) Christ was raised from the dead and you are united to Him; (b) you already possess God's Spirit who assures you that God will do for you all that He has promised. In the same way a young woman looks at the engagement ring on her finger and is assured by it that she is soon going to be married to the man who gave it to her. The ring, which she has already received, 'belongs' to her marriage which has not yet taken place; and so the Spirit belongs to the new age which our bodies have not yet entered, but will enter in the future.

2. **Your spirits** (v. 10)—these words should probably be translated '*the Spirit* is life because of righteousness'. When a person has faith in Christ, he is *immediately* united with Christ, he has His Spirit, he has righteousness, he has life. Although he still lives in the old age, he *now* belongs to the new age of the Spirit.

As for *the future* (v. 11) he has certainty because of the Spirit who dwells in him.

THE SPIRIT OF SONSHIP (VV. 12–17)

1. A child lives his life under his parents' control. It is *right* for him to do this, because he receives food, shelter, clothing, and protection from them.

2. A sensible man decides that it is more *fruitful* for him to work in his fields than to spend all his time in the beer-market. He therefore lives in the way which is most fruitful for him.

Paul gave two similar reasons why Christians should live according to the Spirit:

1. *Because it is right* (v. 12). We receive our life from Him (vv. 10, 11); therefore we are his 'debtors'.

2. *Because it is the most fruitful* way to live (v. 13).

V. 13b: Instead of saying 'if you live according to the Spirit', Paul said, 'if by the Spirit you put to death the deeds of the body'. These words:

(a) tell us *how* to live according to the Spirit;

'When a person has faith in Christ, he belongs to the new age of the Spirit' (p. 105).

Malay youths hailed the 'new age' of freedom when their country gained its independence. What else would independence bring them, besides freedom?

(b) remind us that the Christian life is a conflict in which there are two sides. The Christian is on the winning side, but he has a responsibility to fight (i) by remembering that he has died to sin and lives to God; (ii) by working this out in his life by actually killing ('put to death') the evil thought, word, or deed which he finds readily comes to him. Paul had given similar teaching in 6.11–14, but here in chapter 8 he added the important words 'by the Spirit'. The Christian does not fight alone. The battle is his, but it is also God's. It is important to understand this teaching—it means that we need not despair, because victory is certain ('you will live'). But we must not be idle, because if we are, defeat is certain ('you will die'). The people of Tanganyika rebelled many times against their German rulers, but were defeated partly because different tribal groups tried to fight alone. On the few occasions when they united with one another they were victorious, until disunity again weakened them. Christians, too, should recognize the importance of their union with the Spirit of God in their conflict against evil.

Vv. 14–17: Paul here introduced the idea of sonship and made four points about God's sons:

1. When we fight in this spiritual conflict, we show that we are God's sons (v. 14).

2. There is a connection between having the Spirit and being God's sons, because it is the Spirit who makes us God's sons (v. 15); therefore Paul called Him 'the Spirit of sonship', just as he called Him the Spirit of life in 8.2 because He brings us life.

3. The experience of being God's sons gives us confidence (i.e. the opposite of fear) in our relationship with God (v. 16). We get this confidence directly from Jesus Himself. The Jews never called God 'Abba', because this word was used chiefly by young children, and then only when talking to their own father, with whom they had a close personal relationship. It was like the word 'Daddy'. The Jews did not think it was a suitable name to use when speaking to the Lord God of heaven and earth. But Jesus, God's own Son, usually said 'Abba' when He spoke with God. He also taught his disciples to follow His example and to pray to 'Our Father'. When we do this, it shows that the Spirit is at work in us and that we are God's children. If children are playing together in a quiet street, and a big lorry comes round the corner, each child will at once cry out for its own father, and run to him for safety. It will not run to anyone else. In the same way God's children cry out confidently to Him. Paul was not thinking only of the way in which we repeat 'Our Father' together in Church, but of the way we really feel in times of need.

4. God's sons will receive an inheritance (v. 17). Paul said three things about them:

(a) They share Christ's sonship (see Additional Note, Sonship, p. 218).

(b) They share Christ's suffering (see Additional Note, Suffering, l.c., p. 220).

(c) They will share Christ's glory. This is the meaning of the word 'glorified'. See 5.2 and Additional Note, Glory, p. 208. When the Emperor Claudius adopted Nero as his son (p. 218), Nero had a right to the inheritance. A share in Christ's glory is the certain inheritance of those who have become God's sons through Christ.

STUDY SUGGESTIONS

WORD STUDY

1. The word 'spirit' can refer to man himself (or his mind), or to the power which comes from God. Which of these two meanings does it have in each of the following verses? (a) Ps. 32.2 (b) Isa. 31.3 (c) Acts 10.38 (d) Rom. 1.9

REVIEW OF CONTENT

2. (a) If a man is 'not condemned', which of the following descriptions are true of him?
   Not sinful   not guilty   acquitted   justified   unjust
   (b) What condemns a man before God?
   (c) Why does it condemn Christians no longer?

3. What is the meaning of 'the law' in v. 2?

4. (a) How can a person get free from sin and death?
   (b) What word did Paul regularly use to describe the state of freedom from sin and death?

5. Why is the new principle which controls Christians described as the law of *the Spirit*?

6. (a) What did the law offer to do for men?
   (b) Why was the law unable to do what it offered?
   (c) What did the law actually do to men?
   (d) How can men now obtain what the law offered?

7. Why would it have been *less* accurate if Paul had written in v. 3 either 'in the likeness of flesh' or 'in sinful flesh'? (See Heb. 4.15.) If you can, give examples from the life of Jesus to support your answer.

8. 'Those who are in the flesh cannot please God' (v. 8). Why not?

9. (a) What is the result of living 'according to the flesh'? Is this true of anybody who lives in this way? (See 1 Cor. 6.9–11; Eph. 5.3–10.)
   (b) What is the result of living 'according to the Spirit'?

10. What four gifts, or blessings, of the Spirit are described in vv. 11, 13, 14, 15–16?

BIBLE

11. 'Paul distinguished three stages in what God did' (p. 102). These three stages could be called (a) what Christ was; (b) what He did; (c) what His purpose was in doing it. How are all three stages described in 2 Cor. 5.21?

12. The Spirit is continually at work in the Christian believer. Make a list of the different kinds of work He does in us, according to the following verses: Rom. 8.11, 26; 1 Cor. 12.3, 11, 13; Gal. 5.22, 23. What else can you add to this list?

13. What sort of 'fear' do you think Paul was referring to in 8.15? How does the Spirit deliver Christians from such fear? (See Rom. 7.7–13; Gal. 3.23–26; 1 Jn. 4.18.)

14. (i) In what ways do Christians share Christ's sufferings (see p. 108) according to: (a) Luke 9.23; (b) Mark 10.30; Acts 14.22?
    (ii) What is the final result of sharing His suffering, according to these verses?

15. People have regarded God as 'Father' in three chief ways:
    (a) as their tribal ancestor;
    (b) as in Exod. 4.22 and Hosea 11.1;
    (c) as in Deut. 32.6 and Mal. 2.10.
    In which of these three ways do Christians regard God as their Father?

APPLICATION, OPINION, AND RESEARCH

16. 'Set their minds on the things of the Spirit' (v. 5). What do you think Paul meant by these 'things of the Spirit'.

17. Describe any modern teaching you may have heard about the Holy Spirit which is different from Paul's teaching in vv. 9–11. In what ways is it different?

18. (a) What are the 'deeds of the body' which we are to put to death? Colossians 3.5 names some. Give examples of some others.
    (b) What practical advice would you give about how to put them to death?

19. It is sometimes said that Christians do not speak enough about the Holy Spirit and His work.
    (a) What is your opinion?
    (b) What sort of guidance in speaking about the Holy Spirit do we get from John 15.26 and 16.12–15. (See Additional Note, Spirit, p. 219.)

20. What answer would you give to:
    (a) a Christian who said, 'God has promised victory; therefore I will leave it to Him alone to get the victory over evil in my life'?

(b) a Christian who said, 'The conflict is so tough that I do not think that I shall ever get the victory. I despair of ever reaching heaven'?

8.18–39
Free from Death (2)

OUTLINE

'The fact that we have a new life in Christ does not mean that life has no problems. Like Jesus, we suffer, but in our suffering we have true comfort. First, we look forward confidently to heaven. Secondly, we are always in close touch with God through His Spirit who helps us to pray. Thirdly, we know that God has chosen us, and that He does not change His mind. If we belong to Christ, therefore, we may be sure that nothing will ever cut us off from Him.'

INTRODUCTION

In this second half of chapter 8, Paul discussed the suffering which is present in the world, and offered some help to his readers. All of them were, like us, to some extent faced with this problem. He showed that in suffering Christians have three sources of encouragement: (a) a future hope (vv. 18–25; (b) a present help (vv. 26, 27); (c) the past election of God (vv. 28–30). The chapter closes with a passage which is rather like a hymn, describing how, if God is our friend, nothing can cut us off from His love (vv. 31–39).

INTERPRETATION AND NOTES

THE FUTURE: THE SPIRIT OF HOPE (VV. 18–25)

V. 18. I consider: Paul was not afraid to discuss unpleasant things like suffering. In order to triumph over these things we need first to *consider* them carefully, as Paul did here and in 5.3, so that we may have the right attitude towards them. The Christian should be like a traveller going home, who is prepared to endure many hardships on his journey because (a) he knows his journey will only last for a limited period of time (b) he is thinking of the joyful welcome awaiting him on his arrival home.

Vv. 19–25: Paul encouraged his readers by showing them that their present suffering is only part of the suffering which 'the whole creation' is enduring. They, like creation, can hope for future glory. Such teaching would have been familiar to Paul's Jewish readers.

Many Jews of Paul's time taught that the universe which God had created had become disorderly for two reasons:

(a) When man rebelled against God, the whole creation suffered, just as a whole nation will suffer if the head of the nation does evil.

(b) God punished man's sin, and part of that punishment was the cursing of creation (Gen. 3.17–19), bringing suffering, misery, and death. These Jewish teachers also looked forward to a time when God would renew His creation. This hope was shared by many writers in the Old Testament (see question 10, p. 121), and by Jews who suffered for their faith in the years between the Old and New Testaments. One of them wrote:

'The vine shall yield its fruit ten thousand fold, and on each vine there shall be a thousand branches; and each branch shall produce a thousand clusters; and each cluster produce a thousand grapes; and each grape a cor of wine. And those who have hungered shall rejoice; moreover, also, they shall behold marvels every day.' (The Apocalypse of Baruch, 29.5, written about AD 90.)

See p. 75. Such teaching as this formed the background of Paul's thinking.

Paul's own teaching can be considered under four headings:

1. *The disorder in the world* (vv. 20, 21). Anyone who thinks about the universe can see that it has an orderly pattern. It is equally clear that there is a great deal of disorder in it as well. Paul used two words to describe this disorder:

(a) Futility (i.e. the idea of frustration, or failing to achieve one's aim);

(b) Decay (i.e. the idea of weakness and death).

2. *The cause of this disorder* (v. 20). This verse suggests that Paul held the Jewish view described above, i.e. that this disorder is connected with man's sin and with God's curse. God was ready even to 'subject to futility' what He had created, in order, first to punish man's sin, and then, secondly, to bring men back to the right way ('in hope'). In using the word 'futility', Paul may have been thinking of:

(a) Evil powers which seem to control created things (Acts 14.15; 1 Cor. 12.2; Eph. 6.12). Even today, people are often afraid of the forces of evil, partly because they themselves have turned from the true God, and followed false gods (Rom. 1.21).

(b) Frustration (see 1(a) above). The result of this is that creation cannot attain the purpose for which God intended it. All things were created 'good', but it is often very difficult to see that they are 'good' now. For example, lands which were fertile in the past, and offered the prospect of good harvests for many years, have become desert. Sometimes this results from changes of climate, sometimes from people's

'All things were created good, but it is often very difficult to see that they are good now . . . sometimes this is due to people's selfishness or ignorance; but God has not lost control of the world' (pp. 111, 113).

Children in Minamato, Japan, suffered mercury poisoning in their mother's wombs, because waste from factories was allowed to get into the city's water supply. Tomiko Uemu is 16 years old, but she cannot stand or walk or use her hands, and she is deaf and dumb and blind. She will never get well. But now the poisonous waste is dealt with in other ways: there is hope that no more children will suffer as she does. In what ways, if any, is her suffering (and her mother's) connected with their future safety?

use of destructive weapons, sometimes from their selfishly or ignorantly over-grazing the land with too many cattle, or cutting down too many trees.

3. *The end of this disorder* (vv. 20b–22). Paul knew that God's word of judgement upon creation was not His last word; it was a step on the road to restoring and repairing what had gone wrong. Therefore when God subjected the creation to futility, He did so 'in hope'. God had not lost control of the world; on the contrary, He was going to renew it and had actually begun to do so. In these verses Paul looked forward to:

(a) The freedom and deliverance of creation (v. 21a).

(b) The 'liberty' of Christians (v. 21b). Christians are *already* free from many of the things which troubled them (chs 5—8), but this liberty is *not yet* complete. Paul looked forward to the time when nothing will any longer spoil either the lives of Christians or the creation of God (see Rev. 21.3, 4).

(c) 'The redemption of our bodies' (v. 23b). Paul was here thinking of God's promise that Christians' bodies will share in the final deliverance of the new age (see 8.11 and Notes on p. 105).

(d) 'The revealing of the sons of God . . . glory . . . adoption as sons' (19, 21, 23). At that time we shall share His glory, we shall be like Him, and it will be clear that we are His sons. See Additional Notes, Glory, p. 208, Sonship, p. 219.

4. *Our hope for the future* (vv. 23–25). Throughout this passage Paul had discussed the creation as if it were a person, who can feel pain, disappointment, desire and hope. Paul used a series of word-pictures which indicate hope for the future:

The creation 'waits with eager longing' (v. 19), like the father who looked out for his returning son in Luke 15.20. We also should wait eagerly for the new age.

It 'groans in travail' (v. 22), like a woman who is in pain before she gives birth, but is happy when she thinks of the new baby she will have (see John 16.21). In the same way our present suffering is a sure sign of blessings to come.

We (and the creation) 'wait for' the future 'in hope' (vv. 23, 24). We are just one part of God's whole creation which is moving towards the new age.

We 'have the first fruits of the Spirit' (v. 23). The Jews observed a custom of presenting the first fruits of the harvest to God in the Temple. In doing this they (a) looked forward to the coming harvest (b) showed that the whole harvest really belonged to God. The Jewish teachers of Paul's time looked forward to the coming age as the time when God would pour out His Spirit, as He had promised in Joel 2.28. But Paul knew that God had *already* poured out His Spirit, first on Jesus, then on Jesus's new family. In v. 23 he was saying that God has given us the

Spirit as the first fruits of the new age, to show that (a) for us the new age has already begun; (b) all its blessings belong to us. See Special Note, p. 124.

The value of Paul's teaching for us today can be summed up as follows:

1. Man's rebellion against his Creator affects not only man himself but the world in which he lives. There are countless examples of this (see p. 111, 2), and Paul taught that it had been true since sin came into the world. God intended men to have a leading part in ruling creation for God's glory, but they failed to play their part.

2. God's purpose has not failed. God has already begun to put the situation right, and He still does so by means of man. The Man through whom God has acted is Christ (1 Cor. 15.47–49). Through Him men are set right with God. The creation in its turn will be renewed and share in the glory of the new age which God's children have already begun to enjoy. The chief part of God's creation was man; man also leads the way in God's work of redemption.

3. Paul summed up the aim of chapters 1—11 in 11.32. The whole creation is 'futile' (see Rom. 1.21 and 8.20) until God in His mercy steps in to put things right. This passage is therefore an accurate description of things as they are and of what God is doing to put them right.

4. Many Jews told stories about a perfectly orderly universe before sin came to spoil it, but Paul did not explicitly teach this. He was teaching neither history nor science, as we would think of these subjects today. He was showing his readers why they experience suffering now, and assuring them of God's purpose to deliver them from it in the future.

THE PRESENT HELP: THE SPIRIT OF PRAYER (VV. 26, 27)

In 8.18–25 Paul had told Christians to look forward to blessings which they have *not yet* received. Now he reminded them of a great blessing which they *already* enjoy. They already *have* fellowship with God, as Paul had fully explained in chapters 3—5. He had mentioned in 8.15, 16 how they *experience* this fellowship when they pray. But it is not easy to pray. In vv. 26, 27 Paul was probably thinking of three main difficulties which we experience in prayer:

1. *Our weakness.* This was well expressed by John Bunyan, when he wrote, 'I find that my heart is slow to go to God; and when it does go to Him it does not seem to want to stay with Him; so that very often I am forced in my prayers, first to beg of God that He would take my heart and set it on Himself, and then when it is there, that He would keep it there.' Christians everywhere often find that as soon as they start to pray they are distracted by remembering a letter they ought to write or a job they ought to do. So it may be helpful for us, too, to pray as Bunyan did. We should remember that it is just because we are

114

weak that we need to rely on God in prayer. He has promised the help of His Holy Spirit to those who recognize their weakness.

2. *What we should pray for.* Our weakness is also seen in our ignorance about what we truly need. A small child will reach for a lighted match, not realizing that it will burn him. So we, who do not know the future, nor even God's present plan for us, are like children who need to have their prayers guided and corrected by a loving Father. God has sent the Spirit to do this work in us. Therefore we should not think that prayer is persuading God to do what we want; on the contrary, it is the Spirit in us leading us to ask for the things which God approves. God the Spirit in us prays to God the Father in heaven.

3. *How to pray.* The world is full of books of prayers. Some of these prayers are very beautiful, and can help Christians in their worship together in Church. But Paul's teaching here shows that the words which we use are of secondary importance. Indeed, they are of no importance at all to God. A small child, afraid of the sound of thunder, runs to throw his arms around his mother's knees. He does not need to say any words. In the same way Christians, led by the Spirit, offer prayers 'too deep for words'. God knows what they mean, because God knows both 'the hearts of men' and 'the mind of the Spirit'. In the same way, too, Christians should be ready to turn to God in prayer at any time, bringing to Him all the affairs of their day-to-day life (including those very things which distract them when they pray—see 1, above). A young child chatters to his mother about all the little things which seem important to him. They are important also to her, because *he* is important to her; she is interested in them, because she is interested in him. God wants us to treat Him with a similar freedom and trust.

V. 26. Sighs: This word is similar to that which is translated 'groan' in v. 23. Some people think it refers to speaking in tongues, which was common among the first Christians (1 Cor. 14.5) and also occurs today. More likely it refers to the deep desires and feelings of Christians, which they cannot explain clearly (see 7.15; 8.23).

THE PAST: GOD'S PURPOSE FOR HIS ELECT' (VV. 28-30)

V. 28: There are three ways of translating this verse (see RSV mg), but they all give us the same fundamental meaning. Many people take the attitude to life that 'everything will turn out all right in the end'— often without thinking about the problems which exist. But Paul faced up to the problems, and came to the conclusion, 'We know . . .' (see v. 18).

God works for good: When Paul wrote 'good' here, he was not thinking about our comfort or prosperity or happiness. He was talking about 'man's greatest good', which is salvation, or life with God (see

Additional Note, Salvation, p. 217). In v. 29 he described it as being 'conformed to the image of his Son' (i.e. being like Christ). This is God's purpose for us, and it should be our purpose for ourselves (see 6.11b).

In everything: Most Christians agree that they are travelling along the road to heaven (i.e. towards the good), but regard some things as helping them along that road, and other things as hindering them. But Paul wrote that *everything* helps us along that road. This is a surprising statement, and his meaning was probably as follows:

1. In this whole section he was thinking about suffering. Thus he meant that suffering (which often seems to us to be evil) can help to prepare us for our life with God and to make us more like Christ (see pp. 65, 65).

2. The whole of our life now in this age is a life of tension and conflict. God uses this conflict—and even perhaps the sin against which we fight—to prepare us for the 'good' which He purposes for us.

Three illustrations may help us to see how this can work out in life:

(a) Job was blessed by God. Partly for that reason, he began to experience suffering. He felt that his suffering was an evil and terrible and unjust thing, and he complained bitterly to God. But in the end God spoke to him, and he got to know God in a new way which would not have been possible for him apart from his suffering. Suffering became for Job the way (and the only way) of blessing.

(b) An athlete deliberately suffers pain in the course of his training in order to equip his body for the contest which he hopes to win (see p. 66).

(c) A young student knew that he should serve God, but he decided that he would just live for his own pleasures while he was young, and think about God when he became older. But he fell sick, and the doctors said that he could not get better. He became worse, until he could not leave his bed. All this time his mother nursed him. In his sickness he turned back to Christ, whom he had been trying to avoid for so long, and his mother herself put her trust in Christ. Although he died as a young man, the 'good' was realized in the life of these two people—but as a result of suffering.

Those who love him: Christians cannot always see *how* God is using unpleasant experiences to prepare them for the good. But they believe it to be so. Only those who trust and love God as their own loving Father can accept all that happens to them as His will for them. A man who has been bitten by a mad dog is told by his doctor that he must have injections in his stomach every day for 15 days. If he is wise, he trusts the doctor, follows his advice, and gets better; but some patients find the treatment unpleasant, refuse to trust the doctor's advice, and eventually die in great pain. In the same way it is only the person who

116

turns to God in trust and confidence who can fully experience the blessings which come from suffering.

We know: This knowledge comes from faith. As Paul looked back on his life, he could see that events which at the time appeared to be disasters really worked out for good. If this has been our experience in the past, it gives us confidence for the future. Paul also knew that God was in control of the affairs of the world. He has a purpose in all events—especially He has a purpose for His people (v. 28b).

Who are called according to his purpose. God works for our good, *not* because we love Him, but because our good is 'his purpose', which cannot fail. This is His purpose for us because He loves us, as Paul went on to show in vv. 29, 30.

Vv. 29, 30: God's eternal purpose for His people has five stages:

1. **He foreknew** His people. This does not mean simply that God knew *about* them, nor that He knew what they would do. 'Know' here has the same meaning as in Amos 3.2: 'You only have I known of all the families of the earth.' Clearly God knows *about* all His creatures, but with His people He has a close relationship, and a special love for them. Paul's meaning is therefore that God loved His people before everything—His love is the basis of everything which He does for them (see Eph. 1.5).

2. **He also predestined:** This word means He 'set apart' His people (see p. 118, (b) below). But, in His own purpose, God set apart His people *before* they loved Him; before they started to look for Him; before Christ came to die for them; even before He created the world (see Eph. 1.4; 1 Cor. 2.7).

3. **He also called:** The first two stages took place long ago ('fore-', 'pre-'). Paul then showed how God fulfils His purpose in the lives and experience of human beings now. First, God 'calls' those whom He has set apart (see p. 11). Through the announcement of His good news, God draws them to Himself and they respond by having faith in Jesus (see p. 207. 3).

4. **He also justified:** See Additional Note, Justification, p. 210. See question 6, p. 121. (The order of events is always the same: (i) God calls, (ii) man believes, (iii) God sets the believer right with Himself.)

5. **He also glorified:** This is the final stage in the Christian's experience. It does not take place in this life but in the future (see p. 65, and Additional Note, Glory, p. 208). But instead of writing 'He *will* glorify', Paul used the *past* tense in order to show how certain it is that God will glorify His people—it is as if He has already done it! In the same way, prophets in the Old Testament often used the past tense to indicate the certainty of events which they prophesied would happen in the future.

These five great acts of God show in what way God saves mankind.

They show how God is fulfilling His eternal purpose for us, and they can be a real encouragement to all Christians. From these verses we can learn the following lessons about our salvation:

(a) Our salvation is not a matter of chance, nor does it depend on us. Of course, we respond to the Gospel, and we ourselves believe. But when a Christian looks back over his experience, he knows and sees that God was really doing all the work in him. God Himself led him to faith in Christ.

(b) Our salvation involves our becoming like Christ. No one can be confident of being loved, set apart, and called by God without also being challenged about what he is like in his own life. God did not simply set us apart; He set us apart *to be like His Son*. If we are not beginning to be like Him now, no confidence about our predestination nor hopes for future glory are of any value. Our predestination is to be like Christ; only those who are like Him will share His glory.

(c) Our salvation is the 'good' for which God works, and therefore everything in our lives works towards this end.

(d) Our salvation is a certainty. This chapter shows how a Christian can be sure, and it reminds us that God began laying His plan for us before the world began. and His plan will not be completely fulfilled until after it ends. But it *will* be fulfilled, and our certainty therefore lies in what God has done and is doing—for us and in us.

A HYMN OF ASSURANCE (VV. 31–39)

This section can be divided up into three paragraphs, with a closing summary. In each paragraph Paul first reminded his readers of what God had done, and then asked a question in order to assure them that they had nothing to fear:

Vv. 31–33a: If God is for us, who will stand up against us to accuse us?
Vv. 33b, 34a: If God says we are righteous, who will say that we are not?
Vv. 34b–37: If Christ loves us, what has the power to cut us off from His love? A list of possible answers is suggested. These terrible things really exist (v. 36). But these are the sufferings which lead us along the path to glory, and so in fact they bring us nearer to Him. Therefore 'in these things' we are more than conquerors.
V. 34. Who intercedes for us: In vv. 26, 27 Paul had said that the Spirit intercedes for us—*within us*, in our own prayers. In v. 34 Paul said that Jesus *in heaven* is constantly praying for us. Paul did not say more on this subject, but the writer of the letter to the Hebrews did so, i.e.:

(a) Jesus is not now asking God to bless us, as we do when we pray for others.

(b) The basis of Jesus's prayer for us is the fact that He now sits at God's right hand in glory, as Lord of the universe (Heb. 10,12, 13). He is in the position not of a beggar, but of a king.

(c) But He is there *for us*, who belong to Him (Heb. 2.10, 13). His kingly presence in heaven, therefore, is His prayer for us. It is certain that God will bless us, because Jesus, our Leader (see also Rom. 8.29: 'firstborn'), has already reached the place of victory and power. We are certain to arrive there too.

See also 1 John 2.1, and especially Hebrews 7.25.

CLOSING SUMMARY (VV. 38, 39)

Some people are afraid of dying; some are afraid of living; some fear the future; some fear the present; some fear spirit-power. But God's love for us began before the world or any of these things existed; it was revealed to us in Christ; it will never end. Therefore we need never fear anything. God's love for us is a fact which nothing can ever alter.

It is clear from Romans 8 that Paul thought that all Christians should be sure of their final salvation. But a matter about which many Christians are unsure is whether they are true Christians, i.e. whether they truly belong to Christ. Some people say, 'You can never be sure about this; you can only hope.' Other people say that you certainly belong to Christ if you have been baptized; or if you have accepted Christ into your life as your Saviour; or if your life is good enough to please God.

But Paul, in this chapter, said that Christians can be sure, not through anything which they have done, but if they have the Spirit (see v. 9). He suggested that a Christian can test himself by taking the following steps:

1. By asking himself, 'Do I hate sin in my own life—so that I even find that I sometimes hate myself for displeasing God?' If the answer is 'Yes', this shows that he sets his mind on the things of the Spirit and so has the Spirit of God (v. 5).

Many people make the mistake of asking, 'Do I have victory over sin in my life?' But this is the wrong question to ask, because the more sincere a person is, the more conscious he is of his own failures and defeat. A hymn-writer expressed this well:

> Those who want to serve you (God) best
> Are conscious most of wrong within.

Such a person would probably answer 'No' to this question—but for him it would be the wrong question.

2. By asking himself, 'Do I find myself turning readily to God as my Father in times of need?' If so, then he has the Spirit, who leads him to cry 'Abba' (v. 15).

This sort of self-examination can be helpful, but it will not always take away all doubt. Some people are by nature unsure of themselves, others are naturally confident, and these characteristics affect their Christian life as well as their ordinary behaviour.

But very many Christians, whatever natural characteristics they may possess, do have an inward assurance that they belong to Christ, which they cannot clearly describe. Some Christian writers have called this 'the inward witness of the Spirit'. It seems likely that God intends all Christians to have this assurance, not only for their own comfort, but also in order that they may serve Him more confidently. Those who do not yet have this assurance may be able to gain it by testing themselves along the lines suggested above. But the testing should be done if possible under the guidance of a Christian counsellor or pastor. This is because we can easily fall into the danger of either examining ourselves in the *wrong* way, or of spending far *too long* in self-examination while neglecting work which we ought to be doing. No one can expect to have assurance unless he is honestly trying to do the things which he believes that God wants him to do (see, for example, 8.13).

STUDY SUGGESTIONS

WORD STUDY

1. The Greek word translated 'futility' in the RSV is translated differently in other English Bible versions, e.g.:
frustration, purposelessness, meaninglessness, inability to attain its purpose; and the word 'decay' (RSV) is differently translated: mortality, change, decadence, the power of death.
Which of these translations do you think best conveys the meaning in each case? Do you know of words in any other language which do so better?

2. Which three words in vv. 19–22 suggest the idea of looking forward to something better?

3. In what ways does the 'hope' of vv. 24, 25 resemble faith? (See 2 Cor. 4.18; 5.7.) What, if anything, can we learn from vv. 18–25 concerning (a) the present condition, (b) the future prospects, of:
   (i) God's whole creation;
   (ii) Christian believers;
   (iii) mankind as a whole?

4. Notice the meaning of the word 'know' as used in Hos. 13.5; Matt. 7.23; Gal. 4.9. Then read Amos 9.7, 8 and say which of the people there mentioned were 'known' by God in this sense?

REVIEW OF CONTENT

5. (a) What is our part in prayer, and what part does the Spirit play? (b) How will our prayerful 'sighs' (v. 26) eventually be answered? See also the word 'groan' (v. 23).

6. What is the connection between 'calling', 'faith', and our right relationship with God? (See 8.30; 1 Cor. 1.2, 9.)
7. What did Paul mean by 'all things' (v. 32)? (See 1 Cor. 3.21–23.)
8. How does the Holy Spirit affect our attitude towards the future, according to this chapter? How does He affect our life now?

BIBLE

9. 'It has been granted to you that you should . . . suffer' (Phil. 1.29). In what ways is suffering a 'privilege' granted to Christians? See this chapter and Rom. 5.3; Col. 1.24; Heb. 12.3–11.
10. (a) What orderliness can be seen in (i) the universe described in Gen. 1—3 and (ii) the world today?
    (b) What disorder can be seen in (i) Gen. 3 and (ii) the world today?
    (c) What did the Jews believe about the disorder and about the renewal of creation, according to the following passages? Ps. 107.33–35; Isa. 11.6–9; Isa. 24.5–13; 41.17–20; 65.17–25.
11. (a) What do you think Paul meant by 'the redemption of our bodies' (v. 23)?
    (b) What did he believe about the future state of the body? (See 1 Cor. 15.44; 2 Cor. 5.4, 5; Phil. 3.20.)
12. Luther wrote, 'It is certain that where there is no distress, there is no prayer; or if there is prayer, it is feeble and powerless. That is why troubles are so necessary.' How is this illustrated by Jesus's words in Matt. 6.7 and Luke 18.10–14?
13. Prayer is not 'persuading God to do what we want' (p. 115). What conditions did Jesus lay down for effective prayer? See Matt. 7.11; Mark 7.11; Luke 11.13; John 14.13, 14; 15.7; 16.23, 24. Compare 1 John 5.14, 15.
14. 'Events which at the time appeared to be disasters really worked out for good' (p. 117).
    (a) Of what events in Paul's life was this true, and what good resulted from these events? (See, for example, Phil. 1.12–18; 2 Cor. 12.7–10.)
    (b) Give examples of such events from your own life or experience.
15. 'Conformed to the image of his son' (v. 29). In the following verses, which words indicate that we are already like Christ, and which indicate that we are not yet like Him?
    (a) 2 Cor. 3.18 (b) Eph. 4.13 (c) Phil. 3.21 (d) Col. 3.10
    (e) 1 John 3.2

APPLICATION, OPINION, AND RESEARCH

16. Socrates said, 'The best thing of all is not to be born into this evil world, but, failing that, to leave it as soon as possible and to die in infancy.'
    (a) What is your opinion?

121

(b) How would you answer someone who asked: 'How could a good God have created a world like this?'

17. John Bunyan wrote, 'When you pray, let your heart be without words, rather than your words without heart.' In what ways can books of prayers help Christians? In what ways can books *hinder* us from true prayer? Discuss the right and wrong ways to use such books.

18. Read again the story of the prisoners at Buchenwald (p. 51), and Rom. 8.31–35. In what ways was the death of the Christian priest like the death of Christ, and in what ways was it unlike?

19. 'Therefore we need never fear anything' (p. 119). Does this mean that none of the troubles described in v. 35 will ever happen to us? if not, what does it mean? (See 2 Cor. 13.5; 2 Tim. 1.12; 4.8.)

SPECIAL NOTE F:
PAUL'S TEACHING ABOUT THE NEW AGE

The Jews looked forward to 'the Day of the Lord' (see p. 68), when God would, through His Messiah, bring in the new age of righteousness. They often called this new age 'the Age of the Spirit', or 'the last days' (see Jer. 31.31–34; Ezek. 36.22–32; Joel 2.28—3.3; Micah 4.1–7). They expected that at that time there would be judgement and wrath for the nations; but salvation, righteousness, redemption, and glory for God's people, the Jews. (Scholars sometimes call such ideas as these 'eschatological' because they have to do with the 'eschata', i.e. last things.) Thus the Jews thought of history as divided into two chief parts:

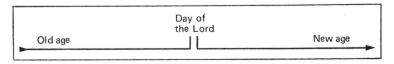

Old age | Day of the Lord | New age

Paul, however, believed that God's Messiah had *already* come (Rom. 1.3), that He had brought in God's new age, and had sent God's Spirit. God's righteousness has been revealed (1.17; 3.21), redemption and justification are *now* experienced by Christians (3.24; 5.9), because God the Judge already declares them righteous through what Christ has done. Therefore the last days are here; the new age has already begun (see p. 68). But, on the other hand, Paul also taught that there is a future judgement yet to come (2.5), a future verdict of justification (2.11), a future redemption of the body (8.23), and our salvation is yet to be brought to fulfilment (5.10). This seems to show that Paul thought of history as divided not into two parts, but into three. Acts 17.30 is a good example of the way in which he thought:

The old age: 'The times of ignorance God overlooked . . .'

Now: 'But now He commands all men everywhere to repent . . .'

The new age: 'Because He has fixed a day on which He will judge . . .'

Thus some scholars have said that Paul taught that Christians now live 'between the ages'. This can be a helpful way of looking at Paul's thought, but as far as Romans is concerned, it would be more accurate to say that Paul thought of Christians as now living 'in both ages'. This can be illustrated by a diagram:

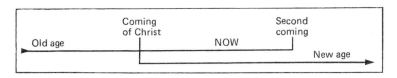

This diagram can be used to illustrate how God acts in history to save men. The old age is the time before Christ's Second coming in glory (i.e. the day of the Lord); the new age is the time after Christ's first coming; 'now' is the time in which we now live, between Christ's first and second comings, when the new age has already begun, but the old age is *not yet* ended. Or the same diagram can be used to illustrate the difference which Christ's coming makes to the life of a person, i.e. a person belongs to the old age of this world; through Christ he belongs to God's new age; but *now* he is involved with both the old age and the new age (see John 17.15–18). In Romans 5.9, 10 Paul expressed this three-part view very clearly (see p. 64):

In the past: we were enemies; *Now:* we are justified; *In future:* we shall be saved.

In 7.14–25, Paul spoke about the conflict which Christians experience (see p. 97). We can better understand his meaning if we remember this three-part view. The Christian *already* belongs to the new age, is a new man in Christ, and has righteousness, life, and peace (see 7.22). But he is *not yet* saved from the old age and this world, where evil and sin are present, even in his own body, which is not yet redeemed (see 7.21, 23). Therefore he cannot *now* escape the sort of conflict which Paul described in 7.25 and Galatians 5.17—and he will not escape it until the full revealing of God's glory at Christ's second coming (see 8.18–25).

Paul used the word 'now' many times in his letter to the Romans (see pp. 47, 69). In these passages he was referring to blessings which Christians *already* experience. It is clear from chapter 8 that the chief of these blessings is the presence of the Spirit of God (just as the chief characteristic of the old age is 'the flesh', see p. 98). In this Paul was giving teaching similar to that of Jesus and the other apostles (see Luke 4.18; Matt. 12.28; John 1.33; 15.26; Acts 1.8; 2.16, 17, 33, 38). The Spirit is the sign that (a) God's new age has come; (b) we *already* belong to His new age (8.9–11); (c) we *shall* receive all the other promised blessings which we have *not yet* received. See 8.23, Notes on pp. 113, 114 and Additional notes on Flesh, p. 208, and Spirit, p. 219.

At the present time there are many things which remind Christians that they still live in the old age, e.g. suffering; just as there are many other things, besides the Spirit, which signify the new age, e.g. prayer.

STUDY SUGGESTIONS

APPLICATION, OPINION, AND RESEARCH

1. (a) Make two lists, (i) of things which are characteristic of the old age, and (ii) of things which are characteristic of the new age. (See especially Romans 8.)

   (b) From which of the things mentioned in your first list are Christians *already* delivered, and from which are they *not yet* delivered?

   (c) Which of the things mentioned in your second list do Christians *already* experience, and which do they *not yet* experience?

   (d) Which of the things mentioned in your first list did Jesus experience in His life on earth?

2. (a) Describe, in your own words, the sort of conflict, or tension, which a Christian experiences as a result of belonging to two ages at the same time.

   (b) What sort of conflict, or tension, if any, would you expect to experience in the future life of glory in heaven? If possible, support your answer by passages from Paul's letters.

3. Read Mark 1.15; Luke 11.20; 17.21; 22.18; Matt. 25.34. What similarities do you notice between Paul's teaching that we already belong to the new age, but have not yet received its full blessings, and Jesus's teaching about the kingdom of God?

4. Draw your own diagram (similar to or different from the one on p. 123) to illustrate Paul's three-part view of 'salvation-history'. Using your answer to 1 (a) above, insert words or headings to describe the chief characteristics of each part (e.g. you may wish to write 'guilt of sin' under Part 1, etc.).

PART 4

THE NATION OF GOD

Chapters 9—11:
God's Plan for Jews and Gentiles

INTRODUCTION

Some scholars have written that Paul ended his explanation of the Gospel with the hymn of 8.31–39, and that chapters 12—16 contain the practical teaching which follows on from 8.39. They think that in chapters 9—11 Paul was discussing a problem which seemed important to him but which is not relevant for us today. But this is probably not the correct way to interpret Romans 9—11. In these chapters Paul continued his discussion of the promises and purposes of God which he had already mentioned in 8.28–30, and in doing so he considered at length some questions which he had already briefly raised in 3.1–8 (see pp. 38, 39). Thus the climax of Paul's whole explanation of the Gospel which had begun at 1.16 comes in 11.32–36, where he:

(a) summed up his teaching about men's disobedience and God's mercy (v. 32),

(b) offered praise to God for the wonderful way in which He saves men (vv. 33–36).

Even so, the contents of chapters 9—11 may appear strange and irrelevant to many modern readers. It will therefore be helpful to consider these chapters as a whole before turning to them in detail.

I. THE JEWISH PROBLEM, AS PAUL SAW IT

In Romans 8 Paul expressed his joy and assurance in what God had done for men through Christ. Yet immediately afterwards he went on to write about his 'great sorrow and unceasing anguish' (9.2), because his own people, the Jews, had rejected these blessings. Men are always most concerned for their own family and people. A Masai theological student in East Africa prayed fervently and constantly for the conversion of members of his tribe. He loved all men, but God had made him a Masai, so it was natural that he should be specially concerned for his own people. Paul felt the same way about his fellow-Jews, but for him the sorrow was far greater because they had been in a special sense God's chosen people, and even God Himself had come to earth as a Jew. See p. 130.

But Paul had a second reason for discussing the Jewish problem. In 8.28–30 he had spoken of God's promise to bring to glory all those whom He foreknew, pre-destined, and called, and of his own certainty that God would do all He had promised. But could Paul—could anyone—be so certain, after what had happened to the Israelites? God had foreknown, chosen, and called them (11.2, 28, 29) to be His sons and to experience His glory (9.4), yet they were disobedient and unbelieving, and therefore God rejected them (11.20). If God rejected the Israelites, can Christians to whom God has given the same blessings (8.16, 29, 30, 33) be any more sure that God will fulfil His promises to them? If God's 'elect' are unfaithful, then will not His promises fail, and all Paul's assurance of chapter 8 be meaningless?

2. PAUL'S ANSWER

Paul's answer has three different parts, all of which are connected, and all of which are necessary in order that we may understand the ways of God and men's response to Him. We shall consider them one by one on pp. 133–152, but it will be helpful to summarize them here as follows:

(a) God is sovereign, and free to follow His own will. His word has been effective in the lives of those whom He has chosen (9.6–29).

(b) All men have a responsibility to have faith in God, but Israel as a nation has not had faith (9.30—10.21).

(c) God is fulfilling His plan, which includes: (i) the conversion of some Jews even at this time (11.1–10); (ii) the conversion of many Gentiles, who came to hear the Gospel as a result of the Jews' rejection of it (11.11–24); (iii) the conversion, in the end, of the nation of Israel, which will take place as a result of God's work among the Gentiles (11.25–36).

Throughout chapters 9—11 Paul was not thinking so much of the way in which God saves individual persons. He was thinking chiefly of the way in which God uses nations as well as individuals, unbelievers as well as believers, in order to fulfil His purposes.

3. THE JEWISH PROBLEM AS IT AFFECTED CHRISTIANS IN ROME

It is likely that disagreements between Jewish and Gentile Christians had arisen in the Church in Rome. Perhaps chapters 14 and 15 indicate a disagreement of this kind (see pp. 183, 184). Jews and Gentiles were unfamiliar with one another's customs and outlook, and were in danger of forming themselves into two separate groups (see p. 12). They needed, therefore, to understand one another better, and discover what is the true relationship between Jews and Gentiles in God's purposes. This relationship is explained in Romans 9—11 in greater detail than in any other passage of the New Testament.

'God had chosen and called the Jews, yet they were disobedient and unbelieving.' ...
If God's 'elect' are unfaithful, will not His promises fail? (p. 126).

Posters and information about political candidates help voters in Swaziland to
decide whom to choose. What happens when chosen leaders fail to obey the will of
those who elected them? Does God treat his 'elect' as voters treat their representatives?

Of *Jewish Christians*, Paul said:

(a) They should not rely on Israel's special religious privileges. Israel, like everyone else, has been unbelieving and disobedient, and so God has at present rightly rejected them.

(b) They should not despair of their nation; God will keep His promises and bring Israel in through His mercy. Their own conversion is a sign that He will bring in the rest also.

(c) They should not despise their fellow-Christians of the Gentiles, because through the Gentiles God purposes to save the nation Israel.

To *Gentile Christians*, Paul wrote more directly (11.13), saying:

(a) Do not despise the Jews for their unbelief, for your salvation has come from Jews—from the patriarchs, from Jesus of Nazareth, even from the unbelieving Jews through whom you got the opportunity to hear and believe (see questions 9 and 10 on pp. 152, 153).

(b) Do not neglect the opportunity now of bearing witness to Jesus among the Jews—they need this good news, and God has promised to save them, through you.

To *all the Christians* in Rome Paul wrote that there is no room for rivalry or jealousy among Christian people, because all are really alike (10.12; 11.32). All need one another (11.11–14); all together are indebted to the mercy of God (11.30, 31); all together should glorify Him (11.33–36; see 15.5–13).

4. THE RELEVANCE OF THIS TEACHING TODAY

(a) Throughout these chapters Paul emphasized the importance of faith. Many Christian people today are in danger of relying, as the Jews did, upon their religious knowledge, privileges, and activities, instead of having a living faith in God's mercy. See pp. 34, 38. Paul himself saw that this would be a danger for Gentile Christians, just as it had been for Jews (see 11.17–24).

(b) Other Christians are despised and persecuted by those amongst whom they live, and nothing seems less likely than that they are God's elect people who will inherit all things. These chapters remind such Christians that God's purpose for His people will not fail, however unlikely its fulfilment may sometimes seem.

(c) In many parts of the world, Christians of different tribal or national or racial backgrounds have come into conflict with one another. Paul's teaching here reminds us that all Christians are similar in God's sight, and the unity which He has given us is more important than the outward differences which sometimes divide us. Often when we cut ourselves off from Christians of other groups, we are cutting ourselves off from blessings which God wants to give us through them.

(d) God's plan for Jews and Gentiles is also relevant for us today.

In the last 1,900 years large numbers of Gentiles have become Christians, but what has been happening to the Jews over this period?

(i) When Paul wrote this letter, many Jews had left Judaea and had settled in different parts of the Roman Empire. After the two great Jewish rebellions of AD 70 and 135, the Romans made Jerusalem into a Roman city which no Jew was allowed to enter. Thus the Jews lost their land, and were scattered through the countries of Europe and the Middle East.

(ii) Jews have been severely persecuted since that time, e.g. in Germany from 1933 to 1945, and, to a lesser extent, in Russia at the present time. Frequently Christians have persecuted them in the name of Christ. Chrysostom preached a series of sermons against them in AD 387, saying that God hates them and wants to destroy them; and that it is the duty of Christians to hate them too. Holy men of the Church led attacks on them in the Middle Ages and, although the Popes usually tried to protect them, Pope Innocent III declared in 1205 that 'all Jews must be slaves for ever because they crucified Jesus'.

(iii) In 1948 the nation of Israel was created in Palestine, and Jews from all over the world went back to their ancient land. It is amazing that the nation of Israel was able to survive 1,800 years of dispersion and persecution, and many people have called it one of God's miracles. In 1965, the Ecumenical Council of the Roman Catholic Church condemned the past persecutions of the Jews and declared that the Jews as a race are not guilty of killing Jesus, and that they are not rejected nor cursed by God. In 1967, as a result of the six-day war between Israel and the Arab nations, the city of Jerusalem and the west bank of the Jordan river were occupied by Israel, for the first time since AD 70. Some Christians believe that this return of the Jews to their land fulfilled many prophecies in the Bible. Many other Christians do not agree.

(iv) Now that there is once more a nation Israel in its own land, we can more easily think in terms of Israel as a whole, or of 'all Israel' (11.26), as Paul could. This passage suggests that when God has completed His purposes of showing mercy to the Gentiles, He will then bring to Himself, through faith in Christ (11.23), large numbers of Jews. This means that God's word for Israel has neither failed nor changed (9.6; 11.2, 11, 29); that God's mercy is for all men, including the Jews (11.32); and that the Church has a special responsibility to minister to Jews. This ministry consists both of preaching the Gospel, and of giving Jews the sort of practical help which Christians should have given them in the past but usually did not give (11.18, 23, 24).

9.1-5

The Problem of Israel's Unbelief

OUTLINE

'But the Jews have rejected this Gospel which I preach, and this both grieves and perplexes me, in view of all the years of blessings which should have prepared them to receive their own Messiah.'

INTERPRETATION

In spite of his hymn of assurance (8.31–39), Paul could not forget the fact that his own fellow-Israelites had rejected their Messiah. This fact raised in Paul's mind important personal and theological problems, i.e.:

1. For hundreds of years God had been preparing the Israelites to receive the blessings of His new age. They had been looking forward to this new age, and were confident that when it came even the Gentiles would come to them to receive God's blessings through them. But now the Messiah had come, the new age was here—yet the Israelites would have nothing to do with it. On the other hand, large numbers of Gentiles had accepted the Israelite Messiah as their Lord and God. God was now pouring out all His greatest blessings, yet the very nation which He had prepared to receive them was not interested. Paul felt that this situation brought deep shame upon the nation of Israel.

2. There was, however, a further, and greater, danger that this situation might bring shame upon God Himself, because it seemed as though God was failing to fulfil His purposes for Israel.

3. Perhaps the Jews' rejection of Christ also made Paul doubtful whether his own message could really be true. A Christian leader in Africa, when he passes a spring on the hillside, feels doubts inwardly even today, because as a child he had been taught that such springs are the homes of evil spirits. He quickly dispels all such doubts, however, by recalling what he *knows* of Christ and His saving work. So too, Paul, if he *did* feel any uncertainty, probably did not feel it for very long. As soon as he considered Jesus of Nazareth, he had no more room for doubts, because he knew that Jesus was the Messiah who had come and fulfilled God's promises made over the years to Israel. Therefore Paul's final thought in this passage was the same as that in 8.31–39, i.e. praise to God for what He had done through Christ (v. 5b).

NOTES

Vv. 4, 5a. Israelites: Paul used this name to describe the Jewish nation as a whole, specially chosen and blessed by God. He then went on to list their special privileges.

Sonship: See Additional Note, Sonship, p. 219.

The glory: The Israelites experienced God's glory at certain times in their history (Exod. 24.16, 17), and especially in their worship (Exod. 40.34, 35; 1 Kings 8.10, 11). See Additional Note, Glory, p. 208.

The covenants: Writers in the Bible often used this word to describe an agreement which establishes a relationship between two people, often with a special sign. In Israel's history, God came to His people over and over again, and made His covenant with them. There is really only one covenant, because the relationship which it establishes between men and God is always the same (see questions 10, p. 43 and 2, p. 60), but it can be called 'covenants' because it was repeated many times in different places, and with many different signs.

Paul then used five words, all of which were connected with God's covenant with Israel:

1. **The law:** See Exodus 20; 24.7. The Israelites knew how God wanted them to live. See Additional Note, Law, 3, p. 210.

2. **The worship:** In the Temple, where God revealed His glory and was specially present with His people.

3. **The promises:** Paul had discussed the most important of these in 4.13–21. God's word to Abraham and all Israel's privileges were, in part, promises which offered hope for the future. They are all in some way fulfilled in the Gospel.

4. **The patriarchs:** These were Abraham, Isaac, and Jacob, the first people to receive the promises.

5. **The Christ:** The Messiah had been promised to the Jews, and Jesus was Himself a Jew.

V. 5b: For hundreds of years scholars have discussed the meaning of these words and have asked, 'Did Paul here call Christ "God", or not?' The Greek is not clear, and can be read in two different ways:

1. 'Of their race . . . is the Christ. God who is over all be blessed for ever' (RSV). Some scholars reject this reading for two reasons. (a) Paul usually wrote 'Blessed be God', not 'God be blessed', and he usually linked such a phrase closely with the previous sentence (e.g. 1.25). (b) We might expect Paul, after describing Christ 'according to the flesh', to add a description of Him as He is 'according to the Spirit', as he did in 1.4.

2. 'Of their race . . . is the Christ, who is God over all, blessed for ever' (RSV mg). The grammar and style of this reading are what we should expect from Paul. But in no other case did Paul actually call Christ God, and some scholars reject it for this reason.

It is difficult to decide between these two possible interpretations, but the second seems preferable. Paul *could* have called Christ 'God' in view of what he said about Him in Col. 1.15, 19; 2.9; and Phil. 2.6. Also, it seems better to accept the interpretation which agrees with Paul's usual style and grammar.

STUDY SUGGESTIONS

WORD STUDY

1. 'My brethren' (9.3). In what sense were Jews Paul's 'brethren'? What other brethren did Paul have? (See Gal. 2.15; Mark 3.31–35.) Today many political leaders and preachers call their hearers 'brethren'. What do they mean by it? Do you think they are right to do so? Of whom do you think Christians should use this word?

REVIEW OF CONTENT

2. (a) Which of the Jewish privileges listed in vv. 4, 5a do each of the following phrases describe? (i) God's presence; (ii) the fathers; (iii) adoption; (iv) future blessings; (v) Temple ceremonial; (vi) agreement; (vii) God's revealed will.

(b) All these privileges involve promises which offer hope for the future. In what way is each one fulfilled in the Gospel of Christ? (See Rom. 3.21; 3.25; 4; 5.2; 8.16; 1 Cor. 11.25.)

BIBLE

3. With what great event in Israel's history were the privileges of v. 4 originally connected?

4. In what way does the attitude of the Jews, as shown in the following passages, confirm what is said about them on p. 130?
Acts 7.54–60 13.44–50 17.5–13

5. Compare with 9.3 Moses's words in Exod. 32.32. In what ways was Paul's wish like that of Moses, and in what ways was it different? (See also Luke 13.34.)

6. In a covenant, there are usually two people (or groups of people), an agreement, and a sign (see p. 131). In the following four examples of covenants in the Bible, say in each case:
(i) which two people (or groups of people) were involved;
(ii) what was the agreement established between them;
(iii) what was the sign of the covenant?
(a) Gen. 31.44–54   (b) Gen. 17.1–14   (c) Gen. 9.8–17   (d) Matt. 26.26–28

7. (a) In what ways is Paul's teaching in 9.1–5 like (i) Jesus's teaching as recorded in Matt. 21.33–43 (compare also Matt. 22.1–10; 23.29–39); and (ii) Stephen's speech in Acts 7?

(b) In what ways is something which Paul emphasized in Rom. 9–11 similar to the conclusion of Jesus's parable in Matt. 21.43?

APPLICATION, OPINION, AND RESEARCH

8. 'In many countries . . . Christians . . . have come into conflict with one another?' (p. 128).

   (a) Give examples of conflict among Christians from your own experience or from what you have heard or read.

   (b) What can cause and increase such conflict among Christians?

   (c) What are the likely consequences of such conflict for the Church and the Gospel of Christ?

   (d) When such conflicts arise, what steps can be taken to bring peace?

9. 'Jews have been severely persecuted' (p. 129). When the people of Zanzibar revolted against their Arab masters in 1964, they murdered hundreds of Arabs, no doubt remembering how the Arabs had led the cruel African slave trade in the nineteenth century.

   (a) In your own country, what minority groups, if any, are badly treated by the majority, and what form does this bad treatment take?

   (b) What reasons do the majority give for such treatment? Do you think that these are the *real* reasons for it? If not, what are the real reasons?

10. To what extent, if at all, and for what reasons, do Christians in your country:

    (a) keep themselves separate from certain groups of people?

    (b) fear such people?

    (c) succeed in loving and caring for such people?

    (d) help to prevent such people from being treated badly by others?

11. What groups of people today enjoy religious privileges similar to those of the Jews in Paul's time? In what ways are such people making the most of their privileges; or in what ways are they squandering them?

9.6–29

God's Sovereignty

OUTLINE

'Throughout Israel's history, God chose some of Abraham's descendants, and not others. It is difficult for us to accept this fact, but we shall understand it better if we remember that: (a) God created the world, so He is free to do as He wishes with those whom He has created; (b) all men deserve God's wrath; the wonder is that He saves any—yet He does, both Jews and Gentiles; (c) God is perfectly just, and no human being can ever accuse Him of doing wrong.'

INTRODUCTION

Paul began his discussion of the Jewish problem by strongly denying that God's promise had failed (9.6a). Perhaps he had not fully thought out the solution to the problem, but was feeling his way towards a solution as he dictated chapters 9—11 to Tertius, his secretary. He was at any rate certain that God's word *could* not fail, and he went on to consider this fact in the light of the Jews' unbelief. Paul's argument had three chief parts, described on p. 126. Here in the first part (9.6–29) he argued that:

(a) God has fulfilled His promise to save His chosen people, e.g. Isaac, Jacob (vv. 6–13).

(b) The cases where His word seems to have 'failed', e.g. Pharaoh and unbelieving Israel, have in fact helped to fulfil His purposes to save those whom He has chosen and called (vv. 14–23).

(c) God has fulfilled His promise to save Gentiles (vv. 24–29).

INTERPRETATION

In 9.15 Paul used the word 'mercy' for the first time in this letter. He went on to use it very frequently in the rest of chapter 9 and in chapter 11. Its meaning is similar to that of 'love' and 'grace', but Paul usually wrote 'mercy' when he was referring to God's general plan to save mankind, both Jews and Gentiles. Chapter 8 (e.g. vv. 28–30) was mainly about individual salvation. Chapters 9—11 are mainly about God's purpose for nations and groups. This is clear in all three sections of 9.6–29, as follows:

(a) **Vv. 6–13:** The words 'might continue' (v. 11) show that Paul was thinking mainly of God's *continuing purpose*, which He fulfils through nations and groups of people. Like Malachi (1.2–5) whom he quoted in v. 13, Paul was thinking not so much of Jacob and Esau as individuals, but rather of their descendants, the nations Israel and Edom. However, nations are made up of individuals, and God chooses and calls individuals in fulfilling His purpose, not because of their family background or good character (v. 11), but because of His mercy. Whether He is dealing with nations or individuals, He is the sovereign King who does not have to save anyone, but through His free mercy chooses and calls some—none of whom deserve it. See p. 68 (c).

(b) **Vv. 14–23:** In this section Paul continued his explanation of how God fulfils His purpose of saving mankind. In doing so He uses individuals, like Pharaoh whom He used at the time of the Exodus, God's great act of salvation in the history of the Israelites. Paul used the word 'harden' of Pharaoh (9.18), a word which he used again in 11.7, 25 in order to show the part that Israel's disobedience played in the salvation of mankind. Such 'hardening' is a step on the road to the salvation of both Gentiles and Jews (9.24; 11.25, 26).

(c) **Vv. 24–29:** Many Jews despised the Gentiles, like the author of 2 Esdras, who wrote: 'Thou hast said they are nothing and are like spittle' (see also Psalm 9.5). But Paul pointed out that this was not how God regarded them. On the contrary, God had from the beginning purposed to show mercy to those who seemed to the Jews to be 'outsiders' (vv. 25, 26). He had now fulfilled this purpose, as the prophets had foretold, not through the nation of Israel as a whole, but through a small but faithful 'remnant' (vv. 27–29; see Additional Note, Remnant, p. 215).

NOTES

Vv. 6, 7. Not all who are descended from Israel belong to Israel: In 4.12 Paul had shown that Abraham's true children are those who, like him, have faith in the promise. But there is something which comes even before faith, i.e. God's choice. Paul illustrated this by the examples of the two sons of Abraham and the two sons of Isaac.

Vv. 10–13. Jacob . . . Esau: Notice *when* God chose one rather than the other (v. 11). See p. 134 (a) and question 3 on p. 138.

Election: See Additional Note, Election, p. 204.

His call: See p. 117, 3.

'Jacob I loved, but Esau I hated': This is a Hebrew way of saying, 'I preferred Jacob to Esau.' To say simply 'God hated Esau' would not give the correct meaning of Malachi's words.

Vv. 14–18. Is there injustice? Some people, on reading v. 11, might think that God acts unfairly. We should condemn anyone who rejected a child before it was born. But Paul showed here that God cannot be unjust, by taking two examples from Israel's history:

1. An example of God's *mercy* from Exodus 33.19. Instead of destroying those who turned against Him by making the golden calf, God had mercy on them. But His mercy does not depend on anything that men do, and we should thank Him that this is so.

2. An example of God's *hardening the heart*, from Exodus 4–17. This is the story of a man who thought he was all-powerful in Egypt. But the story shows that (a) Pharaoh's power came from God; (b) God used Pharaoh to show His own power in saving His people; (c) God intended that this salvation should be 'proclaimed in all the earth'.

Both examples show that God is free to use any means that He wishes, in order to fulfil His purpose. But His nature is to have mercy, and no one, neither rebellious Israelites nor proud Pharaoh, can defeat His purposes of mercy for mankind.

Vv. 20–23: In these verses Paul considered the question of v. 19, but did not really answer it. Instead, he rebuked the imaginary questioner, saying that God, as Creator, has a right to use what He has created as He wishes. Just as the important thing about pots is their usefulness in fulfilling the purpose for which they are made, so for Paul here the main thought is God's overall purpose of mercy in spreading the Gospel throughout the world (vv. 17, 24). But there are some problems connected with the teaching of these verses, e.g.:

1. Man is not clay, but is made in God's image, and has been given a mind which asks questions and worries about the answers.

2. Paul may seem to be a little unkind in silencing the questioner in this way, but we should remember that the question was probably Paul's own, and this 'debate' was taking place in his own mind as he tried to work out the answer.

3. However, there are times when it *is* right to refuse to answer certain kinds of questions (see 3.8). Job and Jeremiah, and even Jesus Himself at times, could not understand why God acted as He did. They called out 'Why . . .?' or 'How long . . .?' All the same, these men knew that God was righteous—that is why they asked their questions. But there are many people who try to accuse God of being evil or unjust, and in doing so they 'turn things upside-down' (Isa. 29.16), because they put themselves in the position of God as judge, and God in the position of a creature. This is a great sin, and for such a questioner there is only a stern reminder of man's true position as a part of God's creation.

4. **Vessels of wrath:** This expression comes from the Hebrew idea of wrath as something that is poured out, as into a cup or vessel. (Compare Jer. 42.18, Rev. 14.10.) It means those on whom God's wrath rests, like 'children of wrath' (Eph. 2.3). Paul seems to have been making the following main points in vv. 22–24:

(a) God would have a perfect right to create some people in order to destroy them in the fulfilment of His purposes. Notice that Paul did not say that God actually does this; he simply defended God's right to do so ('What if God . . .?').

(b) Paul emphasized not God's destruction of such people, but His patience towards them (Rom. 2.4; 2 Pet. 3.9). As they are, they are 'due for destruction' (NEB), but God gives those who are children of wrath today the opportunity to become children of God tomorrow (Eph. 2.3–5). His judgement is 'not yet'.

(c) Paul's chief point was that all men are sinners who deserve God's wrath. The wonderful thing which needs explanation is not that God will destroy some people, but that He has mercy upon anyone. Paul went on to show later in his argument just how amazingly wide God's mercy is.

However, the teaching of this passage does raise a problem which no

'Has the potter no right over the clay?' (Rom. 9.21). 'God, as creator, has the right to use as he wishes what he has created . . . in the fulfilment of his purposes' (p. 136).

The vessel this Indian potter is making may be used for a common purpose or for decoration. If it turns out badly, or cracks in the firing, the potter is free to destroy it and make another. Do you think that God ever does 'destroy' human beings, as a potter might destroy his pots?

scholar has ever fully solved, or ever will. On the one hand it appears that God leaves some people under His wrath (as we all deserve), without showing them His sovereign mercy. On the other hand, all men are still responsible to turn to God in faith, and it is their own fault if they do not do so (9.30—10.21). This is indeed a mystery which we shall not be able to explain in this world. Theologians call it the problem of 'God's sovereignty and man's responsibility'.

STUDY SUGGESTIONS

WORD STUDY

1. 'God's sovereignty and man's responsibility' (p. 138). In the following list which words mean almost the same as 'sovereignty', and which words almost the same as 'responsibility'?
Duty   control   rule   obligation   lordship

REVIEW OF CONTENT

2. (a) Who are 'children of Abraham'?
(b) What is God's intention for them?
3. Jacob was weak, deceitful, and cowardly; Esau was strong, honest, and brave. (See Gen. 25 and 27.)
(a) In which incidents in their lives did they show these characteristics?
(b) Which of these two young men would *you* have chosen as your heir? Give your reasons.
(c) Why do you think that God chose Jacob?
4. (a) On what grounds do some people today wrongly claim to be favoured by God?
(b) On what basis and for what reasons does God show people His favour?
5. (a) What two reasons can we find in Rom. 9.6–29 to suggest that God was not 'unjust' in hardening Pharaoh's heart?
(b) What words in this passage indicate that God's chief purpose is to show mercy rather than wrath?

BIBLE

6. Abraham was concerned about who would inherit his possessions. (See Gen. 15 and 17.)
(a) Whom did he expect to be his heir?
(b) How did God correct Abraham's expectations?
(c) Why was Isaac called the 'child of the promise'? See Gal. 4.23–28.

7. Read Isa. 10.5–15 and Acts 2.23; 7.51–53. As God used Pharaoh to fulfil His purposes, so He used the King of Assyria and those who helped to put Jesus to death.
   (a) What was the intention of these men in acting as they did?
   (b) What part did God play in these actions?
   (c) What do we learn from these events about how God uses evil for His own purposes?
8. Read Isa. 45.1–13; 44.28. Like Paul, Isaiah used the illustration of the potter to describe God's activity.
   (a) What was Cyrus's relationship with God?
   (b) What was God's ultimate intention in using Cyrus?
9. 'The wonderful thing, which needs explanation, is . . . that God has mercy' (p. 136).
   (a) How was God's mercy illustrated by Jesus in the parable of the Labourers in the Vineyard (Matt. 20.1–15)?
   (b) Give examples of how God exercises mercy today.

APPLICATION, OPINION, AND RESEARCH

10. (a) What is the difference between the attitude to God as shown by the imaginary questioner in 9.19, and the attitude of the following, when they complained to God:
    Jesus (John 12.27, 28; Mark 15.34)   Jeremiah (15.18; 20.14–18)
    Job (7.19–21)?
    (b) What kind of questions, if any, do you think it is *wrong* to ask about God?
11. Do you think that God uses national leaders today to fulfil His purposes, as he used Pharaoh, Cyrus, and other leaders mentioned in the Bible? Give examples to support your answer.
12. What answer would you give to someone who said: 'I cannot believe in God when I think of the history of the Jewish people. How can it help His purposes that some of them should experience such suffering, and not others?'

9.30—10.21
Man's Responsibility

OUTLINE

'But whoever you may be, Jew or Gentile, you cannot achieve a right relationship with God through your own efforts or religious position, but only through faith. God has always called on people to trust in Him alone, and He does so today, through the preaching of the Gospel. If Jews refuse to do this, it is their own fault.'

INTRODUCTION

Not only Paul, but many other religious leaders have taught that God is in control of all things, and that He is free to act as He wills. Muhammad in the Quran taught that God created men and their actions also, so that all that happens happens because it is God's will. Consequently many Muslims (forgetting that Muhammad also taught human responsibility) believe that if a person is sick, 'it is the will of God'; if a friend is murdered, 'it is the will of God'; if a man is poor or hungry, 'it is the will of God'. They claim that man cannot do anything about such evils—he must accept and submit to God's will. This attitude has often led to much unhappiness for those who suffer, and to backwardness for whole nations. It is characteristic of the way in which many people approach life's problems. A young man one day accidentally dropped his house-keys into a big water-tank. He walked away, sadly shaking his head, and saying, 'It is the will of God'—until a friend showed him how to get them out by using a long pole and a piece of bent wire.

Paul did not only teach that God is in control (9.6–29). He also taught that people are responsible for their own actions, and, especially, for they way in which they respond to God. God invites all men to believe in Him, and if they do not, that is not His fault but theirs. This is the Theme of 9.30—10.21, and Paul's second answer to the problem of 9.6; i.e. *God's word* has not failed, but *Israel* has failed to have faith in God. Paul described the Jews' failure as follows:

(a) They tried to reach God by way of law instead of by way of faith (9.30—10.4).

(b) The way of faith is easy, and is now clearly revealed in Jesus (10.5–13).

(c) Israel has had every opportunity to believe but has refused to do so (10.14–21).

'People are responsible for their own actions, and for the way in which they respond to God . . . if they do not believe, that is not His fault but theirs' (p. 140).

An official in Fiji prepares a report on people's reactions to a recent health campaign. Whose fault will it be if those who refused to co-operate continue to suffer from crippling diseases?

INTERPRETATION

The subject of this section is *righteousness* (i.e. a right relationship with God, see Additional Note, p. 215), and the two ways of attaining it, i.e. the way of law and the way of faith. Paul had discussed these in 4.13–17 (see pp. 57, 58 and Additional Note, Grace, p. 209, 2). Here in 9.30—10.4 he described the Jews' great efforts to achieve righteousness through obeying the law. They were like an athlete running hard to win his race, who strikes his foot on a stone and falls down. The Jews encountered God's righteousness in Christ, but were striving so hard to gain *their* ideal of righteousness that they rejected the righteousness which He revealed and offered to them. Thus Christ was, to use Isaiah's words, a 'stumbling-stone' to them (see p. 143, below). Those who believe in Christ, however, find that He is 'the end of the law' in the following ways:

1. Christ possesses a perfectly right relationship with God, and thus has fulfilled the law (see Additional Note, Righteousness, p. 216, 5).

2. Christ brings believers into the same relationship with God, and so brings the law to an end as a way of approaching God, as Paul had already shown in 3.21 and 7.4–6 (see p. 93).

In 10.5–13 Paul went on to show that the way of law is difficult. Even today, just as in Paul's time, many Jews make special efforts to fulfil the law, as they understand it. They will not light a fire, nor switch on the light, nor lift a load, on the Sabbath. We must admire their 'zeal'. Theirs is not an easy religion, but they believe it to be right (see also examples given on p. 92). On the other hand, the way of faith is easy, because Christ has done what is difficult.

The first European explorers of Africa had to struggle for many months to reach the interior, but today's traveller relies on a skilfully engineered aeroplane and its crew to take him there without any effort on his part. Yet sometimes it is difficult to believe that we really can travel so far so easily. In the same way, and for all sorts of different reasons, many people find it difficult simply to rely on what Jesus Christ has done. For example, Martin Luther once wrote, 'I find myself wanting to come to God bringing something in my hand for which he should give me His grace. I cannot attain to casting myself on pure and simple grace only.' Another scholar has written, 'God held out helping hands to His people, hands full of His gifts, but the hands of the people were full of their own works. They disregarded the gift and turned away.'

But those who do rely on Christ and what He has done have no reason for boasting, and are all equal in their relationship with God (vv. 11–13). When a railway train arrives at a distant city, the engineers who built the train and the driver and fireman who ran it have achieved a great deal. But the passengers have not achieved anything, and are all alike in that they have all reached their destination through relying on the efforts of others.

Before people can accept a message, however, they must have a chance to hear it. This means that the Church has a responsibility to preach the good news—and if it has not done so, then the Jews cannot be blamed for their unbelief. Paul brought this section to a close in 10.14–21 by showing that in fact the Jews had no excuse, as follows:

1. The Jews had heard the Gospel clearly (v. 18). Paul used Psalm 19.4 to show that God's Gospel is being heard everywhere, just as the things which God has created are everywhere seen. Even had the apostles stayed in Jerusalem, Jewish people everywhere would have heard about the Gospel (Acts 2.5–11). But the apostles travelled and so made sure of this (see Gal. 2.7, 8).

2. The Gospel was not difficult for the Jews to understand (vv. 19, 20). Even Gentiles had understood and believed, as the Scriptures had foretold.

3. The Jews themselves refused to believe (v. 21; see also v. 16). Paul discussed their unbelief and jealousy again in 11.11–16.

NOTES

V. 33. A stone that will make men stumble: Paul here combined two verses from Isaiah which refer to a stone. In 8.14 Isaiah said that God was a sanctuary, i.e. a place where men can be saved, and also a stone over which men can stumble and fall. In 28.16 Isaiah was probably referring to the faithful Remnant (see Additional Note, Remnant, p. 215), and called on the nation to have faith. These two quotations were very popular with the earliest Christians, and may have formed part of a booklet of quotations from the Jewish Scriptures which they believed referred to the coming Messiah and were fulfilled in Christ.

V. 1: Although Paul said many stern things about the disobedient Jews in these chapters, this verse shows that his personal attitude to them was one of love. A famous minister was once speaking to a young preacher who had just delivered a sermon at a big meeting:

'Well, what did you preach about?' asked the minister.

'I preached on "The wicked shall be turned into hell",' replied the young man.

'Oh, very good,' was the reply, 'and were you able to preach about it with love?'

V. 3. Being ignorant: The Jews' ignorance was no excuse (see v. 19), because they had been told often enough that faith was the way to gain salvation. But they refused to believe and to recognize true righteousness in Jesus, perhaps partly because they *preferred* to 'establish their own righteousness'.

V. 4. Christ is the end of the law: See p. 142, above. This does not mean that the law is no longer of any use to Christians, but simply that Christ has shown that it cannot set people right with God.

V. 9. Jesus is Lord: This was the first creed which Christians used. They confessed it when they were baptized (1 Cor. 12.3). It showed that they were disciples of Jesus.

Confess with your lips . . . believe in your heart: This verse suggests that in order to be a Christian it is necessary:

(a) to accept certain historical facts about Jesus, especially the facts of His death and resurrection (see 1 Cor. 15.3, 4);

(b) to have a personal relationship to Jesus, as a slave to a Master;

(c) outwardly to confess this new relationship.

Those who respond to the Gospel in this way have a right relationship with God and are thus on the way to final salvation (see Additional Note: Salvation, p. 217).

V. 14: A wise man will not buy a car which he has not tested, nor a cow which he has not seen. In the same way Christians have no right to expect people to call upon Jesus as Lord unless they for their part have clearly presented basic information about who He is and what He did.

V. 15. How can men preach unless they are sent? No one should 'decide' to be a preacher. If the Church needs preachers, it should not go round recruiting them from schools and colleges. God must call and send His preachers. Without such a call, no one should preach (although all Christians should be ready to bear witness to Jesus as Lord).

STUDY SUGGESTIONS

WORD STUDY

1. 'The Jewish nation was like an athlete running hard . . .' (p. 142). Write down the words and phrases which Paul used in this section to describe the making of a great effort in trying to approach God.

REVIEW OF CONTENT

2. Paul before his conversion was just like the Jews whom he described in this section. See Gal. 1.13, 14; Phil. 3.4–6; Acts 21.20; 22.3–5. What do you think can be said in favour of the Jews (and of Paul before his conversion), and what can be said against them?

3. Hundreds of years before Paul wrote these words about the Jews' rejection of Jesus, the Greek philosopher Plato wrote, 'If perfect goodness appeared among men as a stranger from another world,

all men would fall down and worship it.' Why was people's response to Jesus so different from what Plato had expected?

4. Many people (of all religions) believe that God will count up their evil deeds on the one hand, and their good deeds on the other, and will punish them if the evil deeds exceed the good, and reward them if the good exceed the evil. How does this common belief differ from Paul's teaching in this section?

BIBLE

5. In what ways can Jesus be both a stumbling-stone to people, and a rock which can save people? (See Luke 2.34, 35; John 3.17–19; 2 Cor. 2.15, 15.)

6. How does Rom. 9.30—10.21 help us to understand Jesus's parable about the tax collector (Luke 18.14)? Why could the Pharisee not be justified?

7. 'The Church should not go round recruiting preachers from schools and colleges' (p. 144).
(a) Why not? What should it do instead?
(b) What do the following passages teach us about how God calls people to be preachers? Amos 7.14, 15; Matt. 9.37, 38; Acts 6.2–6.

APPLICATION, OPINION, AND RESEARCH

8. 'God's Gospel is being heard everywhere' (p. 143), and see Col. 1.6, 23. In what sense was this true in New Testament times? To what extent do you think it is true today?

9. 'All that happens happens because it is God's will' (p. 140).
(a) What effect does this sort of belief have on people's behaviour towards people who suffer?
(b) According to Luke 13.1–5, John 5.5–9, and John 9.2 how did people regard those who were suffering?
(c) How did Jesus regard them and their suffering?
(d) Give some present-day examples of different attitudes towards people who suffer. What are the results of these attitudes?

10. Paul said that true religious privileges (e.g. the law) are an advantage to people (3.1). In what ways can such privileges sometimes turn out to be a *dis*advantage? Give examples from present-day life.

11. 'Jesus is Lord' (10.9).
(a) Do you think that this very short creed would be sufficient for a Christian convert today? Give reasons for your answer.
(b) Do you think this creed is more, or less, satisfactory than the creed which Christians often say: 'Jesus is my Saviour'?

12. (a) What did Paul mean when he said that the way of faith is easy?
(b) In what ways do some people find it difficult?

13. Some Church leaders suggest that the Church should not en-

145

courage Muslims who believe in Christ to confess their faith
openly in baptism, because if they do they are cut off for ever from
their own people: instead, these converts should simply go back
quietly to live amongst their own people as witnesses for Jesus.
What is your opinion?

14. Romans 10.9 'suggests that in order to be a Christian it is necessary'
to do three things (p. 144). (See also 1 Cor. 15.17; Phil. 2.9, 11;
Matt. 10.32, 33.)
(a) What are these three things?
(b) Is it really necessary for a person to do all these three things
before he can truly be a Christian?

15. 'Call upon the name of the Lord', wrote Paul. 'Decide to follow
Christ', say many Christian leaders today. What is the difference
in meaning between these two phrases? Which do you prefer,
and why?

11.1–36
God's Plan

OUTLINE

'But in fact God has not rejected all Israelites. Many, myself included,
have already obtained righteousness. Many more, it is true, have been
rejected, but this has resulted in many Gentiles hearing and believing
the Gospel. Thus we apostles learned the lesson that God accepts
anyone who believes, Jew or Gentile. Then what if the nation of Israel
should believe? They would be saved—and they will be, because that
is God's plan for them. You must not despise them, for we have all
turned against God, and any of us whom He accepts are accepted only
because of His mercy to us and His wonderful loving purpose for
mankind. Praise His name!'

INTRODUCTION

In chapters 9 and 10 Paul had taught that God is in control of all things,
and that human beings are responsible to Him—two important truths
which we must not forget if we are to understand anything of how God
works amongst men. But Paul had not yet given a satisfactory answer
to his chief problem, which was, 'What about all God's promises to
Israel—are they going to be fulfilled or not?' Paul faced this problem
in chapter 11, and gave a clear and reasoned solution to it. We should,
however, interpret what he said with care. Some of it is not clearly

taught anywhere else in the New Testament, so we cannot easily compare it with the teaching of other passages.

The three main sections of this chapter are described on p. 126, 2(c). In these three sections Paul opened up to his readers the wonder of God's plan for mankind. He ended the chapter with a hymn of praise to God for His great wisdom and mercy.

INTERPRETATION

Although the Israelites 'failed to obtain' a right relationship with God, because of their unbelief (9.30—10.21), yet God had not rejected them entirely. Paul used two examples to prove that God always preserves a faithful remnant, even when the situation seems hopeless (vv. 1–5). We who live 1,900 years later may be able to think of other examples of this from Christian history. E.g. the Church in Japan grew rapidly for 30 years after the arrival of the missionary Francis Xavier in 1549. Then the political leaders expelled all missionaries and began to persecute Christians. For 300 years Japanese people were not allowed to become Christians. But in 1859 missionaries were again permitted to enter Japan, and when they opened a church in Nagasaki in 1865, about 10,000 Japanese joined them, announcing that their families had been Christian ever since those far-off days in the sixteenth century. The same was true of Israel in Paul's time, so he reached the conclusion that 'there is a remnant, chosen by grace' (v. 5).

Paul then took up the two words 'chosen' (i.e. elect) and 'grace', and used them to show that he was not merely describing the way in which people respond to God, in faith or in unbelief. He was describing the way in which God does His work in the world, by choosing some and rejecting others, so that in the end all nations may receive His blessing (vv. 6–10).

In v. 11 Paul began his explanation of how God planned to extend His salvation beyond Israel to include the whole world, and then, in the end, to bring Israel in as well. The nation of Israel stumbled (see 9.32) but this did not mean that the nation was for ever lost. On the contrary, God had a definite purpose in allowing them to stumble. In vv. 11–16 Paul described the three stages in this purpose, first of all in outline (vv. 11, 12), then in detail (vv. 13–16, see question 3, p. 152):

Stage 1. Through Israel's unbelief, salvation comes to the Gentiles.

Stage 2. The Jews will be stirred up to envy when they see Gentiles enjoying the blessings which they themselves could have had. It often happens that those who most bitterly oppose the Gospel are really very near to accepting it. On 13 December, 1904, a young Indian, Sundar Singh, was angrily burning a Bible. Three days later he came

'Paul opened up to his readers the wonder of God's plan for mankind. . . . God is in control of all things and human beings are responsible to Him' (p. 146).

A senior officer in the Nigerian police explains the department's work plan to a young policewoman, and points out on a map the area she is responsible for. Who will judge her—and who will suffer—if she 'stumbles' in her duty?

to faith in Christ, was baptized the following year, and became one of India's leading Christian preachers.

Stage 3. The final stage will be Israel's full acceptance, so that through it all mankind may receive God's fullest blessings.

Before Christ, Israel had been God's people, and the Gentiles were outside.

Now Gentile believers, together with the chosen remnant of Israel, are included among God's people, and national Israel is outside (stage 1, above).

In the end, God's people will include both Gentiles and the nation of Israel as a whole (through faith), and none will be left outside (stage 3, above).

Paul went on to discuss the final stage of God's plan in vv. 25–32, but first he supported his teaching by an illustration (vv. 17–24). A farmer breaks off some of the branches of a cultivated olive tree which are not bearing fruit, and grafts on in their place some shoots from a wild olive tree. Later on he may even graft back on to the tree those branches which he had previously cut off. In fact, it is very unlikely that any good farmer would do just this, and Paul showed that he recognized this fact by the words 'contrary to nature' (v. 24). But the story does serve as a good illustration from daily life of the three stages of God's plan. Paul's particular aim, however, was to use the illustration as a warning to his Gentile readers, that they should not think that God specially favours them rather than the Jews. He was saying:

(a) It was the Jews' *unbelief* which caused them to be rejected, and the Gentiles were only accepted through *faith* (v. 20). The Gentiles' greatest danger was of becoming proud of their acceptance or of their faith. 'The faith of which a man boasts is faith no longer,' wrote one scholar; i.e. as soon as a person begins to rely upon *his own faith*, he is no longer humbly depending upon 'God's kindness' (v. 22). Every Christian believer needs warnings to 'continue in God's kindness', and the Bible is full of such warnings (e.g. Mark 13.13; 1 Cor. 10.24–27; Heb. 2.3). These warnings are the means by which God stirs us up to persevere in fellowship with Him (see Phil. 2.12, 13).

(b) Israel can be accepted again by God if they believe (v. 23). Not only *can* they, but they *will* be so accepted, because it is easier for God to accept an Israelite as one of His own people than a Gentile (v. 24). The experiences of the Jews described on p. 129 (d) remind us how little notice the Church has taken of Paul's warning, and how Christians have often acted as though the Jews are God's greatest enemies.

In ending his description of God's plan, in vv. 25–36, Paul emphasized three points which he regarded as of special importance:

1. God's plan is a mystery (v. 25), so we need not be surprised if we cannot understand the details of how it will be fulfilled. We need not

even be surprised if it seems to us unlikely to be fulfilled at all. See Additional Note, Mystery, p. 212.

2. God's plan involves the salvation of 'the full number of the Gentiles' and of 'all Israel' (vv. 25–27). By these expressions Paul probably meant each group as a whole. Perhaps he expected that very soon (even within his lifetime):

(a) He, together with others, would complete the mission to the Gentiles (see 15.18, 19);

(b) As a result, large numbers of Jews would come to faith in Christ;

(c) Finally Christ would return, to bring all His people to the experience of complete salvation.

We know today that all this did not happen as soon as Paul may have expected. But even today we should interpret these words in the way he intended, i.e. they probably refer not to every Gentile or every Israelite, nor even to the great majority, but to very large numbers of each group. The fact that even larger numbers had *not* believed made no difference to Paul's view of the matter—his mission had been *completed* (15.19).

3. The keynote of God's total plan is *mercy* (vv. 28–36). It is important to notice that Paul never suggested that God had in any way *altered* His plan. God planned to bless all nations through Israel, and He has done so. He planned to call Israel also, and He will do so. The whole plan is God's, and God's alone. No nation nor any man did anything at all towards thinking of it or accomplishing it. On the contrary, Jews and Gentiles alike (whether considered as national groups as in this chapter, or as individual persons, as in 3.19–23) were in a state of disobedience (v. 32). From that state God in His mercy rescues them; and He does so by this amazing plan which includes all men without distinction. God's mercy comes to men after their disobedience and condemnation under His wrath have left them unable to do anything at all except call upon His kindness and mercy. Mercy is man's only hope—and this is why Paul was so sure about final salvation. Human beings have no right to criticize God for anything at all. The only suitable response from them, and the only suitable ending to these chapters (1—11), is a hymn of praise, whose chief thought is the same as that of the hymn-writer who wrote:

> A debtor to mercy alone;
> Of covenant mercy I sing.

NOTES

V. 2. Foreknew: See p. 117.

V. 5. A remnant chosen by grace: See Additional Notes, Election, p. 204.

Grace, p. 209). The remnant had faith and did not serve Baal, but this did not mean that they earned for themselves God's mercy. The word 'grace' shows that God's mercy in choosing them came first.

V. 7. Hardened: This word seems to suggest that Israel refused to believe *because* God had purposely hardened them. It may be difficult for us to accept this idea, but see the discussion of this problem on pp. 135 and 136.

V. 14. To make my fellow-Jews jealous: Paul had already experienced both the anger and the jealousy of the Jews, because of their opposition to the way in which he accepted believing Gentiles as truly God's people. He realized that this jealousy could eventually lead many Jews to have the same faith in Christ as the Gentiles, and he drew two conclusions from this:

(a) He would work all the harder in his mission to the Gentiles, because by this means not only Gentiles but also Jews would achieve salvation.

(b) Those few Jews who believed as a result of his ministry at that time were 'first fruits' (see p. 113), i.e. they were an indication that the whole nation belonged to God, and would be accepted by Him in the end, through faith.

V. 15. Reconciliation: See Additional Note, p. 213.

Life from the dead: These words may mean that the final stage in God's plan (i.e. the acceptance of Israel as a whole) would be immediately followed by the resurrection of the bodies of those who had died, and by the other events connected with the end and the return of Jesus.

V. 18. Do not boast over the branches: All religious people tend to think of themselves as God's chosen people, and to regard as God's enemies all who are not like them. Gentile Christians at Rome probably shared this tendency, especially in view of the disputes which they had had with Jews in the past, and the misunderstandings which may have arisen between Gentile and Jewish Christians. See pp. 11, 12 (c) and (d).

V. 25. The full number of the Gentiles: The Greek word for 'full number' is the same as that translated 'full inclusion' in v. 12, where it must mean the same as 'all Israel' (v. 26), i.e. the group as a whole, not just a remnant.

V. 26. All Israel: Jewish writers used this phrase to mean the nation as a whole, not every single Israelite. One of them wrote, 'All Israel has a share in the world to come'—but not, he added, Sadducees, heretics, magicians, and a long list of others.

As it is written: Paul here combined two passages from the Jewish Scriptures (Isa. 59.20; Jer. 31.34) to support his teaching that God will save Israel in the end.

V. 32. Have mercy upon all: The word 'all' may suggest that Paul thought that in the end everyone in the world would believe in Christ;

but it is more likely that he meant that *all kinds* of people will be saved. God purposes to abolish the old distinctions between Jew and Gentile, and to bring all into a right relationship with Him.

V. 36. To him are all things: The idea is the same as that found in Psalm 103.20–22: all things exist for God and His glory. 'My soul' must see to it that it, too, lives for God and His glory. But how do we give glory to God? Not just by singing hymns of praise (though that is part of it). Paul told his readers how in the next four chapters.

STUDY SUGGESTIONS

WORD STUDY

1. What four words, in addition to the word 'grace', did Paul use in 11.1–7 to show that it is God rather than man who does the work of setting men right with Him.

2. What is meant by 'the elect' (v. 7)?

REVIEW OF CONTENT

3. In 11.13–16 Paul repeated the teaching of 11.11, 12.
   (a) What details did he *add* in 11.13–16?
   (b) What ideas did he simply repeat in slightly different words?

4. If Paul had not explained God's plan for Israel, why might the Gentiles have been 'wise in their own conceits' (v. 25)? What attitude does this phrase describe?

5. (a) Some people, on reading 11.32, might think that Paul taught that in the end everyone would be saved. Was this his teaching? Give reasons for your answer. (See 2.5–10; 5.18; 11.20, 23.)
   (b) What has been the result of Israel's disobedience?

6. In what ways are Jewish and Gentile Christians dependent on one another?

BIBLE

7. (a) Why did Elijah feel discouraged?
   (b) What similar experiences of discouragement did Paul have?
   (c) What causes of discouragement and what remedies for it are suggested in Rom. 11.1–5; Phil. 1.12–26; 2.3–5; and how can Christians today be helped by these passages?

8. (a) In what ways are the following passages similar to v. 8?
   Mark 4.11, 12   John 12.40   Acts 28.26–28
   (b) To what different groups of people do the above passages refer?

9. Read Acts 13.44–50, 17.5–15, and 18.5–13. Which verses in these passages refer to:
   (a) the rejection of the Gospel by the Jews;
   (b) the acceptance of the Gospel by the Gentiles;
   (c) the resulting jealousy of the Jews.

10. Read Matt. 28.19; Acts 1.8; 11.1–8; 11.19–23; 15.6–11. What were the chief reasons which led the earliest Christian preachers to offer the Gospel to Gentiles as well as Jews?

11. Why were many of the Jews made angry and jealous by the way in which the early Church thought of itself, as described in Gal. 6.16; Phil. 3.3; 1. Pet. 2.9, 10; Rev. 2.9?

APPLICATION, OPINION, AND RESEARCH

12. (a) In what ways was Sundar Singh's experience as described on p. 147 (2) similar to that of the apostle Paul?
    (b) If you can, give from your own experience or from history any similar examples of anger and jealousy leading to a person's conversion.

13. Paul believed that his preaching to the Gentiles would lead in the end to the conversion of the Jews. Ministry to one group may also have a great influence on other groups.
    (a) How was this true of Jesus's ministry (John 4.22, 23; Matt. 8.5–12; 15.21–28; 27.54)
    (b) Give examples of how this can be true of the Church's ministry today.

14. How would you reply to a person who said, 'God has His plan for everyone, and will not change it whatever *we* do. So there is no point in trying to have faith or to please Him.'?

15. In many countries today, as in ancient Israel, there is a strong spirit of national pride, which we call 'nationalism'.
    (a) What is the Christian 'nation', and what kind of 'nationalism' should Christians have? (See 1 Pet. 2.4–10.)
    (b) Can Christian 'nationalism' be combined with political nationalism? Give examples to support your answer.

16. In what circumstances does religious 'faith' sometimes lead people *away* from God rather than *towards* Him? How does that kind of 'faith' differ from what Paul meant by faith? How can we guard against having the wrong kind of faith?

17. For what sort of purpose do human beings 'elect' each other? What are the chief differences between this sort of 'election' and 'election' by God? (See Rom. 8.29, 30 and 11.5–7.)

PART 5

THE BEHAVIOUR OF GOD'S PEOPLE

12.1–8
Christian Conduct and the
Common Life in the Body of Christ

OUTLINE

'Because God, in His mercy, has done all this for you, you should now live your lives for Him. Christians must not have too high an opinion of themselves, nor live as isolated individuals. Because we belong to Christ, we belong also to one another like different parts of the body, and we should each do what we can for the good of the whole Christian community.'

INTRODUCTION

All groups of people everywhere observe a certain way of life. A people's way of life can be described as their 'code of behaviour', or 'code of conduct', or 'ethics'. Julius Nyerere, in his booklet *Socialism and Rural Development*, has described traditional African ethics in terms of three basic principles: respect for every individual person; the sharing of basic goods; the obligation of all to work. In ancient times Jewish ethics were governed by the law of Moses. For many centuries Buddhists have followed an 'Eight-fold path' which they believe will lead them to a perfect state of freedom from suffering and desire. Here in chapter 12 Paul began to give his statement of *Christian* ethics. Verses 1 and 2 form the introduction to this statement, which is contained in 12.3 to 15.13. For the main divisions of this statement, see 'Plan of Romans', p. 5. For a summary of its teaching, see pp. 189, 190.

Paul based his 'appeal' to his readers (12.1) on the doctrinal teaching which he had given them in chapters 1—11. The word 'therefore' refers to all this teaching, and the phrase 'the mercies of God' is a direct link with the theme-word of chapters 9—11: mercy (see p. 134). *Because* of God's mercy towards us, we owe Him a duty. Paul had already expressed this thought earlier in the letter, when he spoke of:

(a) Christian obedience (1.5; 6.16, 17), which includes both responding to the Gospel with faith and living righteously (see Additional Note, Obedience, p. 213);

154

(b) The exhortation to live for God (6.11–14) because of what He has done for us (see pp. 85, 86).

(c) Praise and thanksgiving (11.32–36) from those who understand God's mercy.

As the Church grew during the 30 years after the death of Jesus, Christians handed down to one another many traditions, some of them probably written, some spoken, which they valued very highly. Some of these concerned the life and teaching of Jesus (see p. 190); some concerned Christian doctrine (see pp. 7, 9); some concerned Christian conduct. Paul referred to such a tradition of Christian conduct in 2 Thess. 3.6. Probably some such tradition is partly preserved in Rom. 12.3—13.14.

INTERPRETATION

The earth contains a great variety of different forms of life. Animals, birds, insects, fish, human beings—all have different ways of life. Even amongst individuals there are great differences. It is said that no two people are exactly alike. This is how God has made the world—a world of diversity. Yet all the differences have their origin in one God. The same pattern is found in the Christian Church. Therefore two of the most important lessons which Christians can learn are found in this short paragraph. They are:

1. The *unity* of all Christians in Christ. Christians sometimes think so much of themselves as individuals and of how they differ from one another that they forget their basic unity which comes from Christ. The Christians at Corinth made this mistake (1 Cor. 12.4–13), and so did those at Rome (12.3; see p. 3, e). Paul tried to correct this mistake in his letters to both groups by comparing the Church to a human body (Rom. 12.4, 5; 1 Cor. 12—where the comparison is much more extended). Like the many parts of a body, so Christians are united to Christ and share His life. A young minister was once preaching about the different gifts which God has given to Christians, and said, 'I have a great preaching gift—but the lips that do the speaking belong to a man called Billy Graham—but it is my gift, because we are members one of another. I am a great theological scholar—but the mind that does the thinking is in the head of a man called Karl Barth—but the gift is mine to rejoice in, because we are members one of another.'

2. The *diversity* of Christians. The diversity is as much God's intention for us as the unity, because it helps the whole body to work properly. All the many parts of the body are interdependent. Often the Church has laid down rules which every Christian must follow. Sometimes it may be right to do this, but we must recognize that not all Christians are the same. What is right for one may not be right for all. We all need the help of Christians who are different from ourselves. Paul wanted his

'Because we belong to Christ we also belong to one another. We all need the help of Christians who are different from ourselves' (pp. 154, 155).

Fans applauded Pele, 'King of soccer', as he left the football ground. But victory belonged to the *whole* Brazilian team; *all* the members were needed, each in his different place, to make sure of winning the match. What sort of 'matches' can Christians help each other to win in everyday life?

readers to understand this when he wrote Ephesians 4.1–16. A small group of students in a college were given the opportunity of doing an advanced course of English study. Others in the college complained, saying, 'Why are they preferred to us? We all have a right to do the course. We should all be treated the same.' But Christians are *not* all the same. They are different, and possess different gifts, some natural and some spiritual, all of which must be developed in different ways. It is the responsibility of each Christian (a) to discover what gifts God has given him; (b) to make sure that he has the opportunity of using those gifts. It is the responsibility of every Christian minister to help all the people to do this.

NOTES

V. 1. Present your bodies . . . your spiritual worship: Paul was here using the language of sacrifice. For Christians, true worship does not consist of animal sacrifices as offered by Jews and by pagans. Nor does it consist only in the offering up of the human spirit to God, as some Greek philosophers taught; nor only in praising God in church services—though both of these are part of it. Christians must worship God with their bodies, i.e. in all the activities of body and mind in daily life. They must do so by carefully considering what sort of behaviour is in conformity with God's will, and then making this behaviour the pattern of their lives. This kind of worship is both 'spiritual' (i.e. consisting not in outward ceremonies but in the devotion of the whole person to God, see 1 Pet. 2.5; John 4.23), and 'reasonable' (the translation which some scholars prefer). A college student who spends his holiday travelling round to attend Christian meetings may not be worshipping God as truly as he would be if he went home to build a house for his widowed mother, or to keep her company. Indeed, his attendance at Christian meetings may be completely unacceptable to God if it means being absent from his mother who needs him.

V. 2. Conformed . . . transformed: People live in this world (i.e. this 'age') and belong to it. They think more about their next meal than about God, more about their own advantage than about serving Him. It is natural to do so. Paul had described this situation in 1.18–32. But people who belong to Christ belong to God's new age, and should live in a way suitable to the new age. This is not easy, because we still live in this age, and tend to think and behave like those around us. Therefore we are involved in a continual conflict. For an explanation of the two ages, see Special Note, pp. 122–124. Paul also used the word here translated 'transformed' in 2 Cor. 3.18, to describe how believers are changed into the likeness of Christ.

The renewal of your mind: Christian believers have *already* been changed.

When they belonged to this age only, they had a 'base mind' (1.28), but now their minds have been renewed and serve God's law (7.25). Those who have been so renewed should live new lives in accordance with God's will (see 6.11–14, and the explanation on pp. 85, 86). The mind which God has renewed can recognize and discover God's will, but may still need a good deal of practical help to do so. Paul went on to give this kind of help in the sections which follow.

Prove: The Greek word translated 'prove' is connected with the one translated 'character' in 5.4 (see p. 65). Paul was describing how we are led, first to discover the will of God, then to do it, and finally to prove from our own experience how good and satisfying His will is. This process goes on throughout our lives and is part of the excitement of following Jesus Christ. There are new discoveries every day. A similar process took place when an agricultural expert was sent to a group of villages in Tanzania. He planted one field of crops in the traditional way, and another field using modern methods of cultivation. The villagers had first to *discover* that the modern methods were better; then to *do* it for themselves; then to *prove* from their own experience of cultivation that it was a better method for them to follow.

V. 3. The grace given to me: See 1.5. The grace of apostleship was a gift from God which Paul had to use for the benefit of all the Christians to whom he ministered.

Everyone among you: Every individual Christian needs to be warned not to think of himself simply as an individual Christian.

Sober judgement: The Greek word here is difficult to translate into English, but Paul's more educated readers would have been familiar with the idea, i.e. that people should never follow any extremes of behaviour, but should be moderate in everything, as the Stoic philosophers taught (see p. 65).

According to the measure of faith: These words show that Paul meant that we should consider ourselves as we truly are. By so doing we shall fit in well in our Christian community and the result will be peace and harmony, The word 'faith' in this verse seems to mean 'spiritual power', as in 1 Cor. 13.2.

V. 6. Prophecy: Paul described this gift in 1 Cor. 14.3, 24, 31. He was not referring to the gift of foretelling the future, which Agabus possessed (Acts 11.28; 21.11). Today we should probably use the word 'preaching', but Paul was thinking particularly of that sort of preaching which is (a) directly inspired by the Holy Spirit, bringing a word from God (see Acts 13.1, 2); (b) for the benefit of Christian believers, and (c) aimed at strengthening them in faith and life. Such a gift may have been more needful in the first century, before Christians had the books of the New Testament, than it is today. But there are no good reasons for saying (as some scholars have done) that the gift does not exist today. Perhaps

Christians have forgotten it, or are afraid of what might happen if they allow all sorts of people to speak in the Church. But groups which do allow it often find that their worship is enriched, although there may be dangers of disorder as well. Christians in East Africa exercise a similar gift when they meet in fellowship groups and are all free to speak some word which they feel can be helpful to their fellow-Christians.

In proportion to our faith: This is a difficult phrase, but here is one possible interpretation:

Christians should live every part of their lives in faith. We should therefore use our gifts to the extent we believe God enables us to do so (see v. 3b). For example, many preachers go on speaking long after they have finished giving God's message, or stand up to speak without having taken the trouble to listen to God first. On the other hand, some who have a word from God are too shy to speak it as they should. But, by using our minds, we should keep control of the way we use the gifts which God has given us.

V. 7. Service: This means helping those who are in need. Although every Christian is called to do this, yet some are specially gifted for this work, and should make sure that they do it. Some people think that service is 'unspiritual' work, or that it can be done by anyone without any special gift. For example, in modern society the best nurses often do not nurse, and the best teachers often do not teach. Because they have been successful at nursing and teaching, they have been 'promoted' to other jobs of administration and leadership which are regarded as more important. The Church must not make this mistake, because service is a special gift possessed by few. Each Christian must fully use his own gift. As we acquire greater skill and gain experience we become capable of exercising more responsibility, and perhaps directing the work of others. But we should not move on to another job for which we may not be suited, simply to gain in status. There is no such thing as 'promotion' in the Christian Church.

Teaching . . . exhortation: It is customary today for these gifts to be exercised in the Church by ordained or appointed preachers. But there may be lay people also to whom God has given the special gift of explaining Christian truth (like the Church teachers appointed by John Calvin in Switzerland in the sixteenth century), or of exhortation (like Howell Harries who, although he was never a pastor, held many meetings in Wales in the eighteenth century, where he stirred up Christians to live in accordance with God's will).

V. 8. Liberality: All Christians should give money or other gifts for Christian work, in accordance with principles such as those stated in 2 Cor. 8 and 9 and 1 Cor. 16.1, 2. But some are able to take special responsibility for this work. John Wesley told Christian businessmen to try to be as successful as possible in their business, so that they could support God's work generously. This, too, is a gift (or 'grace') which comes from God (see 2 Cor. 8.6, 7). Not everyone has it.

Gives aid: A better translation would be 'he who presides' or 'he who administers'. Perhaps Paul was thinking of those who had to decide how to use the money which had been contributed. Perhaps these men were church leaders of some sort, but we should notice that administration is a gift which is possessed by some, but not by all. Not all leaders are good administrators, and some ought, perhaps, to be released from administrative work. For example, the administrator of a college may be a different person from the Principal; and the chief administrator of a diocese need not be the bishop—yet he often is.

Acts of mercy: These words may mean the same as 'service' (v. 7), but probably refer especially to showing love and care for the suffering. In any ministry to such people, it is important to be 'cheerful'. We must be truly sympathetic (see v. 15), but must not allow ourselves to become depressed by their sad condition. Our task is to lead them to joy in Christ, not to increase their misery.

STUDY SUGGESTIONS

WORD STUDY

1. Explain in simple language the meaning of the word 'ethics'. If you know a language other than English, how would you translate 'ethics' into that language?

2. Which *four* of the following words would you expect to find regularly used in connection with sacrifice?
   faith   offer   present   mercy   spotless   consecrated   law   righteous

REVIEW OF CONTENT

3. (a) Make a list of the gifts which Paul mentioned in Romans 12.1–8.
   (b) Classify the gifts you have listed into groups, e.g. gifts of speaking, etc.
   (c) List the gifts again in a different order, this time beginning with the one which is most common in your Church, and ending with the one which is most rarely exercised. In what ways, if any, do you think your Church needs to change the way it exercises the various gifts?

4. How would you describe the relationship between the different members of Christ's body?

5. What is the connection between Christian faith and Christian conduct?

6. After his teaching about faith (chapters 1—11) Paul went on to write about Christian ethics (chapters 12—15). In a similar way, divide the letter to the Ephesians into two sections, one about ideas, the other about behaviour. At what point does the division come, and in what ways is the first verse of the ethical section similar to Rom. 12.1?

7. 'For Christians, worship does not consist of animal sacrifices' (p. 157). What sort of sacrifices do Christians make, according to the following passages?
   Rom. 12.1; 15.16; Heb. 13.15; 13.16; 1 Pet. 2.5

8. Read 1 Cor. 12.12–26; Eph. 4.15, 16; 5.23–30.
   (a) In what ways are these passages like Rom. 12.4, 5?
   (b) In what ways are they unlike?

APPLICATION, OPINION, AND RESEARCH

9. What is 'spiritual' (or, 'reasonable') worship? Give examples of such worship. Is the worship of your own Church 'spiritual'? In what ways, if any, could it be made more 'spiritual'?

10. (a) If Christians have been renewed through the Gospel, possess the Holy Spirit, and have the fellowship of the Church and the example of Christ, why do they still need detailed instruction of the sort which Paul gives in chapters 12 and 13?
    (b) For what sort of people is such ethical teaching *not* suitable? What do they need first?

11. What is likely to happen in the Church, if Christians think of themselves too much as isolated individuals?

12. Read again the story of the young minister on p. 155. How does the illustration of the body help Christians to conquer (a) pride, (b) jealousy?

13. Some of the 'gifts' which Paul mentioned in this passage (e.g. contributing), and some of the examples used in this chapter of the Guide (e.g. the study of English, p. 157) seem to have more to do with natural abilities than with spiritual powers.
    (a) Do you think it is possible to classify gifts as 'natural' or 'spiritual'?
    (b) What is the relationship between the natural abilities which people have and the spiritual gifts God gives His people? Give examples.

14. How would you answer a Christian who said:
    (a) 'I am only an ordinary person and have no gift of any value'?

(b) 'Everyone, not just the pastor, should have a chance to preach in this church—let us all take turns.'?

15. (a) Make a list of the gifts which you possess. (1 Cor. 12.28 and Eph. 4.11 may give you further ideas.) What makes you think you possess them?

(b) Are you using these gifts? If not, why not? If so, how do they benefit the Church? How could you use them more?

(c) Do you think you are doing some work for which you do *not* have the gift?

16. 'There is no such thing as "promotion" in the Christian Church' (p. 159). What is your opinion?

17. This passage has suggested that there is work for every Christian to do in the Church.

What do you think is the *special* responsibility, if any, which the pastor has in the local congregation? Eph. 4.7–16 may give you some ideas.

18. In some areas Church leaders seem reluctant to allow ordinary Christians to use their gifts. What is the reason for this?

12.9–21
The Life of Love

OUTLINE

'Be active in good deeds, and care sympathetically for one another, even for those who oppose you. Kill evil with goodness.'

INTRODUCTION

In 12.3–8 Paul had shown how Christians differ from one another—each has a different function. Here he told his readers how *all* Christians should behave all the time. We should distinguish between Christian teaching about behaviour which applies to every Christian, and other teaching which may apply only to certain classes of Christians, perhaps depending on what gifts they possess.

INTERPRETATION

The basic theme of this passage is *love*. All the instructions which Paul gave here arise out of the command to love (v. 9, 10). Paul said more about this in 13.8–10. The word 'love' is used today to mean many different things. It is important that Christians should understand clearly the meaning of the word as Paul used it. See Additional Note, Love, p. 211.

It is not enough to tell Christians simply to 'show love'. Some modern Christian teachers say that you can do anything you like as long as you do it in love. This may be true; the real problem is that we find it very difficult to know how much our actions are being governed by selfishness and how much by love for others. In any case, it is difficult today to know exactly what love is in any particular situation. Therefore, in our human weakness, we need special instructions of the sort which Paul gave here. All of them explain what love is, and how it should show itself in various circumstances. Much of Paul's teaching here is based upon the teaching of Jesus. See Special Note, p. 190, 4, 5.

NOTES

V. 9. Genuine: This word means 'not hypocritical'. Our love for others should be like God's love for us. See Additional Note, *Love*, p. 211, 3. A good example of this sort of love is seen in the story on p. 49 of the Chinese.

V. 10a. Brotherly affection: This word reminds us of how we should regard other members of Christ's new family.

V. 10b: See Phil. 2.3 and Rom. 12.3.

V. 11, 12: In v. 11 Paul spoke of what we do; but in v. 12 gave a reminder of how we need to rely on what God has done and will do for us. What we *do* forms only a small part of God's plan for us.

V. 13a: Paul described how some Christians did this in 15.25–27.

V. 13b. Hospitality: This is a very important duty in many parts of the world, including the areas where the apostles worked. Writers in the New Testament wrote a good deal about hospitality for the sake of Christ, and Christians need these reminders, because hospitality is forgotten in many modern societies.

V. 15: It is obvious that it is difficult to love one's enemies (v. 14), but it is equally difficult to show true sympathy as described in v. 15, and is only possible for those who do not put themselves first in their life and thinking.

V. 16: Associate with the lowly: An African pastor asked to be provided with a car because, he said, 'the Europeans in my parish will not respect what I say unless I drive a car as they do'. See Luke 14.12–14.

Conceited: See 11.25 (a special warning to Gentile Christians); 12.3.

V. 17b. In the sight of all: Compare Luke 2.52; Acts 2.47; 1 Peter 2.12.

V. 19–21: If we do have an enemy (and it is not always possible to avoid this), there are three principles here which should guide us in our dealings with him:

1. Like Jesus, we should never try to pay him back for his wrong deeds (v. 19; see 1 Pet. 2.23). Such repayment is 'vengeance' and must be left to God. God's wrath is good and right; ours will probably be wrong

in some way. God shows His wrath against wrong-doers in three chief ways:

(a) In the laws of nature, which often cause suffering to the man who goes against those laws.

(b) In the laws of nations, where God uses rulers and judges to punish those who break the laws. The similarity between the words of v. 19 and those of 13.4 suggest that this thought was in Paul's mind here, even before he discussed it in detail in chapter 13.

(c) In His final judgement at the last day (see Additional Note, *Judgement*, p. 209). See Additional Note, *Wrath*, pp. 221.

2. We should actually try to help our enemy, because this will achieve the result of causing him burning pain (v. 20). Paul was here quoting from Proverbs 25.21, 22, but he left out the last line and put in his own words (v. 21) instead. This shows that he was giving a new meaning to the proverb, i.e. 'Acts of kindness towards an evil man will lead him first to recognize the goodness of these acts and the evil of his own life; secondly to resist the goodness; finally perhaps to the painful experience of repentance and change.'

3. If this happens, we have succeeded in changing an enemy into a friend (v. 21). By this means evil is destroyed and turned into good. This is how God Himself acted towards us. God has shown us that love is the most powerful force in the world. The great French Emperor Napoleon recognized this at the end of his life, when he said, 'Alexander, Charlemagne, and I built great empires by force. Jesus built His empire by love. Now I am forsaken by all, yet there are millions who would gladly die for Him.'

STUDY SUGGESTIONS

WORD STUDY

1. In what different ways is the word 'love' used today? Give examples to show the different meaning it can have. In what ways are these meanings like Paul's idea of *agape*, and in what ways are they different?

REVIEW OF CONTENT

2. Write, in your own words, a more detailed outline of this passage than the one given on p. 162.

3. (a) How should we treat our fellow-Christians?
(b) How should we treat those who hate us—and perhaps hate Christ also?

BIBLE

4. Which of the following passages give teaching which is for every Christian, and which give teaching for particular groups only?

'Love is the most powerful force in the world, but sometimes it is difficult to know whether our actions are governed by love for others or by selfishness' (pp.163, 164).

The Soviet Union sends gifts of relief goods to a famine area. Some people say that the powerful nations give help to weaker ones for political reasons. What is your opinion?

(a) Col. 3.18–4.1   (b) Gal. 5.16–23   (c) 1 Cor. 14.26–36   (d) 1 Pet. 2.13–17.

5. 'Practise hospitality' (12.13). What did the writer of 3 John say about hospitality? Why was this such an important duty?

6. Read the words of Jesus in the following passages: (a) Luke 6.27; (b) Luke 6.28; (c) Matt. 5.9; (d) Matt. 5.39; (e) Mark 9.50. In which verses of Rom. 12.9–21 does it seem that Paul was following the teaching of Jesus in those five passages?

7. 'Live in harmony with one another' (12.16). In Philippians 2.1–5 Paul told his readers to be of 'one mind'. Does this mean that Christians should always agree about everything? If not, what does being of 'one mind' mean?

8. (i) In what three chief ways does God show His wrath against wrong-doers?
   (ii) Which of these ways is described in each of the following passages:
   (a) Rom. 13.1–7   (b) Rom. 1.27   (c) 2 Cor. 5.10

9. 'Our love for our fellow human beings is . . . an extension of God's love for us' (p. 212). In each of the following passages,
   (i) What word is used to describe God's love?
   (ii) How are we told to respond to, and also to imitate, His love?
   (a) Rom. 12.1   (b) Rom. 15.7   (c) 2 Cor. 5.14   (d) Eph. 4.32—5.2.

APPLICATION, OPINION, AND RESEARCH

10. Most people like to be respected by others; they do not like to appear foolish. What should be the Christian's attitude to honour and respect? See Rom. 12.10, 14–16, and 1 Cor. 4.10–13. How, if at all, should Christians obey this teaching today?

11. In what ways, if any, did the African pastor mentioned on p. 163 (v. 16) have a mistaken attitude?

12. (a) 'Noble . . . in the sight of all' (v. 17). What is the reputation of Christians in your country today? (See also Acts 2.47.)
    (b) What sort of things does the community as a whole ('all') in your country regard as 'noble' or 'honourable'? To what extent is it *right* for Christians to follow 'public opinion' in the way which Paul seems to suggest? To what extent would it be an advantage for them to do so, and to what extent a disadvantage?

13. Read again the instructions which Paul gave in this passage, one by one. In what practical ways should a Christian of today obey each instruction?

13.1-7
Christian Citizenship

OUTLINE

'Submit to the laws of the land, because governments have been set up by God, and they do His work in the world. Therefore give to the government all that it has a right to demand.'

INTRODUCTION

These verses come in the middle of a passage about showing love (12.14–21 and 13.8–10). They are connected with the ethical teaching of chapters 12 and 13 in the following ways:

1. God rules His world in love, and also in justice. He punishes evil (12.19) and one of the ways in which He does this is by using governments and their laws (13.4; see p. 164 (b). In doing so He shows both love and justice towards mankind. Christians can do the same, and work for the good of their fellow-men, by supporting the government and helping to preserve it.

2. Some Christians may have thought that, if they had died with Christ to the powers of this age, then they need no longer obey the pagan governments and laws of this age (see Rom. 7.4–6; 12.2). Paul showed that such thinking was mistaken, because God wants us to continue to live in His world as it is until He takes us out of it, as He will (13.11–14).

3. Ethical teaching which is meant to guide individual Christians (e.g. 12.19) is often unsuitable for governments; and behaviour which may be right for a government (e.g. 13.4) may often be wrong for an individual in his personal relationship with people. But the existence of a strong and just government to control people's behaviour makes it easier for individuals to be kind and forgiving to one another.

NOTES

V. 1. Be subject to: This word does not mean simply 'obey', though it includes the idea of obedience. It means 'submit to'. The first Christian teachers told slaves to be subject to masters, children to parents, wives to husbands, the Church to Christ—but also everyone to everyone else, because of the supreme authority of Christ over everyone (see Eph. 5.21). Those who acknowledge Christ's authority have a duty to honour, to serve, and to care for other people. Paul emphasized this idea in chapter 12 (see vv. 10, 16, 17; also Phil. 2.3, 4), and continued it in chapter 13, i.e. Christians have a duty to serve and to preserve the government *because of* the supreme authority of God. To be subject normally means to obey, but there may be occasions when it involves disobeying—because we recognize that God's authority is supreme. See below, pp. 172.

The governing authorities: When Paul wrote this letter, the Emperor Nero was ruling well, with the help of his Provincial governors, army, and magistrates. He had not yet begun to persecute Christians. Most people were ready to obey such an Emperor, even though they had not chosen him and could not depose him or influence his decisions. He ruled by force because he controlled the army, and no one could resist his power.

Instituted by God: Paul had had no experience of democracy, and did not distinguish between various forms of government, nor did he consider the way in which rulers were appointed—in the Roman Empire often through bribery, deceit, or murder. But he did teach that God has ordained that there should be government in human society, and that no one can be a ruler except by God's permission and direction. This was true of Nero, of Pontius Pilate, and of the Council of the Jews in Jerusalem—even though these men at times disregarded God and misused the authority He had given them.

V. 2. Resists what God has appointed: These words seem to mean that revolution or even disobedience is always wrong. This is certainly so, if vv. 3 and 4 are a true description of the government. But if the government opposes good conduct and supports bad, then it may be our duty to resist, in order to submit to God. Those who do so will certainly be punished by the government; but Paul did not say that to resist the government is necessarily to resist God Himself, but only the authority which He has appointed.

V. 3. Not a terror to good conduct: It is generally true that governments punish those who steal, kill, and disrupt the peace of society. But also governments are often guilty of these crimes themselves. Paul could have named many evils done by Rome, but in spite of this Rome became famous for the justice and peace which her government brought to the world. Both Paul and Peter were eventually condemned and put to death by the government for doing good. But Peter taught that even if that happens, there is still no need to be afraid, because to suffer punishment for the sake of righteousness is really to receive God's blessing (1 Pet. 3.13–17; 4.14–16).

V. 4. God's servant for your good: Both Jews and pagans in Paul's time recognized that governments were a part of world order and were necessary for human prosperity. Paul was able also to see that the government benefited the Christian Church. Christians have always

'The problem is how to apply Paul's teaching (about the relationship between Christians and the Government) . . . sincere Christians disagree sharply about these matters' (p. 171).

A bishop of the Orthodox Church in Kurdistan is a member of the local Revolutionary Council. He inspects soldiers whose aim is to overthrow the present government. Do you think he can fruitfully serve both the Revolution and the Church?

prayed for the government of their country. In North Africa in AD 197 Tertullian wrote, 'We Christians are always interceding for all the Emperors. We pray for them long life, a secure rule, a safe home, brave armies, a faithful senate, an honest people, a quiet world—and everything for which a man and an Emperor can pray. . . . We must respect the Emperor as the chosen of our Lord. So I have a right to say, Caesar is more ours than yours, appointed as he is by our God.' Some scholars have interpreted vv. 4 and 6 to mean that rulers are only God's servants in so far as they act justly. This interpretation is mistaken: according to Paul they are God's servants not because of the way in which they rule, but because they are appointed by Him.

The sword: Governments have power of life or death over their subjects, but Christians today hold different opinions about whether or not it can ever be right for a government to put a person to death, even for a serious crime like murder. Paul's teaching in this pasage does not help us to decide this question.

To execute his wrath: See Special Note on p. 175.

V. 5. In this verse Paul gave two reasons for being subject to the laws of the state:

1. Because we shall be punished if we are not.

2. Because God exercises His authority, in part, through the governments which He has appointed; if we disobey them, our conscience will accuse us of rebelling against God's authority (see Notes on 2.15, pp. 37, 38). This second reason is more important than the first, and can itself be a reason for *breaking* unjust laws when they go against God's own will for mankind.

V. 6. You also pay taxes: Governments need a lot of money in order to administer the state and maintain their armies. By paying taxes, we help the government to do the job of governing which God has given it. Rulers have a *right* to demand taxes from their subjects; but they also have a *responsibility* to use these taxes for the good of the whole country, and not to spend them on luxury living for themselves or on special privileges for certain groups.

V. 7. Dues: Paul took the view that the government had the right to demand certain things from its subjects, but he did not suggest that they should obey it when it demanded things (e.g. worship) to which it had no right.

Respect . . . honour: See 1 Pet. 2.17. When Peter wrote, Nero was beginning to rule badly, and cruelly to persecute Christians. It must have been difficult to honour such a man.

INTERPRETATION

The chief points of Paul's teaching in this passage are clear. But the chief problem is how to interpret and apply his teaching to the very different circumstances in which Christians live today. We face different problems from his, and we have opportunities to influence the government which Paul never had. Some of the problems which have confronted Christians in recent years are listed below, together with a short description of some of the solutions different people have tried to give to these problems. Sincere Christians disagree sharply with one another about most of these matters, and it is important to remember to respect and love as brothers those whose opinions are different from our own.

1. *Are all governments appointed by God*, and do they have a right to make laws for their subjects? Karl Marx wrote that capitalist governments have no right to govern and will be overthrown by the workers. Some Christian revolutionaries have expressed a similar opinion, but most Christians think that such a view is clearly contradicted by this passage and other passages in the New Testament. See p. 168.

2. *Can a government become so evil that it no longer has the right to govern?* Pastor Dietrich Bonhoeffer thought that this had become true of the Nazi regime in his own country, Germany, in 1944 (see below, p. 173).

3. *Should Christians always support the government?* Some Christian revolutionary scholars have written that God is active in changing His world for the better, and He does so by revolutionary methods—therefore Christians have a duty to discover how God is working in His world and co-operate with Him. This sort of argument can be used to support freedom fighters who try to overthrow the oppressive and racist regimes in their countries. But it can also support the action of anyone who wants to oppose by force the government in power—and it does not offer any guidance in distinguishing between those actions and events in the world which God approves of, and those which He does not. Most of the evidence available in the New Testament suggests that God is at least as much 'on the side' of existing governments as He is on the side of revolution. In any case, a Christian's conduct should be guided by what God has revealed as just and righteous. It should not depend on 'what is happening' in the world (which would be no help in making a decision whether to support Pilate, or Jesus, or the Jewish high-priests).

4. *Which is the legitimate government of a country at any one time?* It is sometimes difficult to decide this question in times of war or of revolution. Mr Ian Smith's government does in fact control Rhodesia, but many other countries regard it as illegal. Sheikh Mujibur Rachman heads the government of Bangladesh, but it would be difficult to say on what date he really began to do so. Some countries, like Guinea-Bissau, are controlled partly by one government and partly by another.

5. *On what occasions should Christians refuse to obey the government?*
There are three possible answers to this question:

(a) When it commands things which are forbidden by God, or forbids
things commanded by God. Most Christians would agree with this
answer. For example, Pastor Wang Ming-tao of Peking continued in
1955 to preach about the Kingship and the Return of Christ, although
the Communist authorities had forbidden him to mention these
doctrines. An African government forbade doctors to treat the wounds
of refugees from a certain tribe, but Christians said that they could not
obey this order. Some Christians who were ordered by a government
official to plant a tobacco crop refused to do so, because they con-
scientiously believed that it was (for them) wrong to cultivate a crop
which could endanger the health of others.

(b) When it is guilty of tyranny, i.e. when it makes it impossible for
people to live with proper human dignity. Some Christians agree with
this answer: others are more doubtful. At the conference of Common-
wealth Prime Ministers at Ottawa in 1973, President Nyerere of
Tanzania pointed out that it was not sufficient for there to be peace in
the world; we must aim at justice for all mankind. For example, in
Russia people are not free to worship God as they want to, and many
governments in Africa discriminate against certain groups of people on
the grounds of colour or of race or of tribe. Martin Luther King
wrote that 'To disobey such a law is to show the highest respect for
law.' And Augustine had written long before, 'An unjust law is no law
at all.' At the time of the American struggle to gain independence
from Britain, an American wrote, 'Rulers are bound to rule in the fear
of God and for the good of the people; and if they do not, then in
resisting them we are doing God service.'

(c) When it passes a law which we disagree with, or when it demands
from us more money than we are prepared to pay. For example, in
England in 1972 a bill was passed by Parliament and became law, but
many Trade Unions disagreed with it, would not recognize it, and
refused to obey it. But most Christians would not agree with this
answer, and would reply that simply disagreeing with a law is not
sufficient reason for disobeying it.

6. *In what ways should Christians oppose unjust government?* There are
three possible answers to this question:

(a) *Disobedience.* In 1937 Pastor Paul Schneider was told by the
German government to preach only those doctrines which were
approved by the government, because, they said, 'you must be subject
to the governing authorities.' Schneider declared that he would
disobey, saying, 'We must obey God rather than men' (Acts 5.29). But
Schneider showed respect to Hitler, the Head of the government, and
continued to pray for him. Other Germans at the time helped Jews to

escape when the government was trying to arrest and execute Jewish people. For other examples of disobedience, see 5(a), above.

(b) *Active protest.* In 1963 Martin Luther King led a civil rights march in Alabama, USA, in peaceful protest against racial discrimination in that state. In doing so, he broke the law which forbade such marches, and he was put in gaol. He defended his action by pointing out that 'justice is never *given* by the oppressor; it must be *demanded* by the oppressed'.

(c) *Violent revolution.* In 1944, near the end of the Second World War, Pastor Dietrich Bonhoeffer and other Christians felt that it was their duty to Christ and to their country to pray for their country to be defeated in the war, and even to plot to kill their evil rulers. Others believe that violent revolution is 'absolutely prohibited' for Christians, on the grounds that it is wrong to use immoral means to achieve moral aims. Both Schneider and Bonhoeffer belonged to the Confessing Church in Germany, whose members began to disobey the government in 1932; then actively protested; finally some of them plotted violent revolution. One scholar who believes that it may sometimes be right for Christians to use violence has written that they may do so *only* on the following conditions;

(i) after peaceful protest has completely failed;

(ii) if they are opposing a tyrannical rule for the sake of obedience to God;

(iii) if they aim to set up a flexible, democratic government which can itself easily be reformed and changed;

(iv) if they are tolerant of other Christians who are opposed to violence;

(v) if they use as little violence as possible, and never use it against innocent civilians as some Palestinian liberation groups have done;

(vi) if they recognize that a perfect society is beyond the reach of sinful mankind. See Special Note, p. 29.

7. *How should Christians support the government?* In Paul's time they could not do much more than submit, pray, and pay taxes. Today they can and ought to do more, i.e. to vote at elections, to try to understand political issues, to remind politicians of their God-given responsibility, perhaps to join a political party, and perhaps to play an active part in influencing the government in the direction of righteousness for the greater good of the community. William Wilberforce did this patiently for many years in England until he succeeded in stopping the slave trade. Bishop Musorewa, the Chairman of the African National Council in Rhodesia, is attempting to do this now, in 1973.

In all discussion of these problems, Christians should remember the following points:

173

(a) The Church has often tended blindly to support the government in power, and to forget its task of pointing out injustices and trying to correct them. This is why, in the last century, Karl Marx rightly accused it of being 'the opiate of the people', i.e. of keeping the people in a state of submission to their capitalist rulers.

(b) The true function of the Church, *as the Church*, is to proclaim the Gospel, which alone can truly revolutionize people's lives. It is then the task of those people as individual citizens to go out and change society and influence governments. When the Church did this with great success in England through the Puritans in the seventeenth century, many of the rich people and leaders complained that the Church was encouraging ordinary people to regard themselves as 'important' and to think too highly of themselves!

(c) Both the Church and individual Christians should be ready to submit to unjust treatment, but when groups or individuals have the chance of demanding their rights, then they should do so.

(d) It is probably wise these days to avoid using the word 'revolution' unless we explain what we mean. This word is being used with very different meanings in different parts of the world.

(e) In this sinful world there is no possibility of establishing a perfectly righteous government. All governments will always need to be reformed and changed.

(f) Christians will have to work out their course of action in each situation which they face. There are no easy rules which can guide us, and it was certainly not easy for Bonhoeffer and Schneider in Nazi Germany to decide what to do. This means that those who are outside the situation cannot lay down rules of behaviour for those who are actually facing a situation of oppression.

(g) Governments often try to enforce their authority by claiming that they hold supreme power, which no one may resist, just as in the first century many Roman Emperors tried to get their subjects to obey them by claiming to be God. Most communist countries today similarly put themselves or their teachings in the place of God. Christians must always deny and oppose all such claims.

(h) We should remember that the Roman government was not democratically elected. It was imperialist, racist, disliked by the majority of people, often cruel and unjust, especially to Christians, to slaves, and to its subject peoples. It represented a minority rule over the majority. Yet all this time, for 300 years, the Church taught that Christians should submit to it (though not necessarily always obey it), and opposed any idea of violent revolution against it. The writer of the Book of Revelation described a state which was demonic and opposed to God, but did not once encourage Christians to oppose it by violence.

SPECIAL NOTE G:
THE AIM OF PUNISHMENT

What is the government's purpose in punishing those who disobey the law? Christians have given three main answers to this question. It is important to consider all three answers when we think about crime and punishment.

1. Punishment is *reformatory*, i.e. its aim is to reform the criminal, so that he becomes a good citizen. Paul said that this should be our aim in our personal behaviour (12.21), and many people today think that this is the best aim a government can have in punishing criminals. But Paul did not mention this idea in chapter 13. If this is the only aim, or even the chief aim of punishment, there is no certainty that justice will be done. For example, a Russian court in 1973 sentenced Pyotr Yakir to 3 years hard labour followed by 3 years in exile, simply because he had been spreading ideas which contradicted communist doctrine. He had already spent 14 years of his life in prison for similar offences. The government did not aim to punish him as he *deserved*, but regarded him as a sick man who needed to be healed or 'corrected'. He will never finish paying the penalty for his crime until the government considers that he has been 'reformed'.

2. Punishment is *deterrent*, i.e. its aim is to deter or dissuade others from breaking the law by making them afraid of what will happen to them if they do. Paul mentioned this idea in 13.3. But if this is the chief aim, then it might sentence *every* criminal to death or to years in prison, as a warning to others. When crimes of robbery with violence increased in Kenya in 1972, some members of Parliament asked for the death penalty for all such crimes, as a deterrent to violence. In Uganda in 1973 General Amin tried to encourage everyone to obey his government, by executing in public in different parts of the country young men who had been found guilty of plotting to overthrow the government. In all such cases the chief consideration is not what the criminal deserves, but what will deter others.

3. Punishment is *retributive*, i.e. its aim is to repay the criminal with the punishment which he deserves, neither more nor less. Paul emphasized this idea in 13.4. It is important that governments should have this aim, because this is the only way of ensuring that justice is done, and of treating people with the respect that is due to responsible, adult human beings. However, this aim is not adequate by itself—for example, insane people, sick people, children, cannot be punished as if they were responsible adult human beings—and there may be other occasions when we should remember that a person may have been driven to do wrong through circumstances which were no fault of his.

STUDY SUGGESTIONS

1. (a) Who or what was Paul thinking of when he wrote 'the governing authorities'?

   (b) In your own community, who or what could be described thus?

2. Explain the difference between 'sin' and 'crime', and give examples.

3. Write sentences to show the meaning of the following words: authority   due   retribution   deter

REVIEW OF CONTENT

4. What is the relationship between God and national rulers?

5. (a) What would be the result if the government acted according to the teaching of Rom. 12.14–21; or if individual people acted as if they were governing authorities (13.3, 4)?

   (b) 'An eye for an eye, and a tooth for a tooth'; 'If anyone strikes you on the right cheek, turn to him the other also.' How can these pieces of advice found in the Bible both be right? Compare Exod. 21.22–25 and Matt. 5.38–42, noticing the different situations.

6. Why should Christians (a) honour the leader of the nation? (b) obey the law of the land?

7. Which of the following passages supports the teaching that:

   (a) Even unjust governments have been appointed by God.

   (b) Christians should respect and honour the governing authorities

   (c) Governments may make mistakes, and even oppose God.

   (d) Christians should sometimes disobey the government in order to obey God.

   Acts 23.5; Acts 4.29–31; John 19.11; 1 Cor. 2.8.

8. Which of the following sentences best describes, in your opinion, how a Christian should behave? Give reasons for your answer.

   (a) Obey every command of the State.

   (b) Obey the State in everything you believe to be right.

   (c) Obey every command of the State which is supported by Biblical teaching.

   (d) Obey every command of the State which does not contradict God's commands.

BIBLE

9. (a) How did Jeremiah both oppose and respect the government of his country, according to Jer. 37.16—38.4?

   (b) In what ways, if any, was the conduct of (i) Schneider, (ii) Martin Luther King, (iii) Bonhoeffer, similar to that of Jeremiah, and in what ways different?

10. (a) In what ways did the first Christians find that the governing authorities could benefit the Church and its work? See Acts 18.12–17; 19.35–41; 23.10; 1 Tim. 2.1–5; 1 Pet. 2.14–15.

(b) How does the present government in your country benefit the Church?

11. (a) What use did Paul make of his Roman citizenship? See Acts 22.25–29; 25.9–12.

(b) In what ways should *we* make use of our citizenship in the different circumstances in which we live?

APPLICATION, OPINION, AND RESEARCH

12. 'It is a good thing to organize the life of the world, but the only necessary and truly good thing is to change it.'

(a) Do you agree with this statement?

(b) How should Christians in your country fulfil these tasks, and in what ways if any, are they failing to do so at present?

13. 'The task of churchmen is to teach morality . . . their primary function is to teach the Ten Commandments.' This was said by the Minister of Housing and Local Government in Rhodesia. What connection if any, do you see between this statement, and Marx's criticism of the Church, quoted on p. 174? What is your own opinion?

14. In one African country, the Church has been called upon by the government to work 'shoulder to shoulder' with it. To what extent should the Church take this advice? In what ways are the tasks of government and Church similar, and in what ways are they different?

15. A few years ago the government of Malaya allowed Christian missionaries to enter the country to work amongst the Chinese, but forbade them to preach to Malays. Those who disobeyed were expelled. What do you think would be the right action for Christians to take in such circumstances?

16. President Nyerere, addressing a conference of pastors in Tanzania, said, 'You have come here to hear from one who is greater than I.' What is the attitude of rulers in your country to (a) religion, (b) the Christian Church?

17. Should Christians take the same attitude towards those who hold authority in villages, schools, families, churches, offices, etc. as they do to the central government of their country?

18. Suppose that a group of Christian refugees from countries where they were oppressed, have been asked to join some freedom fighters to help liberate their country, and invite you to give them a Bible Reading on Romans 13. What are the main points which you

177

will make, remembering to show sympathetic understanding of their situation.

19. Consider the examples given on pp. 172, 173 of Christians who disobeyed, criticized, or opposed the government. Give any similar examples you can think of. In each case discuss whether, in your opinion, the Christians concerned acted rightly or wrongly. What better course of action could you suggest?

20. 'The aim of punishment is to repay the criminal with the punishment which he deserves, neither more nor less' (p. 175).
How can a government decide how much punishment a criminal deserves?

13.8–14
Brotherly Love and the Coming Day

OUTLINE

'Do not leave any debt unpaid except the debt of loving one another—which you can never fully pay, because "love" sums up the whole of our duty to one another. The darkness of this age is nearly past: therefore prepare for the full light of God's new age by living as those who already belong to it. Let Jesus Christ direct your every action.'

INTRODUCTION

The word 'owe' links this section with v. 7. 'Owe no one anything' can be translated 'Do not leave any dues unpaid'—including those listed in v. 7. Paul here continued the theme of love which he had begun in 12.9–21. He reminded his readers again that

(a) they have a duty, not only to the government, but to all men (vv. 8–10);

(b) they belong not to this dark age which is rapidly passing away, but to Christ's new age of light which is just dawning (vv. 11–14).

INTERPRETATION AND NOTES

V. 8: The debt of love is one which we shall always owe, because no Christian can ever say, 'I have fully paid my debt to my neighbour, and now owe him nothing.'

His neighbour: This word does not necessarily mean a person who lives near you, or comes from the same tribe, or is in any way like you. It includes people who differ from you in every possible way. Paul was probably here thinking of

(a) our Christian brothers, as in 12.9–13, whom we Christians were commanded specially to love, in spite of many differences which may exist between us;

(b) our neighbours who may not be Christians, as in 12.14–21.

V. 9. The commandments: Paul found God's law a valuable guide for Christian behaviour, though this was not its only, or even its chief, value (see Additional Note, Law, p. 210). Christians need detailed explanations to help them to know *how* to love God and their neighbours (see p. 163).

You shall love your neighbour as yourself: This summary of the law was as old as the law (Lev. 19.18) and was repeated by Jesus (Mark 12.31).

V. 10. Love does no wrong: Love always considers other people and wants to preserve and deepen fellowship with them (and Paul discussed a practical example of this in chapter 14). Often this means being more ready to give than to take (see Acts 20.35). But equally often it also means being prepared to receive. Sometimes people are unwilling to receive gifts or teaching from people of another race or tribal group, but this is a wrong attitude, based on pride, which can only be broken down by love. Love is needed both by the 'giver', so that he may not adopt a superior or patronizing attitude, and by the 'receiver', so that he may be ready to take the lowly position which involves saying 'Thank you' (see 1 Cor. 13.7–11).

The fulfilling of the law: Only Jesus showed perfect love and so fulfilled God's law in the way God intended. Through being united to Him, (a) we can share in His fulfilment (see 8.4) and (b) we begin to show love for others (see 5.5). Therefore the law can find nothing to condemn in those who are united with Christ (see Gal. 5.23), even though in practice we often fall short of Christ's example.

V. 11. Besides this: Paul was about to give another reason for holy living.

Hour . . . full time . . . now: Paul used these words of time so that his readers might be fully aware of the times in which they were living (see Special Note, p. 122). They should be wide-awake to the true situation. Paul especially wanted them to understand:

(a) that God had *now* taken them out of the night of sin into Christ's new day—this fact should control their thinking, so that they no longer do the things which belong to the night;

(b) that they have *now* gone further along the road to salvation— therefore it is even more urgent for them to live in the 'light' of that salvation (see Additional Note, Salvation, 3.c, p. 217). When large numbers of Christian refugees entered Burma from south-west China, where they had been persecuted for their faith by the government, it was seen that the most used and most marked part of their Bibles was the

Book of Revelation. These Christians showed that they were fully aware of the times, by turning to a book which was written specially to encourage Christians who were in danger of being overwhelmed by powers of this world.

Wake from sleep: Throughout vv. 11–14, Paul compared the old age to the night and the new age to the day. Just as a person wakes up if he recognizes that the day is near, so the Christian must realize how near his salvation is and live accordingly. He must not live as if it were still midnight, even though other people do so, and think that he is behaving foolishly (1 Pet. 4.4). Noah must have seemed foolish to his fellow-men, to spend so long building a boat, but in reality he was wise because he knew what hour it was, and acted accordingly. A family who are moving to a new house do not spend time trying to improve the old one, because

(a) they know that they will not be living there much longer;

(b) they want to spend time preparing for life in their new home.

V. 12a. The night ... the day: There is here a contrast between the two ages:

1. This is an age of darkness. It seems to be in control of the world, but it will soon come to an end.

2. The new age brings light. It is present now, but hidden; it will soon be fully revealed.

Paul thought that it would not be very long before Jesus returned in power in order to bring this age to an end, and to bring to fulfilment the promised new age of God's reign. Early in his ministry, Paul expected to be alive to see that day. Later in his life, he seemed to think that he would die before it came. But whatever his personal expectation, his teaching about the time of the Second Coming was as follows:

1. We do not know when it will take place.

2. It is unlikely to take place so soon that we should stop living normal lives in order to stand and wait for it.

3. Because it may take place at any time, we should always be ready for it—by keeping awake and watching. In any case, every day may be our last on earth; so the way we live now is a matter of importance and urgency for us all. Many of Jesus' parables were intended to teach this lesson. John Wesley was once asked what he would do if he knew that Jesus would return the following week. He took out his diary, looked carefully through his list of engagements, then closed his diary. Then he replied, 'I should follow the plans which I have already made. I should not make any alteration.' He was living as one who was ready for his Lord's return.

Vv. 12b, 13. The works of darkness: Paul listed these works in three groups in v. 13. All were particularly connected with night-time and were common in Corinth, where Paul was living when he wrote this letter.

And he knew that what was true of Corinth was likely to be true of Rome also, and of any large city.

The armour of light: We should wear the clothes which are suitable for the work we have to do and for the hour of the day. A man does not wear his best suit for playing football or for sleeping at night, nor does he go to Church in football boots. We ought to act in a way that is suitable for the daytime (v. 13b), because we realize how near the day is. If people do the works of darkness, that is because they do not realize that the day is near.

Notice that Paul did *not* tell his readers to live as though this age no longer existed. For example, the governing authorities belong to *this* age only (1 Cor. 15.24), and so does marriage and the family (Matt. 22.30)—but this does not mean that we should abandon our obligations to any of them (Rom. 13.1; 1 Cor. 7.10, 11).

V. 14. Put on the Lord Jesus Christ. All the many instructions which a Christian needs are summed up in these words.

1. The Christian has *already* put on Christ in his baptism, through faith (Gal. 3.27; see p. 1).

2. But we need to put on Christ *every day*, i.e. consciously remember the 'new clothes' which we wear, and do the work for which they are suitable (see pp. 85, 86). Having put on Christ, we should live as He lived (see p. 190).

In some parts of the Church new Christians, when they are baptized, put on a white garment as a sign of their new purity. Of course, they do not then wear it every day, but every day they should remember to live the life of purity which they first accepted at their baptism.

STUDY SUGGESTIONS

REVIEW OF CONTENT

1. In what ways are Christians 'in debt', and to whom? How should they discharge these debts? (See also 1.14.)
2. What is the relationship between God's love and God's law?
3. Which of the many instructions which Paul gave in Rom. 12, 13 apply only to our life in this world (e.g. prophecy), and which will apply to life in the new age also?
4. 'Besides this' (v. 11). What reasons had Paul *already* given in chapters 12, 13 why we should live holy lives?

BIBLE

5. If you could ask Jesus, 'Who is my neighbour?', what answer do you think He might give *you*? (See Luke 10.29.)
6. Read 1 Thess. 5.4–8; Eph. 5.8–18.
   (a) What things connected with the night should Christians avoid?

(b) What did Paul mean when he said that a Christian should not sleep?

7. Paul was not content simply to tell Christians what they should *not* do. He always tried to give them something positively good to do instead. What did he tell the Corinthian Christians to do instead of getting drunk, being immoral, and quarrelling? (See 1 Cor. 6.9–20; 11.17–34; 13.1–13.)

8. What teaching about the time of the Second Coming is given in the following verses, and what practical guidance for Christian living did the writers draw from this teaching in each case? Mark 13.32, 33; Acts 1.7, 8, 11a; 1 Thess. 5.1, 2, 6; 2 Thess. 3.10–12; 2 Pet. 3.11, 12.

9. What do we learn from the following verses, about Paul's expectation of the Second Coming at different times in his life? 1 Cor. 15.51; 1 Thess. 4.17; 2 Tim. 4.6–8.

10. 'Christians need detailed explanations to help them to know *how* to love their neighbours' (p. 179).
(a) Which of the Ten Commandments that God gave to His people through Moses provide explanation on this subject?
(b) Which of these explanations in the Commandments did Paul also give in 1 Cor. 13.7–11, and what *additional* explanations did he give there?

APPLICATION, OPINION, AND RESEARCH

11. (a) To love often 'means being more ready to give than to take' (p. 179). In what way does each of the sins forbidden in vv. 9a, 10a involve 'taking' something?
(b) If two people commit adultery, they may make the excuse, 'We love one another so much'. Do you think this excuse is a valid one? If not, why not?
(c) Love is 'prepared to receive'. How is this true (i) of us in our relationship with God; (ii) of God in His dealings with us; (iii) of Jesus in His dealings with Zacchaeus, the tax-collector whom no one else wanted to know? (Luke 19.5.)

12. Is the Church in your area fully aware of the times in which it is living? If so, what practical difference does this make to the way in which Christians behave? In what ways, if any, is the Church in your area failing in this respect?

13. Read the story about John Wesley (p. 180). What alteration in your plans would you make if *you* knew that Jesus was coming next week?

14.1—15.13
The Weak and the Strong

OUTLINE

'Some Christians observe certain strict rules of behaviour which they regard as important, while others despise them. In fact these rules are of no importance in themselves; what is important is that you should not quarrel about them. Everyone should follow the guidance of his own conscience, and not judge his brother. Your harmony in Christ is a gift from God. Do not destroy it. Christ welcomed you; you must welcome one another.'

INTRODUCTION

Paul ended his teaching on Christian behaviour by discussing one special problem. This problem (or one like it) was causing trouble in the Church at Corinth, where Paul was living (see 1 Cor. 8). We do not know whether the same problem had arisen in Rome—perhaps Paul thought it was likely to arise there. He discussed the problem in quite general terms, without going into details as he did in 1 Cor. 8. We cannot therefore be sure of the exact nature of the problem, but we can be sure of the following:

1. Trouble of this sort was likely to become worse where there was jealousy and suspicion between Jewish and Gentile Christians, as there may have been in Rome (see p. 12).

2. Trouble of this sort is common among Christians even today, and therefore Paul's teaching here is relevant to us.

3. The trouble becomes serious only when Christians start to form themselves into groups who oppose each other.

4. Paul's aim was not that all Christians should think alike about these matters, but that they should respect one another's views and live together in love and harmony.

INTERPRETATION AND NOTES

A. THE CAUSE OF THE PROBLEM

Some Christians refused to eat meat (v. 2), others refused to drink wine (v. 21), others insisted on observing special holy days (v. 5). Amongst all religious people, there have been those who observe strict rules of this kind. For example, Muslims will not eat meat unless they know that it has been killed in a special way. There were even some Christians who thought that keeping such rules was more important than faith in Christ (Gal. 4.10; Col. 2.20–22). But the New Testament writers never laid down any rules of this kind, though some Christian groups have felt it right to make such rules for themselves. At Corinth, for example, some Christians refused to eat meat because much of the meat sold in the market came from animals which had been offered for sacrifice to a pagan god. They thought that eating such meat would be like taking part in pagan worship. Other Christians said that they were free to eat anything, because pagan gods do not really exist, and food is just food, however it has been prepared. See 1 Cor. 8.

No one at Rome said that you had to keep these rules in order to be saved. They simply said, 'Meat (or wine) is unclean—therefore it is sinful to eat it', or, 'God will be displeased with us unless we observe certain holy days (perhaps the Sabbath)'. Other Christians disagreed with these points of view.

Paul referred to these two groups of Christians as 'the weak' and 'the strong' (14.1; 15.1). Perhaps the 'strong' used these names. Paul did not mean that the weak were worse Christians than the others, nor that their faith in Christ was weaker. They were 'weak in faith' simply because they did not feel 'strong' enough to say, 'This rule does not matter to me any more.' Today some Christians think that smoking is, for them, a sin. Others say, 'Beer is sinful'. Others feel that it is essential for them to eat no meat on Friday, or to go without nice food during Lent. These people are not weak Christians. They are called weak only in relation to their particular rules—if they broke them, they would feel guilty. In all other respects they may be strong.

B. THE REAL PROBLEM

This difference of opinion between Christians was not the problem. The real problem was the quarrels and 'disputes over opinions' which arose in the Church as a result of it (14.1). There were two sides to the problem (14.3, 10):

1. The strong *despised* those who observed these rules, probably thinking of them as foolish, ignorant, and narrow-minded.

2. The weak *passed judgement* on those who neglected these rules, probably thinking of them as unspiritual, or even sinful.

It would have been easy for Paul to have said, 'I agree with the strong; the weak are mistaken.' But he did not, because that would not have solved the real problem, which was lack of love amongst the Christians. His solution was very different, and not so simple.

C. THE SOLUTION

Paul's solution to the problem has several parts, and his thought moved forward in six clear stages:

1. **vv. 3–12:** Everyone should decide what he believes to be right and then act in that way, for the 'honour of the Lord' (vv. 5b–9). He should respect his fellow Christians for doing the same thing, even though their views may not be the same as his (vv. 4, 5). But he must not pass judgement on his brother, because:

(a) God has welcomed that man as His servant (vv. 3b, 4);

(b) Each person will have to answer to God (and to no one else) for the way he himself (and no one else) has lived (vv. 4b, 10–12).

2. **v. 14a:** Evil is in people, *not* in the things which God has created and given us to use. Perhaps Paul knew, as we do, the saying of Jesus on this subject—Matt. 15.11. This is true of meat, of wine, of beer, of cigarettes. Therefore, if it were a case of deciding between the two opinions, the 'strong' are correct, and Paul was one of them (15.1). But this was *not* the real problem (see B, above).

3. **v. 14b:** What a person *believes* to be right is important, even though he may be mistaken. If a Christian acts differently from what he truly believes to be right, then that action is, for him, sin against God (vv. 14b, 23), because he is not acting in the way described in v. 6.

4. **vv. 13, 15–23:** But the 'strong' must not be concerned only with his own correct opinion. If a man is involved in a road accident in which two of his own family are killed, it will not comfort him to say, 'I drove correctly; it was the other driver who was in the wrong' (although it might help him in a law-court). The strong must think of others and want to help them, even if they are mistaken. Therefore he must:

(a) not dispute and argue with his weak brother (v. 22a). On the contrary, he must maintain the 'peace and joy' of Christian fellowship (vv. 17–19).

(b) be ready even to observe those rules which his weak brother thinks are important (v. 21). This may mean, said Paul, going without meat if you are with a fellow-Christian who thinks it is wrong to eat meat. If you do eat meat in such circumstances, you are likely to cause your brother to be tempted either to pass judgement on you as a sinner (v. 15a), or else to imitate you by eating meat, although he believes that it is sinful for him to do so (v. 23). In *either* case you are causing him to sin—and Paul used strong language to show how wrong it is to do this (vv. 13, 15, 20, 21).

Paul gave these severe warnings to *the strong* for one very simple reason, i.e. the strong can easily change their way of behaviour, because they do *not* think that these rules are important. Those who think that they *are* important find it difficult to change. Therefore it is the strong who must take care of the weak and be their brothers' keepers.

5. **15.1–6:** Love towards one another is really the only solution to the problem. Very often people want to be 'proved correct' in their opinions

'It is the strong who must take care of the weak and be their brothers' keepers' (p. 185).

Motorists in Kuwait halt their vehicles so that pedestrians may cross the streets in safety. Give some other examples from daily life, of ways in which the 'strong' give way to the 'weak'.

or actions. They like to be able to say 'I told you so'. But the *right* attitude for Christians is to want:

(a) to live in a right relationship with others, not just to hold the correct opinion (14.18);

(b) to maintain peace, not to provoke disputes (14.19);

(c) to build up (i.e. to 'edify') other Christians, not to damage them (14.19; 15.2);

(d) to consider others, not to please themselves (15.1).

The result of such an attitude will be harmony and fellowship which will glorify God (15.5, 6). See p. 190, 3.

6. **15.7–13**: As in everything else, so in this matter Jesus Christ is the example for us to follow. He did not attempt to be proved correct; He did what was truly right by giving up his rights (15.3) in order to be 'a servant' of the Jewish people and also of the Gentiles (15.8–12). Because He loved and welcomed *both* groups, He was a specially suitable example for the Roman Christians to imitate (see p. 215, 'Remnant'). By acting in this way, Christ brought glory to God (15.9–12), and we too can glorify Him if we act in the same way towards one another (15.7).

D. A MODERN EXAMPLE

In 1947 the Anglican, Methodist, Presbyterian, and Congregationalist Churches in South India united with one another to become the Church of South India. All ministers of the uniting Churches were recognized as real ministers of the Word and Sacraments. There were, however, some Christians who found difficulty in accepting as real ministers those who had not been ordained by a Bishop. A paragraph called 'The Pledge' was therefore written into the Union Scheme, which declared that if any Christian congregation felt unable to accept the ministry of (for example) a man who had not been ordained by a Bishop, they would not be forced to do so. It is clear that these Churches were following the principles laid down by Paul in Romans 14.15, as follows:

1. The Church of South India as a whole accepted all the ministers as real ministers, without any doubts. See 14.14a.

2. Some Christians, however, honestly felt that, for them, real ministers ought to have been ordained by a Bishop. See 14.14b.

3. It would have been sinful for these Christians to go against what they thought to be right. See 14.23.

4. It would have been wrong for the Church as a whole to try to compel them to do so (although it thought they were mistaken). See ing the principles laid down by Paul in Romans 14 and 15, as follows:

5. The Church as a whole therefore 'bore with the failings of the weak', not in a spirit of criticism or pride, but in a spirit of fellowship and brotherly love, and welcomed them, writing The Pledge in order to help them to come in. See 15.1, 2.

STUDY SUGGESTIONS

WORD STUDY

1. Explain in your own words the meaning of 'weak' as used in 14.1. In what ways are you, or Christians known to you, 'weak' in this sense?

REVIEW OF CONTENT

2. In view of the teaching of Rom. 14.14a; Mark 7.14–23, and 1 Tim. 4.3–5, do you agree that *nothing* can be itself sinful, or unclean? On the other hand, can any *thing* be 'holy', e.g. a day, a building, or water? How should we interpret the prayer used by some Christians at baptism services, 'sanctify (i.e. make holy) this water, for the washing away of sin', or at meal times, 'bless this food'?

3. (a) What does God regard as sin? Which are more important to Him—our outward actions, or our true intentions and attitude? (See 14.14, 23; 1 Sam. 16.7.)

   (b) If a man, intending to do good, does harm, is it sin? If, on the other hand, he intends to do evil but actually does good—is he still to be blamed? (See Gen. 45.5–8; Isa. 10.6, 7, 12; Acts 3.13–16.)

4. Some Christians are determined to show others that little rules are not important.

   (a) In what ways is this attitude correct, and in what ways is it mistaken?

   (b) Why should we be prepared to keep such rules for the sake of others?

BIBLE

5. 'No one at Rome said that you had to keep these rules in order to be saved' (p. 184). If they had, what would Paul's reply have been? (See Acts 15.1, 2; Gal. 2.4, 5, 11–16.)

6. According to Acts 15.1–21, the Church was even then in danger of splitting into two groups.

   (a) Which of these two groups might have been called 'weak' and which 'strong'?

   (b) How did the Church ask 'the strong' to bear with the failings of 'the weak' on this occasion?

7. We ought 'not to please ourselves' (15.1). Read Rom. 8.8; 15.1–3; 1 Cor. 7.33, 34; 10.33; Gal. 1.10; 1 Thess. 2.4; 4.1; 2 Tim. 2.4. Whom should the Christian try to please, and whom should he not please according to the teaching of these passages? Give reasons for your answers.

8. (a) What would have been the easy answer to the dispute which Paul described?

(b) If Paul had given the easy answer, it would have saved him a lot of thought and trouble. What trouble would it have caused to others?

(c) What is your own reaction when requested to take similar trouble over people's problems? Have you sometimes been lazy in giving a simple answer?

9. Rules about meat are not very important to many Christians today. But what similar rules do some Christians regard as important? What sort of trouble can disagreement about such matters cause in a Christian fellowship? Discuss this question in groups of 5 to 8 people; then let each group perform two short dramas before the rest, the first drama showing how Christians should *not* behave towards one another in such a situation; the second showing how they *should* behave, according to Paul's teaching.

SPECIAL NOTE H:
SURVEY OF ETHICAL TEACHING OF
CHAPTERS 12.1—15.13

There are five chief points which we should notice about Paul's ethical teaching in Romans 12 to 15.13:

1. The Christian Gospel has practical results, which are seen in the way Christians behave. Having taught Christian doctrine in chapters 1—11, Paul began in chapter 12 to teach Christian ethics. Having described what God had done for men, he went on to describe how men should live for God. The letter began with a brief statement of the 'bad news' of men's sickness (1:18—3.20; see p. 22), went on to describe the 'good news' of God's cure (3.21—11.36), and ended with 'good advice'. This is very different from the Greek ethical system which was designed to lead people, through deeds of 'virtue', to attain the 'highest good'. In the Gospel, however, God gives people the 'highest good' (which biblical writers often called 'salvation') as a gift through Jesus Christ— and then calls upon them to practise deeds of virtue out of gratitude to Him. It has been said that in Christianity 'ethics is gratitude'. When Christ becomes the centre of life, then we can offer every moment and every action to God.

2. Christian behaviour depends on the power of the Holy Spirit. As members of Christ's new family, Christians possess the Spirit of Christ,

who leads them to live in a way pleasing to God. Paul did not emphasize this teaching in chapters 12—15, because he had already done so in chapter 8.

3. Christian behaviour is not an individual matter. Like all human behaviour, it involves our daily relationship with others—other members of our own family; other members of Christ's new family (see especially 12.3-13; 14.1—15.13); and other members of the human race who are still outside the Christian family (see especially 12.14—13.7).

4. Christian behaviour does not consist in obedience to a fixed set of laws which tell us just what to do in every situation. In these chapters Paul gave varied instructions, without attempting to make an orderly connection between them (see p. 155 (c) for one possible reason for this). We are told what to do when we are persecuted, but not what to do when the government forbids us to preach the Gospel. We are told to obey the governing authorities, but are given no instructions as to whether or not it is right to fight for national independence. In other words, the Bible does not provide us with an easy answer to all our problems (which is why Christians often disagree about politics and many other subjects), but it does provide us with certain guiding principles.

5. Christian behaviour is based on Christ Himself. Although some scholars have tried to find the basis of Paul's teaching in Greek ethics or in the Jewish law, in fact the teaching of chapters 12-15 remind the reader over and over again of

(a) Jesus's own teaching in the gospels (e.g. 13.8-10);

(b) Jesus's own personal example (e.g. 15.3-8);

(c) Jesus as the centre of the Christian's life and thought (e.g. 13.14). (Paul did not know the written gospels which we know, because they had not yet been written down, but he did know many traditions about the life and teaching of Jesus which had been handed down amongst the Christians by word of mouth, and in some cases in written documents.)

15.14–33
Paul's Ministry and Future Plans

OUTLINE

'I have only been reminding you of what you already know. It is my duty to do this because of the special work which Christ has given me to do for Him. I am looking forward to seeing you soon, on my way to Spain. But first I must take to Jerusalem the gift which the Gentile Churches have collected for the brethren there.'

INTRODUCTION

From 1.16 to 15.13 Paul included scarcely any personal word for his Roman readers. The truths which he was teaching were of equal value for all Christians. But he ended his letter in much the same way as he had begun it—with a personal message:

1. He gave thanks for the state of the Church at Rome (15.14—see 1.8).
2. He described his own ministry to the Gentiles (15.15, 16—see 1.5, 14).
3. He expressed his desire to visit his readers (15.22, 23—see 1.10, 13).
4. He wanted his visit to bring them blessing (15.29—see 1.11).
5. He believed their fellowship would be a blessing to him (15.32—see 1.12).

INTERPRETATION AND NOTES

Paul's graciousness (vv. 14, 15): Paul's readers knew and had accepted the Gospel. But, like us, they needed many reminders about it and about how they should live. Paul praised his readers whenever possible; he exhorted them because he loved them; he taught them boldly because of his commission from Christ (see p. 7); he rebuked them if necessary.

Paul's offering (v. 16): Paul said that he was like a priest who offers the sacrifice which God really wants, i.e. obedience from men (see Additional Note, Obedience, p. 213). The Gentiles who responded to (i.e. obeyed, v. 18) Paul's message about Christ's sacrifice for sinners were:

(a) a sacrificial offering to God, because they belonged to Him through Christ (see 6.1–11) and were now presenting themselves to Him (12.1);

(b) sanctified (i.e. made holy, or set apart) by the Holy Spirit (8.9), even though non-Christian Jews would regard them as still *unholy* because they had not been circumcised.

Paul's humility (vv. 17–19a): Paul never boasted of his own achievements, because he regarded his work as beginning with Christ's grace to him and finishing with the offering of the Gentiles in obedience to Christ. See Matt. 28.20.

Paul's methods (vv. 19b–21): Paul's first preaching was at Jerusalem (Acts 9.28, 29), and he may at some time have gone as far as Illyricum (north-west of Macedonia). Jesus's own plan for the movement of the Gospel (Acts 1.8) can be seen in the movement of Paul's own ministry from Jerusalem, through many cities of the East, and now, as he hoped, to Rome and the West.

When Paul had planted a Church, he expected the Christians of that

Church to reach out to the areas round about (1 Thess. 1.8; see p. 12). After spending only two or three years in each important city, it was time for him to move on. William Carey followed this method in the nineteenth century in India, when he made plans to set up mission centres at selected points along the River Ganges. Paul was happy for others to build upon the foundation which he had laid (v. 20; 1 Cor. 3.6, 10), but was himself conscious of a special call to open up new work in important towns.

Paul's plans to visit Rome (vv. 22–24). See 1.13. Paul did not spend much time visiting friends; he did the work to which God had called him. He gave three reasons for wanting to visit Rome:

1. He wanted to enjoy the fellowship of the Christians there for the first time (vv. 23, 24).

2. He wanted to bring to them and receive from them some blessing (vv. 29, 32).

3. He hoped that they would in some way help his new work in Spain (v. 24; see p. 3). But we cannot be sure just what he meant by 'I hope . . . to be sped on my journey there by you'. Perhaps he was hoping for three kinds of help:

(a) The company, for part of his journey, of travelling-companions from the Roman Church. To supply such companions was considered an important part of the duty of hospitality, as it still is today in many countries (see Acts 21.5; notes on 12.13b, p. 163).

(b) Regular prayer for him and for the new work (see v. 30).

(c) A contribution of money which would enable him to start this new work in the West, just as the Church at Philippi had sent him money when he was working in the East (Phil. 4.15–18). If Paul did hope for this kind of help, he did not mention it to the Romans, but simply told them of the generous giving of Christians in Greece (v. 26). In 1969 there was a severe famine in central Tanzania. Some American Christians who were touring the area met a group of Tanzanian students who had collected some money to help people who had not enough to eat. When they saw what the Tanzanians had done, the Americans wanted to give generously to the same fund.

We do not know whether Paul ever reached Spain. After being imprisoned in Rome, he may have been released and gone either to the East again (Titus 3.12) or to Spain, or both, before he was arrested again for the last time (2 Tim. 4.6).

Paul's journey to Jerusalem (vv. 25–27). Paul mentioned the 'contribution' for the poor Christians at Jerusalem several times in his letters (see also 1 Cor. 16.1–4, written from Ephesus during his visit of Acts 19; 2 Cor. 8, 9, written from Macedonia during his journey of Acts 20.2; and see also Acts 24.17). He clearly regarded it as very important, perhaps for the following reasons:

'Paul's readers knew and had accepted the Gospel. But they needed many reminders about it' (p. 191).

A health worker in Korea reminds a villager that he and his family must come to the clinic for an X-ray before they can receive treatment. Whose job is it to 'remind' Christians about the Gospel today? What happens to them if they forget about it?

1. It was one way in which the Gentile Christians could say 'thank you' to the Jewish Christians from whom the Gospel had first come to them (v. 27).

2. It was one way of showing Jewish Christians that Gentiles really had become God's people through faith in Jesus the Messiah (v. 26).

3. It was one way in which Paul could prove to himself and to others that his mission to the Gentiles had been completely successful (see v. 28, RSV note x—he was setting the seal on (i.e. completing) his ministry).

4. It was one way of showing Christians everywhere, and especially at Rome, the sort of close fellowship which Gentile and Jewish Christians ought to have with one another—helping one another in every way they could (v. 27).

5. It was one way of offering 'service' to God, i.e. worship (v. 27). Giving money is not simply helping others: it is worshipping God (Phil. 4.18). We, like these Gentiles, should be 'pleased to do it'.

Paul's need of prayer (vv. 30, 31). There were three reasons why Paul wanted his readers to pray for him:

1. He was afraid that he would meet with bitter opposition from the Jews at Jerusalem (v. 30; see Acts 21.10-14). This is in fact what happened, and several times Paul was nearly killed (Acts 21.27—25.12).

2. He was not sure whether even the Jewish Christians there would give him a friendly welcome (v. 31b)—but in fact they did (Acts 21.17).

3. He wanted to establish a close relationship with the Roman Christians at once, so that they would continue to pray for him when he went to Spain (v. 24).

If we think that Paul was a great missionary, we should always remember that many Christians were helping him by their prayers. William Carey was one of the greatest missionaries who ever lived, learning many of the languages of India. He translated the Bible into three of them, and so laid the foundations for years of missionary work, which helped to change the history of India. People who read about Carey today are amazed that one man could have done so much. But he had a sister in England who lay paralysed in bed for fifty years. She could not move, and for much of the time could not speak. But she wrote long letters to Carey—and prayed for him, for fifty years. There have not been many missionaries like Carey. But perhaps there have not been many Christians who prayed like Carey's sister.

STUDY SUGGESTIONS

REVIEW OF CONTENT

1. Draw a sketch map to trace, from Acts, Paul's journeys from the time he left Antioch (Acts. 18.23) to the time he arrived in Jerusalem.

Mark on it all the places he visited on the way. Notice also what he said in his letters during that time about the collection he was making for the Jerusalem Christians (see notes on 15.25–27, p. 192).

BIBLE

2. Compare Heb. 6.9; 2 Peter 1.12, 13; and 1 John 2.20, 21 with Rom. 15.14, 15.
   (a) What special teaching do all these passages contain?
   (b) Why do you think each of these writers emphasized that teaching?
3. Why did Paul not like to boast of his achievements? (See 1 Cor. 15.10; Gal. 2.20.) How does 2 Cor. 12.5 help us to understand his attitude? (Read from 2 Cor. 12.1 to 12.10, remembering that in vv. 2–5 Paul was probably referring to himself.)
4. The 'signs and wonders' which Paul did often gave people quite a wrong idea about him (see Acts 14.11; 28.6). What, then, was the purpose of these miracles?
5. How did Paul in fact achieve his purpose of going to Rome? Why do you think God spoke to him the words of Acts 23.11 and 27.24?

APPLICATION AND OPINION

6. (a) What do you think Paul meant by 'I have fully preached' (v. 19)? Has the Gospel been 'fully preached' in the area where you live?
   (b) Paul expected Christians 'to reach out to the areas round about'. What is your Church doing about reaching out? What are *you* doing about it?
7. In what ways could the Gentile Christians help the Jewish ones? In what ways could Jewish Christians help Gentile Christians? In what ways can you help other Christians who live far away from you, and are perhaps very different from you? (Do not make the mistake of thinking that you cannot help anyone unless you have a lot of money!)

16.1–27
Greetings and Hymn of Praise

OUTLINE

'Warmest greetings to all my brothers and sisters in Rome. Take care to preserve your loving fellowship with one another. May this Gospel strengthen you, and to God be the glory through Jesus Christ!'

INTRODUCTION

We know nothing about most of the people mentioned in this chapter. However, we should read it carefully, because it shows us that Paul did not write this letter for scholars. He wrote it to help ordinary people to understand what Jesus had done for them, and show them how to live for Him in all the hurry and bustle of a busy city. The Church is not an organization of bishops and clergy. It is a fellowship of men, women, and children 'in Christ' who are all, in different ways, working hard for Him.

Some scholars have thought it strange that Paul knew so many members of a Church which he had never visited. They have therefore suggested that chapter 16 must have been a separate letter, perhaps one which Paul sent to Ephesus as an 'introduction' for Phoebe (v. 1). But it is very unlikely that Paul would have written a letter consisting of nothing but greetings, and there were probably good reasons why he should have greeted so many people by name in Rome, e.g.:

1. If he wanted to establish friendly contacts with the Roman Christians, a good way of doing it would be to show his interest in them as individuals, as he did in the case of the Colossian Christians, by sending them many personal greetings (Col. 4.7–17) although he had never visited them.

2. People were always travelling to and from Rome, and Paul had met some of them on his journeys in Asia, e.g. Prisca, Aquila, and probably Epaenetus. It was not strange that such people should now have been in Rome.

3. When Christians travel, for example, from Africa to London, they are often asked by other Christians who have never been to London to take personal greetings to Christians in London whom they know about or have met in Africa.

INTERPRETATION AND NOTES

Vv. 1, 2. Phoebe: It was Phoebe who carried Paul's letter to Rome. Because the Christians there did not know her, Paul wrote these few words of introduction. Cenchreae was the sea-port of Corinth. The word 'deaconess' may describe an official job in the Church, or it may simply mean that Phoebe did useful service. Women in the early Church did valuable work, much of which could never have been done effectively by a man. Church leaders today spend much time discussing whether or not women should be given the *same* ministry as men. They might do better to re-examine how writers in the New Testament described the ministry of women, and what *sort* of ministry women should exercise today.

Vv. 3–5. Prisca and Aquila: This Jewish couple had been expelled from Rome by Claudius. They travelled to Corinth and then to Ephesus, where they developed their business (see Acts 18). Like many Jews, they probably returned to Rome after Claudius's death. By then, they perhaps had an extensive business with branches in many cities, which made it necessary for them to continue to travel widely (2 Tim. 4.19). They were well known by many of the Churches of the Gentiles because, wherever they went, they welcomed Christians into their home for fellowship, worship, and instruction. At that time the Churches had no special buildings for worship. Christians met together in each other's houses. Prisca and Aquila therefore set a very suitable example to the Roman Christians of how Jewish and Gentile Christians should care for one another.

V. 7. Andronicus and Junias my kinsmen: By 'kinsmen' Paul meant 'my fellow Jews' (see vv. 11, 21). They had become Christians before Paul, and may have been members of the Jerusalem Church mentioned in Acts 2—6. They were 'apostles'—probably sent out by the Jerusalem Church, not specially commissioned by Jesus Himself, as Paul had been (see p. 7).

V. 11. The family of Narcissus: Tiberius Claudius Narcissus was one of the Emperor Claudius's most important officials. He was put to death when Nero became Emperor, and his property, including his household, i.e. his slaves, was taken by Nero. Perhaps Paul was here referring to these slaves. If so, then they may have been just a few of the Christians who were in 'Caesar's household' (Phil. 4.22).

V. 13. Rufus: See Mark 15.21. Mark probably wrote his gospel for Christians in Rome, and probably mentioned the fact that Simon of Cyrene was the father of Rufus and Alexander simply because his readers knew Rufus and Alexander. Paul may have been referring here to the same Rufus, Simon's son (though Rufus was a common name). Rufus, then, may have had a father who carried Jesus's cross and a mother who cared for Paul as if he were her own son. But he was 'eminent' not because of these things, but because of his own faithfulness 'in the Lord'.

V. 16. A holy kiss: A kiss was a common Christian greeting, which later became part of the Holy Communion service in Rome, as it still is today in some Eastern Churches. In some other parts, it has been replaced by the hand-shake.

All the churches of Christ: At the time of writing this letter, Paul was acting as the representative of the Eastern Churches in taking the collection to Jerusalem (Acts 20.2–4); it was therefore very natural that he should greet in their name the Christians in the chief city of the Empire.

Vv. 17–20: One of Paul's chief aims in this letter had been to show his readers (Jewish and Gentile Christian alike) how much they all needed one another and should work together in harmony. He therefore gave a final warning about how they should treat 'those who create dissensions'. We cannot be sure what these people taught. 'They serve their own appetites' could describe those who were always thinking about rules concerning food (ch. 14, 15), but it is more likely to describe those who said that Christians are free to live as they like (Phil. 3.19). This kind of teaching may have been present in Rome (see 3.5; 6.1), and Paul may have thought that it might spread. But the words which he used are true of anyone who is more interested in his own ideas than in the harmony and peace of the Church. Paul was confident that God, who alone could bring them peace, would defeat all who tried to do evil in the Church in Rome (v. 20; see Gen. 3.15).

V. 22. Tertius: Paul's secretary added his own personal greeting.

V. 23. Gaius: See 1 Cor. 1.14. In 3 John 1, 5–8 we read of another Gaius who was well known for his hospitality.

Erastus: 'Not many of you were of noble birth', wrote Paul to the Corinthian Christians. But perhaps Erastus was. At Corinth he had the important job of *aedile* (Latin for City Treasurer). In appreciation of his appointment to this office, he laid a pavement at Corinth, just as any leading citizen may lay out a garden for the use of the residents of his town. On the pavement he inscribed the following words, which can still be seen today: 'Erastus laid this at his own expense on account of his treasurership'.

V. 25–27: Paul had begun his letter with a short, well-known statement of the Gospel which he believed and preached (1.2–4). Now he ended his letter with a similar statement—a hymn of praise to God (or 'doxology'). This hymn, like 1.2–4, may not have been written originally by Paul, but it does give a summary of the main points of this letter:

Paul's Gospel is the preaching about Jesus Christ (2.16; 1.1, 3).

It is witnessed to by the prophetic writings (1.2; 3.21; etc.).

It is now disclosed (1.17; 3.21).

It is made known to all nations (1.5; 9.24–15.13).

It brings about obedience to the faith (1.5, 16; see Additional Note, Obedience, p. 213).

It is preached according to the command of the eternal God (15.15, 16).

It comes to men always and only through Jesus Christ (5.1, 11, 21; 6.1, 23; 8.39), through whom believers give to the only wise God glory for evermore (11.33–36).

A TEXTUAL PROBLEM

Not all the early manuscripts of this letter end in the same way. Some end after chapter 14, and some after chapter 16. In the different manuscripts, the doxology (16.25–27) appears in three different places, and in one manuscript it does not appear at all. We do not know how this confusion happened, but the most likely suggestion is that some editor (perhaps the heretic Marcion who lived about 150 and did not like references to the Old Testament) cut out chapters 15 and 16, and added the doxology. Others who copied the letter put back chapters 15 and 16, and kept the doxology—but in three or four different places. So the different manuscripts end in different ways. The true story of what happened will probably never be known, but the problem is not important, because it does not affect the meaning of the letter as a whole.

STUDY SUGGESTIONS

WORD STUDY

1. Count up how many times the idea of 'work' and the phrase 'in Christ' or 'in the Lord' appear in this chapter. What do these words teach us about the life of a local Church in the first century? What do they suggest that the life of our Churches today should be like?

BIBLE

2. (a) Tryphaena, Tryphosa, Persis, and Julia are names of women. How many women are mentioned in this chapter?
(b) Read Luke 8.2, 3; Acts 9.36–39; 16.13–15; 18.26; 1 Tim. 5.3–16; 2 Tim. 1.5; Tit. 2.3–5. What special ministry or ministries did women have in the Churches of the New Testament?
(c) What sort of ministry do you think that women should have today?

3. 'The church in their house' (v. 5; see vv. 14, 15, 23).
Which of the gifts mentioned in Rom. 12 were these Christians exercising?

4. Read Acts 16.40; 18.7; 1 Cor. 16.15; Col. 4.15; Philemon 1, 2.
(a) All these seem to refer to 'house-churches'. Name if you can the places where they were, and the people in whose houses the worship and meetings were held.
(b) Are there any 'house-churches' in your area at the present time? How do you think a house-church should function today? Of what value might they be in your area?

APPLICATION AND OPINION

5. 'Avoid them' (v. 17). This advice may seem to us to be rather unkind and even un-Christian when we remember that Jesus was the friend of sinners.

(a) Why do you think Paul gave this advice? (See 2 John 7—10; 2 Tim. 2.23.)

(b) In what ways, if any, should we follow such advice today? (See Matt. 18.17.)

SPECIAL NOTE I:
WHY DID PAUL WRITE ROMANS?

Some possible answers to this question were suggested on p. 3. Now that we have studied the whole letter, we are in a better position to give an answer ourselves. It will help us to do so if we try to answer two other questions first:

1. Do we know of any particular problem which was troubling the Church at Rome at the time when Paul wrote? Although we do not know much about the Christians at Rome, we have already seen that they probably faced one major problem. See pp. 11, 12.

2. Although Paul considered many subjects and discussed many problems in Romans, is there *one* theme which keeps on appearing throughout the letter? One idea which is mentioned in almost every chapter is that the Gospel is for *all* people, and that it abolishes the distinctions between people. It does so because it is not a Jewish idea, but the message of God Himself for all nations (1.1, 5; 16.26). All people need this message because all have sinned (3.23) and can be set right with God only by His grace, or mercy (3.24; 11.32), through faith (3.22; see p. 49). Paul applied this teaching especially to Jews and Gentiles (1.16; 3.9, 29; 9.24; 10.12; see p. 18). The Christians in Rome especially needed this teaching if, as seems likely, disputes had arisen among them. Perhaps these disputes were concerned with whether or not it was right to observe ceremonial rules (14.1–5), perhaps they arose from pride on the part of Jews (2.1–5, 17–20) or of Gentiles (11.17–25). Paul said that there was no room for pride (3.27; 12.4, 16). Jews were as sinful and disobedient as Gentiles (ch. 2; 10.3, 20, 21; see pp. 39–42), and God had accepted Gentiles just as much as Jews (9.30). God's plan to justify mankind through faith started with the father of the Jews, Abraham, who is truly the father of all who believe (4.16, 17). The plan was fulfilled through the Jewish Messiah, Jesus (1.3; 9.5); thus Gentiles owe their salvation to Jews (11.11). Jews, on the other hand, who seem to have been rejected, will come back to God through the ministry of the Gentile Church (11.23–31; see pp. 128, 147–150).

Human beings usually tend to think of themselves as belonging to a special group—a continent, a race, a nation, a tribe, a party—but Paul thought of mankind as a unity (5.12–21; see p. 78). Through His work of reconciliation, Christ restored to mankind unity with God and with one another in God's new family (5.10, 18; 12.5). Christians have a responsibility to live as members of this family who love and care for each other (12.9–16; 13.8–10; 14.13–21). Therefore Paul made it clear that he was writing to *all* Christians in Rome (1.7; 16.3–16), not just one group. Christians all need one another (1.11, 12; 12.6), so Paul rebuked those who thought in terms of groups or parties (16.17–20), and picked out for special mention three examples of brotherly love for others (15.1–13; 15.27; 16.3, 4).

If this is really the main theme of Romans, then it becomes clear:

(a) why Paul included two long passages (9–11 and 14.1–15.13) which some modern scholars have found both difficult and irrelevant (see pp. 125–129, 183);

(b) why Paul sent to the Roman Christians this detailed statement of the Gospel—because there is nothing which breaks down the barriers between different sorts of people as effectively as the Christian Gospel which condemns all men as sinners, justifies them as a free gift of God's mercy, and gives them a truly new life in Christ (see pp. 88, 89) as children of God.

Today, the Jews are involved in racial conflict even more than they were in Paul's time. But theirs is only one example of the hatred and mistrust between nations and peoples which exists in the world. Racial, or tribal, or ideological conflicts have taken place in recent years in Southern Africa, in South America, in the East Asia, in India and Pakistan, in the Soviet Union, Czechoslovakia, Northern Ireland, many African countries, and the United States. Very often people who call themselves Christians have been involved in these conflicts. Sometimes these conflicts seem to be unavoidable—and even right—and Christians differ on these matters (see pp. 171–175). But undoubtedly Christians who believe the Gospel which Paul preached have a vitally important ministry in this world of conflict. They must proclaim Christ as the source of all true reconciliation, who alone can bring true peace to mankind. Hundreds of people, of whom Tom Skinner (see p. 29) is only one, have found that when they believe in Christ their outlook is changed, they begin to see themselves as God sees them. They lose their pride, and they see other people not as rivals or enemies but as equals and as brothers, all of whom share the same need and all of whom can share the same newness of life. This message of God's love, when accepted, can create the peace which people long to have.

ADDITIONAL NOTES
ON IMPORTANT WORDS AND THEMES

Baptism (*Chief references:* Rom. 6.3, 4)

1. In order to become a Christian, a person had to have faith in Jesus Christ and to be baptized into His name (Acts 2.38).

2. There is no definite example in the New Testament of anyone being baptized in Christ's name unless he had expressed faith in Jesus Christ, but everyone who did express this faith was also baptized, for there were no unbaptized believers.

3. In baptism a person went down into the water (a symbol of death and burial) and came out again (a symbol of resurrection to new life).

4. In Paul's teaching baptism signifies two things. In baptism:

(a) The believer's sins are washed away (Eph. 5.26; Acts 22.16).

(b) The believer is united with Jesus Christ.

Therefore Paul taught that Christians are baptized *into* Christ (though many English translations say 'in'), with the result that they are *in* Christ. This was a familiar idea to most of the first readers of the New Testament. To be baptized meant an end of the old life and the start of a new life. To be baptized *into* a person meant to begin a new life in union with that person. Therefore the baptized believer is 'Christ's man'. We belong to Him.

Being united with Christ means to share His death and resurrection. Paul described the 'death' and new life of the Christian in exactly the same way as Christ's (6.10, 11). All that happens to our 'head' or 'representative' (see p. 79) is also true of us. If He died, so did we; if He was buried, so were we; if He rose, so did we; if He ascended, so did we; if He is in glory, so are we. Not only are we His men; He is our man.

5. Baptism is therefore like a funeral combined with a birthday. We who are under God's wrath are condemned to death, as Christ was condemned. But then, having died, we rise again to a new life of fellowship with God.

6. Many Christians who read Romans 6.3, 4 today ask the question: 'Are we saved by faith alone, or by baptism: Which is more important?' This is an important question, because it is clear that many people who have been baptized have ceased to follow Jesus Christ. On the other hand, there are some sincere followers of Jesus who do not accept baptism.

(a) According to the New Testament, both faith and baptism are necessary.

(b) Paul usually mentioned baptism, as he did in this letter, only in connection with the ideas of faith and repentance. These ideas cannot be separated. Paul would probably not have understood our question about 'faith *or* baptism'.

(c) Faith is emphasized much more than baptism in the New Testament (e.g. in this letter). Therefore it is certain that baptism *alone*, without faith, cannot unite a person to Jesus Christ. Baptism is not a 'magic ceremony'.

(d) On the other hand, it is difficult to see how a pagan can be a true follower of Christ without desiring to obey His clear command to be baptized.

(e) If baptism is unobtainable, then there can be no doubt that a man who has faith in Christ is truly united with Him. Those who teach differently may be in danger of making the same mistake as the Jews did about circumcision (see p. 204, 3–6).

(f) Many Christians disagree with the practice of infant baptism. But that is a separate problem, and Paul's letter to the Romans does not help us to solve it.

See also Acts 2.4; Acts 16.31, 33; Galatians 3.26, 27; Colossians 2.12; Questions 14 and 15 on p. 91.

Blood (*Chief references:* Rom. 3.25; 5.9)
See 'Expiation', p. 204. In Jewish custom the blood of a sacrificed animal was offered to God at the altar (Lev. 17.11). This showed that the animal had been given up to God, and that its life had come to an end. The animal had borne the sins of the worshipper. It had died instead of him. In the same way Christ offered Himself to bear the sin of men.

Some scholars say that the Jews thought of the blood as a sign of the life which was released and offered to God at the altar. It was to show that the worshipper repented of his old life of sin and gave it up with the animal's blood. He also gave himself as an offering to God, and God gave him back new life.

According to this second interpretation, Christ offered up His life to God and we, through our repentance and faith, make His sacrifice our own, and receive back from God the new life which we need. Although some scholars interpret Paul's meaning in this way, the shedding of blood seems to indicate life brought to an end rather than life released; and a comparison of Rom. 5.9a with 5.10a seems to show that Paul used the word 'blood' to mean the same as 'death'.

Circumcision (*Chief references:* Rom. 2.25–29; 4.9–12; 15.8)
1. Many tribes practised circumcision in the time of Abraham.

2. Although many of Abraham's ancestors may have practised circumcision, God gave it to Abraham as a sign of His 'covenant'

(i.e. agreement, see p. 131) with Abraham and his descendants (Gen. 17).

3. From that time, the Jews have valued their circumcision very highly because it marks them off as the people of God, and have often referred to themselves as 'the circumcised' (Rom. 15.8).

4. Many Jews became too proud of their circumcision, as if it was the only thing that mattered. 'We are circumcised,' they boasted, 'we are children of Abraham, we belong to God.'

5. Jeremiah told the Jews of his time that although they were circumcised outwardly, they were really just like the pagans around them in their behaviour. Inwardly (in their hearts) they were uncircumcised (Jer. 9.25, 26), and God would not acknowledge them as His people. They must circumcise their hearts by repenting (Jer. 4.4).

6. Paul said the same thing in Romans 2.25–29. Circumcision is a symbol of cutting away uncleanness and sin. Those who are still sinful in their behaviour, therefore, are counted by God as uncircumcised; but those who obey His will are counted as circumcised and as 'real Jews' (i.e. truly God's people). (Gal. 6.15, 16; Phil. 3.2, 3; Rev. 3.9.)

7. Some people may ask: If circumcision is *part* of God's law (see John 7.22, 23), how can a man 'keep the law' without being circumcised? Paul's answer is in Romans 2. Like Jesus he distinguished between the external 'letter' of the law (*written code*, v. 27; *literal*, v. 29) and the inward meaning of the law (*the precepts*, v. 26; *spiritual*, v. 29). The inward meaning of the law is faith, obedience, and love. See also Notes on Romans 4.9–12, p. 57.

Election, Choose (*Chief references:* Rom. 8.33; 9.11; 11.5, 7, 28)
Just as citizens of a country elect, or choose, people to represent them in their country's Parliament, so God chooses men and women to be His own people. This action of God is called His election, or choice. Paul used the word 'election' in Romans as follows:

1. To describe God's choice of the patriarchs as an important step in the process of fulfilling His purposes for mankind (9.11);

2. To describe the status of the nation Israel as God's chosen people (11.28);

3. To show how, within the unbelieving nation Israel, God has chosen some people to have faith in His Gospel (11.5, 7);

4. To describe the secure position of those whom God has loved, set apart, and called (8.33). They, with all believers, have been chosen by God in Christ (see Eph. 1.4).

Expiation (*Chief references:* Rom. 3.25)
1. The English word 'expiation' used in the RSV means 'a way of removing sin' (NEB). It is used in Romans 3.25 in connection with the

word 'blood', which shows that Paul was here using a word-picture from the Temple sacrifices (see p. 203).

2. Sacrifice is an important idea, and is found in most of the world's religions. In every case it is related to men's need for a right relationship with the god (or spirit) to whom they offer the sacrifice. Sacrifice is practised for 3 chief purposes:

(a) Sacrifice is thought to provide the gods with the food which they need, and thus is a way of earning their favour.

(b) Sacrifice is a sign of fellowship between men and God (or gods). For example, Hindu worshippers are offered food and drink from the god's table. Cf. 1 Cor. 10.18.

(c) Sacrifice is a way of transferring sin from a guilty person (or group of people) to an animal, which is then given up to the god and punished by death in place of the guilty person. The Yoruba of W. Nigeria believe that the gods may punish with sickness a person who has offended them. Therefore they take a sheep, rub it against the sick person's body, then kill it and bury it with all the care which they would give to a human corpse. They believe that in this way the gods will accept the death of the sheep in place of that of the sick man, who will then recover.

3. Animal sacrifices, even those once offered by the Israelites, can never really take away the guilt of human sin. Psalm 51 (especially v. 16) shows that David realized this. He therefore appealed only to God's mercy (vv. 1, 2), and asked God to give him the only thing which could please Him: a clean heart (vv. 10, 17). The prophets looked forward to the time when this cleansing and restoration would be accomplished (Jer. 31.33, 34; Ezek. 36.25–27).

4. The writer of Hebrews said that Christ has offered the only sacrifice which can take away sin (10.4, 11–18). This is the sacrifice of which Paul wrote in Romans 3.25. Like the writer of Hebrews, Paul drew his ideas of sacrifice from the Old Testament.

5. Perhaps the best way of explaining the idea of sacrifice found in the Bible is as follows:

(a) A man lays his hand on the head of an animal, confessing his sins, to show that the animal is bearing his sins instead of him.

(b) The man deserved to die as a sinner under God's wrath, but the animal dies instead of him. God 'has given' the animal as a substitute for the man (Lev. 17.11).

(c) The blood is sprinkled on the altar to show that a death has taken place which removes the sinner's guilt, so restoring him to a right relationship with God.

6. The word 'propitiation' is often used to describe this process, because it is a way of turning away God's wrath against sin. It is very likely that Paul had these ideas in his mind when explaining the sacrifice of Christ

in 3.25. If so, 'propitiation' would be a better translation of the Greek word he used than 'expiation'. See Notes on 3.25, p. 51.

7. 'Expiation' and 'propitiation' are not the only two possible translations of the Greek word which Paul used. A third possible (though less likely) translation is 'mercy-seat'. Among the Israelites, the mercy-seat was the golden covering of the ark in the tiny room (called the Holiest Place) in the middle of the Temple. Only the High Priest was allowed to enter it, once a year on the Day of Atonement (see Lev. 16), to sprinkle the blood of the goat to take away the sin of the people. The Israelites believed that there God manifested His presence, showed His glory, met with men in mercy, revealed His wrath against sin, and was presented with the sprinkled blood. All these ideas are present in Rom. 3.21–25. Christ, in His death on the cross, is the true mercy-seat, where men meet with God.

In the middle West of America the farmers are afraid of the fierce fires which sweep across the plains in the dry season, moving faster than a car can travel. There is only one way to escape the fire. The farmer, when he sees the smoke in the distance, starts his own fire, burning a large circle of ground all round his house. Then he puts all his possessions onto the circle of ground which has already been burned. He waits calmly for the fire to pass. The fire burns up everything in its path, but when it reaches the patch of ground already burned, it has nothing to burn and so passes harmlessly either side of the farmer and his possessions. The place where the fire has already fallen cannot be burned again—and that is the place of safety where the farmer must stand, knowing that the fire has already done its work of destruction there. In the same way, God's judgement against sin has fallen at the cross of Christ, and that is now the place of safety provided by God for all those who have faith in Christ.

8. Through faith men come into a right relationship with God, because Christ's sacrifice of Himself becomes effective for all who believe, and actually achieves what animal sacrifice never could.

Faith/Believe: (*Chief references:* Rom. 1.16, 17; 3.21—4.25; 9.30–33; 10:4–17)

The word 'faith' is a noun. 'Trust' and 'confidence' are sometimes used with the same meaning. The verb which corresponds to 'faith' is 'to believe'. Sometimes we use this verb with the meaning 'to know' that something is true; or 'to think' or 'to hope' that it is true. But Paul generally used the word in a different way. Any of the following words or phrases can be used to express what Paul meant: believe in; believe on; trust; trust in; rely on (and sometimes: accept; receive).

1. Faith is a human act. It is people who believe.

2. Faith is one of the chief characteristics of Christians—so in the New Testament they are often called simply 'believers'.

3. Faith is called into action by God's power, which works through the Gospel (Rom. 1.16). A person cannot have faith independently of God (see Eph. 2.8; Phil. 1.29).

4. When a person believes, God's salvation, which is offered to everyone, becomes effective in his life (Rom. 1.16; 3.22).

5. In Greek the word for 'believe' is often followed by the word 'into' —'to believe into Christ'. This shows us an important truth—faith joins us to Christ, so that we are united with Him. So faith has been called 'the hand which grasps the gift of God' and 'man's "Yes" to God's word'. One practical result of faith is that Christ, rather than ourself, becomes the most important one in our life.

6. At other times the word 'believe' is followed by 'on'—'to believe on Christ'. This suggests relying on Christ, particularly in the matter of coming into a right relationship with God, rather than relying on other things (such as our own efforts or religious practices). Its simplest expression is 'I cannot, but Christ can.' This means that the one on whom we rely, or believe, is more important than our faith itself. When a man sits on a chair, he relies on the chair, but the important thing is whether the chair is strong enough to support his weight. If it is not, his faith will not help him. In the same way, truly Christian faith must look to and rely upon Jesus Christ. Those Christians who worry about whether their faith is strong enough would often do better to spend more time considering Jesus Christ and *His* strength.

7. Faith, which looks to what *God* has done, abolishes all distinctions between human beings (Rom. 3.22), because these are always based on what men *are*, or on what men *do*.

8. To believe or not to believe is a decision which each person must make for himself. People will be saved as individuals, not in groups (see Matt. 24.40–42). But in fact no man lives alone, as an isolated individual, because people influence one another. There are many examples of this:

(a) In the New Testament people were usually (though not always) baptized in households, not as isolated individuals. (See Acts 16.33, 1 Cor. 1.16.)

(b) In many African tribes decisions are usually taken, not by individuals, but by the family, or clan. Whole villages have often decided to become Christians.

(c) When a king or a chief believes in Christ (as the Emperor Constantine did in AD 312) it often happens that hundreds follow his example.

Thus when a group of people turn to Christianity, some of them may 'believe' simply because they are in the group, without having a true faith in Christ. John showed how this happened in his time in John 2.23–25; 6.60–66; 1 John 2.19. Paul used the word 'faith' to mean a true faith, not just an outward profession. Every Christian should ensure that he has a true personal faith in Christ, and is not simply following the crowd. This letter to the Romans can help us to be sure.

Flesh (*Chief references:* Rom. 1.3; 7.5, 18, 25; 8.3–13; 9.5; 13.14)
All living people live 'in the flesh'. There is no other way in which a person can live in this world. Christ lived in the flesh (1.3; 9.5). The word 'flesh', in this sense, means the same as 'body'.

But Paul frequently used the word with a different meaning (see note on 7.5, p. 98). One scholar has defined this meaning as 'the lower part of human nature'. But a better definition would be 'human nature as it is before a person becomes right with God through Christ'. 'The flesh' belongs to the old age (see Special Note, p. 122). Therefore to 'walk according to the flesh' (8.4) means to live one's life apart from God, and to 'live in the flesh' (7.5) is to be without Christ. Christians 'are not in the flesh' (8.9); however, some remains of their old life 'in the flesh', apart from God, still cling to them (Rom. 7.25; Gal. 5.17) as long as they live in the body, in this world (see note on 7.17–20, p. 99). In ch. 8 Paul used the word to describe what people without Christ are like: (a) in themselves—they 'are in the flesh'; (b) in their thinking—they 'set their minds on the things of the flesh'; (c) in their behaviour—they 'walk according to the flesh'.

Glory, Glorify (*Chief references:* Rom. 1.23; 2.10; 3.23; 5.2; 8.17, 18, 30; 9.4, 23; 11.36; 15.7; 16.27)
1. The word 'glory' is used to describe the splendour of God's presence and character.
2. God has always been surrounded with glory (John 17.5; Rom. 1.23).
3. God created man to be like Him and to share His glory (1 Cor. 11.7).
4. Man, by turning against God, was 'deprived of the divine splendour' (Rom. 3.23, NEB).
5. The Jews were given signs of God's glory, but God's glory has only truly been seen on earth in the life of Jesus of Nazareth (John 1.14).
6. Jesus's reward for His faithful obedience to God was to be 'crowned with glory' (Heb. 2.9). Christians will share that glory with Him (Rom. 5.2; 8.18).
7. Christ still shows men God's glory through His presence with His people (2 Cor. 3.18), who are called to do everything for His glory (Rom. 15.7) and to acknowledge His glory (i.e. to glorify Him) (Rom. 11.36; 16.27).

Grace (*Chief references:* Rom. 1.7; 3.24; 4.16; 5.2; 5.15–6.1; 6.14, 15; 11.5, 6; 12.6; 15.15)

1. The word 'grace' is used to describe God's love or generosity seen in action on behalf of those who do not deserve it. Grace is seen in every part of God's saving activity—in the gift of His Son (2 Cor. 8.9), in His calling (Gal. 1.15), and in justification (Rom. 3.24). See Rom. 5.15–21.

2. Therefore Christian believers are often said to be 'under grace' (Rom. 5.2; 6.14). This means that they have come to God in the following way:

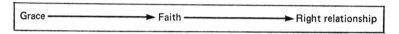

Grace ⟶ Faith ⟶ Right relationship

Grace and faith always belong together because faith is the way in which men receive God's grace (Rom. 4.16). But many people try to approach God in a different way, as follows:

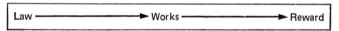

Law ⟶ Works ⟶ Reward

Those who do so are said to be 'under law', but no one can actually come to God in this way because no one can fulfil His law. Therefore this way of approaching God always has the following result (see Rom. 4.15).:

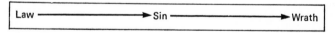

Law ⟶ Sin ⟶ Wrath

3. Because God's grace continues in the life and ministry of Christians (Rom. 1.5; 12.6), Paul often prayed for grace for his readers (Rom. 1.7).

4. The word 'grace' only describes God's loving activity. It does not explain it, or give a reason for it. The idea can never be fully understood or explained by men (see p. 68).

Judgement (*Chief references:* Rom. 2.1–16; 3.6; 5.16; 13.2; 14.10)
God's judgement of the world is one of the central ideas of the Bible. God always judges righteously (Gen. 18.25; Rom. 3.6). God's judgement is described in two ways:

1. In people's lives, when good actions are rewarded and wrong actions punished. But this does not always happen. Sometimes people 'get away with' doing wrong, or are punished for something they have not done. Once a man called Evans was hanged for a murder in London. A few years later new evidence seemed to show that the real murderer

was Christie, who lived with Evans. Christie was hanged for many other murders, but Evans could not be brought back to life.

2. At the last day, when God's final and perfect judgement will take place, there will be no mistakes. All wrongs will be put right; all good deeds will be rewarded; all evil deeds will be rightly punished (Rom. 2.6–11). Many people find this a comforting thought.

In Rom. 1.18–32 Paul was thinking of God's judgement *in people's lives*. In Rom. 2 he was thinking of God's judgement *at the last day*— yet to come. When God judges people, His wrath is often revealed. See *Wrath*, p. 221.

Justify, Justification (*Chief references:* Rom. 2.13; 3.20—4.5; 4.25; 5.1, 9, 16; 8.30; 10.4)

The word 'justify' means 'declare righteous' or 'count righteous'. The word comes from the law-court and describes the action of a judge. To justify the unrighteous is the action of an unjust judge (Prov. 17.15; Isa. 5.23). Because God is just, He justifies only the righteous. Therefore it is the doers of the law who will be justified (Rom. 2.13). Sinners cannot be justified in God's sight (Rom. 3.20).

However, in Romans 4.5 Paul went on to describe God, surprisingly, as 'the one who justifies the ungodly'. i.e. who acquits the guilty. In the passage 3.20—4.5 Paul had shown how this seeming contradiction is a true description of God. Because of Christ's death, God is able to declare sinners to be righteous (3.24). More than that, He does this without Himself becoming unrighteous. God justifies the sinner, yet unlike the unjust judge, He does so in a way that is right (3.26). A person whom God declares righteous *is* 'right with God', i.e. he has a right relationship with Him (see *Righteousness*, p. 215).

This is the Gospel, and the heart of Paul's message. The fullest explanation of how it takes places comes in Romans 3.21–26.

Law (*Chief references:* Rom. 2.12–29; 3.19–31; 4.13–16; 5.13, 20; 7.1–25; 8.2–8; 9.31; 10.4, 5; 13.8, 10)

In Romans Paul used the word 'law' to mean four different things:

1. The Jewish Scriptures (3.19a, where Paul had just quoted from Psalms and Prophets).

2. Part of the Jewish Scriptures, apart from the Prophets—or perhaps just the first five books of the Scriptures (3.21b).

3. The will of God for human behaviour. The word usually has this meaning in Romans. God revealed His will to men in various ways:

(a) Through the system of commandments and regulations given to Moses at Mount Sinai (5.13, 20). Therefore 'adherents of the law' (4.16) is a way of describing practising Jews. Often Paul seems to have been thinking particularly of the Ten Commandments (e.g. 7, 7–12; 13.9).

(b) Through God's general revelation to all men, in their ability to distinguish between right and wrong (2.14—'a law to themselves'). Thus Gentiles, even though they did not have Moses's law, knew something of God's law.

(c) Through the life and teaching of Jesus Christ. The *idea*, without the actual word 'law', is found in 15.3, 5; see also 13.8–10.

In this letter Paul showed that the law does three things:

(a) It shows people that God is holy and righteous, and that they fail to do His will (3.20b);

(b) It restrains them from the worst evils, by threatening them with punishment. This can be seen in the laws which are enforced by governments (13.1–5).

(c) It shows Christians how God wants them to live, though it can never actually help them to live in that way (13.8–10).

4. Principle, or guiding rule (7.21; 8.2; 3.27—where the Greek word for 'law' is actually translated 'principle' in the RSV).

Life, Live (*Chief references:* Rom. 1.17; 5.17–21; 6.4–13, 22, 23; 7.6; 8.2, 6, 11)

1. All living creatures have life because God has given His own life to them.

2. Animals and human beings have this life, and it ends when they die.

3. There is another sort of life which men can have. It is the life of fellowship (or, right relationship) with God. This is the way in which God meant men to live. In John's writings we read that men do not naturally have life in this sense, and the only way to get it is through Jesus Christ (John 5.40; 1 John 5.12). Paul's teaching is similar— through Christ a man has new life now (Rom. 6.4), which he will never lose because it is eternal (6.23).

The chief characteristics of this second sort of life are:

(a) it is lived *for* God (Rom. 6.10, 11);

(b) it is lived *with* God, and is therefore described as the life of the Spirit (Rom. 7.6). Thus the new life of the Christian is quite different from his life (perhaps we should say 'his existence') before he had faith in Christ (see especially Rom. 5—8).

4. All men die, but the bodies of Christians will come to share in this new life which Christ brings. Paul mentioned this in Romans 8.11, and explained it more fully in 1 Corinthians 15.

Love (*Chief references:* Rom. 5.5, 8; 8.28, 35–39; 12.9, 10; 13.8–10: 14.15)

Writers in the New Testament used this word to describe God's attitude to us, and also to describe what our attitude should be towards God and our fellow human beings.

1. *God's love for us.* This was what Paul was referring to on many of the occasions when he used the word 'love' (Greek: *agape*). See pp. 66–69. Notice especially that God's love for us is not caused by anything we can do.

2. *Our love for God.* Paul did not say very much about this. He usually used the word 'faith' in order to describe how we should respond to God. The reason for this is probably that our love for God is always different from His love for us, because our love for Him is always *caused* by His goodness and generosity to us. He is worthy of our love because of what He is. Paul usually kept the word *agape* to describe the special kind of love which comes only from God.

3. *Our love for others.* Paul said a lot about this, and used the word *agape* to describe it, i.e. the same word which he used to describe God's love for us. He used the same word for two reasons:

(a) We should love our fellow human beings, whatever they are like, good or bad, friendly or offensive. Our love is like God's when we love those who have done nothing to deserve it.

(b) Our love for our fellow human beings is really just an extension of God's love for us. His love has been poured into our hearts through the gift of the Holy Spirit. This means that it overflows through us to others, because God's Spirit is always with us, causing us to love in the same way that God loves.

The hymn of 1 Corinthians 13 is a true description of Christ's love to us and of how we should love others, but is not really meant to describe our love for God.

Mystery (*Chief references:* Rom. 11.25; 16.25)
This word is often used to refer to something which is beyond man's understanding. It is used in this way on p. 138 of this Guide. Paul, however, usually used the word to denote a secret which God alone knows, but which He has revealed to men, or will reveal to them in the future.

1. It frequently refers to God's total plan for saving mankind which He has revealed through the Gospel of Christ (Rom. 16.25; Eph. 3.9). People cannot understand this plan unless: (a) it is disclosed to them as it is through the preaching of the Gospel (1 Cor. 2.10–12); (b) they are enabled to understand it by the work of the Holy Spirit in their minds (1 Cor. 2.13–16). In the same way a blind man may be given a carefully wrapped picture, but he is unable to see it until he has both unwrapped it and somehow regained his sight.

2. It often refers to different aspects of God's plan (see Eph. 3·5, 6).

3. It sometimes refers to some future happening of which only God

can know. But God revealed some truth about it through the ministry of Paul, although many details of it still remain hidden (Rom. 11.25).

Obedience, Disobedience (*Chief references:* Rom. 1.5; 2.8; 5.19; 6.16, 17; 11.30–32; 15.18; 16.28)

1. Human beings have a duty to obey God because (a) He is their Creator and Lord; (b) He has revealed His will to them. Because He loves us, His will is always for our good.

2. God rewards obedience and punishes disobedience (2.8), which is called sin.

3. The first man disobeyed God's will, with the result that God regarded all men as sinners: but Christ obeyed God's will completely, with the result that God accepts as righteous all who have faith in Him (5.19). (See also Righteousness, p. 216.)

4. God revealed His will through His law and commanded men to obey it, not with outward actions only, but by personal, willing acceptance of God's will.

5. God revealed His Gospel through Christ and Christ's obedience (3.21, 22; 5.19), and commanded men to accept this Gospel, i.e. to have faith in it. Paul often described this faith as 'obedience', and unbelief as disobedience (1.5; 6.17; 15.18; 16.26;11.30, 31).

6. This obedience includes:

(a) repenting of sin (see Repentance, p. 35),

(b) accepting the truth of the Gospel (6.17),

(c) receiving the gift which God gives (5.17),

(d) personal commitment to Jesus Christ of whom the Gospel speaks (1.5, 6).

7. Those who respond to the Gospel in this way show their gratitude to God by obeying His will in whatever ways He has revealed it (12.1, 2; 13.1, 9; 15.7).

Reconciliation, Reconcile (*Chief references:* Rom. 5.10, 11; 11.15)

1. Men turn against God when they reject His rule over them, i.e. when they sin.

2. This action also turns God against men, because God is opposed to sin. God has 'something against' men (see p. 69), and this is sometimes called His 'wrath' (see p. 23). Occasionally writers in the Bible described God as being 'at enmity' with sinful men (Rom. 11.28; Isa. 63.10; cf. Gal. 3.10). The word 'enmity' is a way of describing the wrong relationship which exists between God and men because of men's sin. The word 'reconciliation' describes God's action in bringing this enmity to an end.

3. Thus we see that God is not really our 'enemy' in the sense in which we usually use this word, because He loves us. Even though He is 'against us' because of our sin, He is, even more, *for us*.

4. By His death, Christ dealt with sin, which had caused the enmity between God and men, with the result that 'we are justified by His blood' (Rom. 5.9), i.e. we are counted not guilty, but righteous.

5. As a result, we have peace (Rom. 5.1), i.e. we are reconciled. God made peace, and because this is the way in which *God* acted, out of love for us, writers in the Bible never say that God 'is reconciled' to us—on the contrary, it is always God who reconciles us to Himself, and we who are reconciled (Rom. 5.10). Some scholars say that this proves that God is never against men, but men who are opposed to God. However, in Jesus's parable about reconciliation in Matt. 5.23, 25, we find that 'enmity' did not exist on one side only. The first man had done wrong, with the result that his brother had something against him. In the same way God has something against us because of our wrong-doing. The relationship needs to be put right, on His side as well as on ours. This is what God does in reconciliation. One scholar has written 'The word reconciliation is less about man and more about God.' It is not that Christ's death changed God from man's enemy into man's friend, but that God's love for us came first, and as a result Christ died for us. God was so opposed to our sin, yet loves us so much, that He dealt with the problem of our sin in this way, even though it was at the cost of the death of His dear Son.

Redemption (*Chief references:* Rom. 3.24; 8.23)

1. The word 'redemption' may sometimes mean simply 'deliverance'. (Rom. 8.23), but its proper meaning is 'deliverance through payment of a price'.

2. It was originally used to describe how prisoners or slaves were set free, and it would have reminded a Jew like Paul of how God had delivered the Jews, first from slavery in Egypt (Exod. 6.6), and later from exile in Babylon (Isa. 41.14).

3. A slave could be 'redeemed' from his master's power; Christians are 'redeemed' by Christ from the ruling power of sin. But when Paul used the word in Rom. 3.24, he was probably thinking of how Christ redeems men from the position of being guilty before God.

4. A redeemer pays a price, sometimes called a ransom (Isa. 43.3, 4). In Paul's day a slave could buy his freedom if he could collect enough money (see p. 50). But men cannot 'buy' their freedom from sin by collecting good deeds for God (see Psalm 49.7, 8). God Himself has paid the price of men's redemption (1 Cor. 6.20, 1 Pet. 1.18).

5. If a slave redeemed himself, he was free. If someone else paid the price, he belonged to that person. The Christian is free from his old master, but now belongs to a new one (1 Cor. 6.19; Rom. 6.16–18).

6. Often, though not always, one person would redeem another because of some special relationship with that person (Lev. 25.47–49).

Men have been redeemed by Christ, but this redemption is effective only for those who come into a new relationship with Christ through faith (see p. 52).

Remnant (*Chief references:* Rom. 9.27; 11.5)

The doctrine of the 'remnant' was developed by the prophets of the Old Testament, particularly by Isaiah. He was distressed at the way in which Israel and her leaders continually refused to have faith in God (Isa. 7.4, 10–13; 8.6), and he saw that God would judge them for their rejection of Him. But there were a few, like Isaiah and his followers, who were faithful. Amongst them, God would preserve His word and maintain His witness, although the nation as a whole would be rejected (Isa. 8.16–18; 10.20–22, which Paul quoted in Rom. 9.27).

When Jesus came as the Messiah, the Jews behaved like their ancestors and rejected Him. There were only a few who had faith and became His disciples. In the end, even they forsook Him. Jesus was left alone, as the only Faithful and Righteous One, whom God accepted as His Child. The faithful remnant was One Man. He was the stone which was rejected by the whole nation, yet accepted and chosen by God (Isa. 8.14, 15; 28.16, quoted by Paul in Rom. 9.33).

Although Jesus alone is the true remnant, men can now be numbered among that remnant through having faith in Him (9.33; see Righteousness, 5, p. 216). Paul wrote that many Jews had in fact believed, and were among the remnant (11.5). Many Gentiles, too, were numbered among the remnant, through faith. The remnant does not now consist of any one nation or of part of any nation. It consists of people of all nations, who have faith in the one faithful and righteous Israelite.

Righteousness (*Chief references:* Rom. 1.17; 3.21–26; 4:1–25; 5.17–21; 6.16–20; 8.10; 9.30—10.6)

1. God alone is perfectly righteous, or just.

2. God gave to His people righteous commands and laws (Rom. 7.12) in order to guide them to live righteously, i.e. in a right relationship with God and one another.

3. People are righteous (or, upright) when they obey God's laws (Rom. 2.13) and unrighteous when they do not do so (Rom. 9.30, 31). As a Jew, Paul had believed that the only way in which a man could be righteous before God was by obeying God's law.

4. Righteousness also describes the activity of God. He always does right (Gen. 18.25). He shows His righteousness chiefly by two kinds of activity:

(a) He condemns the unrighteous (Exod. 20.7) and saves the righteous (1 Kings. 8.32).

(b) He saves His own people whom He has promised to save. This was especially emphasized in Isaiah (e.g. 51.1–8) and some other passages of the Old Testament, where God's righteousness means almost the same as His activity in saving. The RSV clearly shows this by using the word 'deliverance' to translate the Hebrew word 'righteousness' in Isa. 51.5, 6, 8. For example, Psalm 24.3–5 taught that the righteous man who does God's will may suffer now, but in the end God will save and 'vindicate' him. This means that God will ensure that justice (or, righteousness) is done, by saving the righteous man from unjust suffering.

Both these kinds of activity expressed God's righteousness, but they raised a big problem for many writers in the Bible, i.e. 'How can God save His people who are unrighteous?' This problem is expressed in Isa. 59.11–13. How can God justify (i.e. declare righteous) the ungodly (Rom. 4.5), when such an action is hateful to Him (Prov. 17.15; Isa. 5.23)?

5. Righteousness was seen in the life of Jesus of Nazareth. This does not mean simply that He obeyed God's laws. It means also that He had a right relationship with God and lived in accordance with God's will. (1 Pet. 3.18). Therefore God vindicated Him although men killed Him (Acts 3.13–15; 1 Pet. 2.23). This fact offers hope to men. For if one man had a perfectly right relationship with God, then it is possible that others might come to a right relationship with Him through that one man. Through the Righteous One, unrighteous men may become righteous. This is Paul's teaching in Romans.

6. Righteousness is available to men through Christ (2 Cor. 5.21). Men cannot achieve this righteousness by their own efforts, as most Jews believed; it is a gift which God gives to those who believe in Christ. Long ago Jeremiah had said, 'The Lord is our Righteousness'. Paul interpreted this to mean:

(a) Christ saves us (see 4.b).

(b) Christ brings us into the right relationship with God which He had.

In Phil. 3.4–11 Paul showed how this had worked out in his own life— he had received righteousness as a gift from God, through faith in Christ (9b). This righteousness was the way to final salvation (vv. 10–14), which Paul could never have achieved through his own obedience to the law (v. 9a).

7. This righteousness is not 'man's own righteousness', but God's (Phil. 3.9a). Thus it is quite different from any human righteousness. This righteousness: (a) is seen in the life and death of Christ; (b) is a perfect righteousness, which is pleasing to God; (c) is God's gift to men. Because of it, God declares man to be righteous (i.e. justifies him). This is the beginning of the process which leads to salvation, because God is saying that man is 'Not guilty' and is right with God. In Romans Paul taught that *righteousness* (now) leads to *salvation* (in the future).

8. The person who has a right relationship with God ought actually to *do* righteous acts (Rom. 6.13). Because he belongs to Christ, he is beginning to be like Christ. He is beginning to want to do right (Rom. 7.21), and to fulfil God's law (Rom. 13.8–10), although in practice he constantly fails to do so.

Salvation, Save (*Chief references:* Rom. 1.16; 5.9, 10; 8.24; 10.9–13; 11.11, 26; 13.11)
When a man is 'saved' he is delivered from a bad situation and enters into a good situation. Salvation can be called 'man's greatest good'. Human beings aim at salvation throughout their lives, but different people have different ideas of what is the 'greatest good'.

1. *The Romans* called the Emperor Augustus 'saviour' because he brought peace to the world after many wars.

Others, like *the Greek philosophers*, thought that perfect knowledge was salvation.

Most *agricultural peoples* think of salvation in terms of good rains, a fertile soil, and a plentiful harvest. The Israelites held this idea. It is also present in parts of the Old Testament.

2. For *Paul*, salvation was the life of everlasting happiness with God. This life will be perfect in the future, but even now it has already begun.

3. It is possible to think of salvation in the following ways:

(a) Believers *have been* saved from a wrong relationship with God sometimes described as 'wrath' or 'condemnation' (Eph. 2.5, 8).

(b) Believers *are being* saved each day from their own weaknesses and from evil powers which threaten them (1 Cor. 1.18). Salvation, in this sense, is one of the favourite words of the Hausa Christians of Northern Nigeria—salvation that is not only from sin, but also from 'disease, fear, and the aimlessness of life'.

(c) Believers *will be* saved from the presence of evil, suffering, and death (Rom. 5.10).

Through the Gospel, God brings salvation to men in all these ways, and Paul described them all in Romans. But in this letter he almost always used the words 'save' and 'salvation' in the third sense (c), to refer to the future life of perfect blessing which God had promised to all believers.

4. There are two other important ideas connected with the word 'salvation':

(a) Isaiah closely connected 'salvation' with the idea of God's *righteousness* (see Additional Note 4b, pp. 215, 216). God shows His righteousness by saving from misery, humiliation, and defeat those whom he has promised to save, i.e. His people.

(b) Salvation is achieved by *the sufferings of Christ*. Although this idea was rejected by Jews and Greeks (see pp. 16,18), the first Christians saw it clearly in the Suffering Servant passages of Isaiah, especially chapter 53.

Sin (*Chief references:* Rom. 2.12; 3.20–25; 5.12—6.23; 7.7–25; 8.2, 3)
Sin is the name given to any action, word, or thought which goes against God's will. Thus the most important thing to notice about sin is that it is *against God*. We should never think of it except in this way. We may hurt or offend our fellow-men, but we *sin* against God. All the different Greek words used for sin—missing the mark, lawlessness, falling, transgression, unrighteousness, wickedness—emphasize this fact. Paul expressed the idea of sin in Romans 1, 18–32, but he did not use the word itself until 2.12, together with the word 'law'. Sin can only be understood in terms of God's law (i.e. His will revealed to men)—compare 1 John 3.4. and see Rom. 4.15; 5.13. Its results are that it separates men from God and brings God's wrath.

Sin in the life of men can be thought of in three ways:

1. There are sinful *actions* (or, omissions). These are called 'sins' in the plural. A man can sin in this way by thought, word, or deed.

2. There is the *power* of sin. Paul usually called this simply 'sin', and spoke of it as a power which rules over all men. This is why *all* men (not just most men) sin. It is the source (or, root) of men's sinful actions. It sometimes seems as though Paul thought of it as a power outside men, at other times as a corruption, or sickness, within men. We refer to the power of sin when we say that man's *state*, or condition, is sinful.

3. There is the *guilt* of sin. This word comes from the law-court, and refers to men's *status*, or standing, before God. Those who have disobeyed God's law are sinners. God, as the righteous Judge, through His law, declares them to be guilty. He condemns them. They deserve to be punished.

Sons, Sonship, Children (*Chief references:* Rom. 8.14–21; 9.4, 7, 8, 26–29)
The Greek word translated 'sonship' means 'adoption'. When Paul used this word, there may have been two ideas in his mind:

(a) *In Roman law*, adoption was regularly practised. For example, just four years before Paul wrote this letter, the Roman Emperor Claudius adopted L. Domitius Ahenobarbus to be his son, and gave him the new name of Nero Claudius Caesar. When Claudius died, Nero became Emperor in his place, even though Claudius had a son of his own, called Britannicus. Nero was in every way regarded as the son and heir of Claudius, and he lost any rights or inheritance which he might have had in his previous family. He was counted as a new person, and this was shown by his new name.

(b) *In Jewish history*, adoption was unknown, but the Jews did have a real experience of what it meant to be made the sons of God. See Exod. 4.22, 23; Hos. 11.1. So Paul, in Rom. 9.4, could use the word 'sonship' to describe the Jews' relationship with God.

Thus, if we remember both the Jewish and the Roman ideas of sonship, we can see that Christian sonship means:

1. That God has chosen, or adopted, us to be His own sons. This was true of the Jewish nation, and is now true of those who are 'in Christ'. It is *not* true of all men; although all men are God's children in a *general* sense, because He created all men.

2. That our sonship is connected (a) with our union with Jesus Christ, because we share His Sonship, though He is God's true Son while we are His adopted sons (Rom. 8.29); and (b) with the gift of the Spirit, who brings Christ and His blessings into our lives (see Additional Note, Spirit, below).

3. That we have confidence in God as members of His own family (Rom. 8.16).

4. That we, together with Christ, shall inherit all that God has prepared for His sons (Rom. 8.17). Therefore, although we are *already* God's sons, this sonship is *not yet* manifest to all; we are waiting for the time when it will be manifested (Rom. 8.23; see 1 John 3.1, 2; and Special Note, pp. 122–124). This reminds us of Christ's Sonship, which was partly hidden during His earthly life, but was manifested at His resurrection (see pp. 9, 10).

Spirit, Spiritual (*Chief references:* Rom. 1.4; 5.5; 7.6; 8.1–27)

1. The word 'spirit' is often used in Old and New Testaments to mean the *mind* of a person (Mark 2.8; 1 Cor. 2.11a) or the person himself, as he truly is (see Rom. 8.16).

2. In the Old Testament, the word spirit is used for *wind* (with the idea of force and power), and also for something which *comes from God* (with the idea of being greater than man). 'Spirit' was often contrasted with flesh, and the word was commonly used to indicate divine power.

3. The Spirit was seen in the words and works of Jesus, because God was at work in Him. The Spirit is the *Spirit of God.*

4. But Jesus's words and works were continued in the lives of his followers on the Day of Pentecost and afterwards (Mark 16.20; Acts 1.1–5; Heb. 2.3, 4). Thus the Spirit is also the *Spirit of Christ.* Christians today cannot meet with Christ's body, but they can have fellowship with Him through His Spirit. In John 14—16 He promised His disciples that He would not abandon them at His death, but would send them the Spirit, who would be with them and would guide them in the same direction as He Himself had done (14.7, 26; 15.26; 16.7, 13–15). This coming of the Spirit is sometimes described as the coming

of Jesus (14.18), or as the coming of the Father and the Son (14.23). Therefore it can be true to say that in our Christian experience, God is the Spirit and Christ is the Spirit.

5. It is the Spirit who brings God's blessings into our lives and experience, i.e. He applies Christ's work to us personally (see p. 68). Therefore we say that God's gifts come to us from the Father, through the Son, in the power of the Holy Spirit.

6. Thus the Spirit is what makes the Christian different from a person who is 'in the flesh', i.e. without Christ (see p. 103). The Spirit makes us new men. He belongs to the new age and brings to us *now* the blessings of the new age (though we do not yet fully experience them all—see Special Note, pp. 123, 124). It was therefore natural for Paul to describe our new life as the 'life of the Spirit' (7.6), and to speak of the Spirit as the 'law' (i.e. principle) which now controls us (8.2), and to say that it is the Spirit who directs us in the Christian life (8.5–27).

Suffering (*Chief references:* Rom. 5.3–5; 8.12–39)

1. The *nature* of suffering.

(a) Suffering is an unavoidable part of life in this world, both for human beings and for animals. We know what it is to feel pain, sickness, sorrow, weakness of body and mind, and death. No one imagines that Christians escape these things. But many people ask, 'Did God originally intend the world to be like this?'

(b) Suffering is often connected with some form of evil, for example: (i) Evil men may cause suffering to others, directly or indirectly. (ii) Wrong ways of living or wrong use of God's gifts may cause suffering. (iii) Writers in the Bible sometimes suggest that the world is in disorder, that this disorder is one of the consequences of men's turning against God, and that part of this disorder is the suffering which we see around us. See Rom. 8.19–21.

(c) Christians experience suffering in all these ways, but also they very often suffer *because* they are Christians. There are three chief reasons for this:

(i) Becoming a Christian involves saying 'No' to our old life, and this can often be a painful experience (see pp. 88, 89).

(ii) Through Christ God purposes to put right the disorder which is in the world. He has already begun with the Christian Church. This means that we, who have been set right with God, live in a world which is, for the most part, estranged from Him. We therefore experience conflict in our lives.

(iii) For us, as for Christ, this conflict may involve us in open suffering —or at least ridicule—for the sake of Christ.

Therefore suffering is said to be one of the marks of being a Christian (Rom. 8.17, 18). Christians are not promised an easy life in this world.

2. The *results* of suffering.

(a) Suffering is always under God's control, like everything else in this world. We can see this fact most clearly in the sufferings of Christ. It is most difficult to see it when we ourselves are suffering, and we can only do so by faith. But quite often God lets us experience victory over sufferings in various ways (see 2 Cor. 12.7–10). But the resurrection of Christ shows that the final victory is always certain, for those who belong to Him.

(b) One result of suffering should be to make us realize how weak we are. It should drive us to rely more upon God. This is the way of victory. But sometimes, instead of turning to God in trouble, people turn away from Him. This is the way of defeat.

(c) God has promised that those who have become His children through faith in Christ will inherit His glory together with Christ. But the road to glory must pass through suffering, in the ways mentioned above, as it did for Christ Himself.

Wrath, Anger (*Chief references:* Rom. 1.18—2.11; 4.15; 5.9; 13.4, 5)

1. *What is God's 'wrath'?*

(a) Many people who follow *traditional religions* believe that when God was angry with men, He separated Himself from them, and that thunder and death can be a sign of His wrath now. But they believe that God is normally good and kind, and the anger of local spirits is more troublesome than God's anger.

(b) The *ancient Greeks* often called God's wrath 'fate' or 'destiny'. When a man broke the laws of his society, he could not escape God's wrath. In a Greek story a man named Oedipus became king of a city, with hopes of great power, but the wrath of God destroyed him because he had killed his father and married his mother.

(c) Since that time *many thinkers* have written about people who offend against the good order of the world, and yet seem to prosper. But in the end they fail and are sometimes destroyed. Many people today call this 'the inevitable process of cause and effect in a moral universe'. This is true, and it can be seen in history.

(d) *The Jews* called this process 'the wrath of God', because they recognized that God made the world in this way, and its laws are His. They believed Him to be a personal God, who had made His will known and who would, sooner or later, reveal His righteous wrath against all those who go against His will—against the nations who harm His people (Zech. 1.14, 15), against evil powers whose aim is to destroy His work (Ps. 2.5; see Rev. 11.18), and against His own people when they turn against Him (Ps. 78). All men are, in some sense, under His wrath, because all have in their hearts at some time turned against Him who loves them (Ps. 90.7–9).

2. *Is it good to be angry?*

It often seems to be right (2 Sam. 12.5), but in the New Testament human anger is never praised. It is almost always said to be wrong. This may be because men find it difficult to be angry without having wrong feelings. But God's wrath is different:

(a) His wrath does not affect His 'feelings'. He does not feel passion as we do.

(b) He is always good, so His wrath must always be pure and right.

(c) We must use human language in speaking about God because it is the only language we know, but in using it we must never think He is exactly *like us* in His wrath or in anything else.

Most people have at times felt angry through hearing about some cruel deed in which innocent people have suffered—but very often those who do such deeds are not punished. But Christians can rejoice because they know that God has fixed a time when He will put right all the wrongs that have ever been done—and even now He is beginning to do it. See Acts 17.31 and Psalm 73, especially vv. 3–5, 10–13, 16–19.

3. *Is it possible to be angry and loving at the same time?*

Often a father is angry with his child *because* he loves him. If he did not love him, he would not bother to be angry. This is even more true of God (see Ps. 103.8, 9; Heb. 12.5–11). He is firmly opposed to *everything* which harms or spoils the lives of those whom He loves. See Mark 3.1–5, where Jesus's love for the crippled man caused Him to be angry with those who were trying to stop His good work.

4. *What makes God angry?*

There is really only one thing which causes God to show His wrath—our rejection of Him (which can take many forms). In rejecting Him we are rejecting love, and those who will not have God's love have nothing left to them but wrath (Rom. 2.4, 5). This is seen most clearly in men's attitude to Jesus. In Him God's love is perfectly revealed. Therefore those who reject Him are under God's wrath (John 3.36). For this reason the good news of Jesus Christ becomes bad news for those who reject it.

5. *How do men experience God's wrath?*

(a) In their lifetime through the misery and disorder present in the world (Rom. 1.18–32), and sometimes through events in which they see God's judgement (Jer. 32.37).

(b) At the end of their life, through death (Ps. 90.7–12; Rom. 1.32; 5.12). *Unrighteousness* leads to *Wrath*, which leads to *Death*.

(c) At the last day, through God's final judgement when His wrath will be fully revealed (Isa. 13.9; Rom. 2.5, 8, 9). See Additional Note, Judgement, p. 209.)

6. *Whom does God use to exercise His wrath?*

Rulers and others in authority do this when they punish wrong-doers

(Rom. 13.4); at the last day Jesus Himself, with His angels, will exercise God's wrath (Matt. 25.31–46; Rev. 6.16).

7. *How can men escape God's wrath?*

Although several ways are mentioned in the Old Testament (Jer. 4.4, 8; 36.7), the Jews knew that there was really only one way—simply to call upon God's mercy, which they knew they did not deserve (see Dan. 9.4–19). New Testament writers taught that this mercy is revealed in Christ, who delivers us from wrath (1 Thess. 1.10). He achieved this particularly by His *death* (1 Thess. 5.9, 10; Rom. 5.9, 10), but exactly *how* he achieved it remains a mystery. On the cross 'he bore our sins' (1 Pet. 2.24), was 'made to be sin' (2 Cor. 5.21), 'became a curse for us' (Gal. 3.13), and felt that He was forsaken by His Father (Mark 15.34)— all this suggests that He suffered the wrath of God instead of us. But in the Bible Jesus is never actually said to have been under God's wrath. He always enjoyed God's favour, and if we can say that He in any sense experienced God's wrath on the cross, then this confirms the fact that wrath is not something which God personally 'feels' as we do, but rather His constant opposition to what is wrong. In the case of Jesus, God was 'opposed' to our sins, which Jesus was bearing. Thus some scholars have pointed out that the wrath of God is most clearly revealed by the Gospel, because the death of Jesus, when in some mysterious way He took on Himself the world's evil, shows how firmly God is opposed to evil.

Even though all the details of the teaching may not be clear, it is certainly clear that Jesus is the Saviour from present and future wrath. Our freedom comes only from Him. Apart from His Gospel (Rom. 1.16, 17), there is only wrath (Rom. 1.18; John 3.36).

Key to Study Suggestions

1.1–15

1. Missionary; ambassador. See p. 7, 2 (d) and (e).
2. Servant–slave; Gospel–good news; anointed–Christ; Gentiles–nations; saint–holy; barbarian–uncivilized.
3. See pp. 6 and 7
4. (a) See p. 10.
   (b) See pp. 9 and 10.
5. See p. 7, lines 13–23.
6. (i) (b), (c), (e).
   (ii) (a), (d), (f).
7. Point (a): verse (c).
   Point (b): verse (a).
   Point (c): verse (e).
   Point (d): verse (b).
   Point (e): verse (d).
8. (b) See 2 Tim. 2.11–13.
9. (a) Acts 2.16–35; 3.18, 24; 10.43.
   (b) Acts 2.22; 3.13; 10.38, 39.
   (c) Acts 2.24–32; 3.15; 10.40.
   (d) Acts 2.32; 3.15; 10.41.
   (e) Acts 2.38; 3.19; 10.43.
10. See p. 11, lines 10–21.
    The first way: Acts 5.40; 20.17.
    The second way: Acts 2.39; 2 Tim. 1.9; 1 Pet. 2.9.

1.16, 17

1. Life; fellowship with God. See p. 217, 2, 3; p. 19, line 3; p. 211, lines 26–40.
2. Some possible answers are: (a) know; (b) trust, rely on; (c) thinks, expects. See p. 206, lines 36–43.
3. Rom. 1.18 (i) (a) (ii); (b) (iii); (c) (iv); (d) (i).
4. See p. 15, lines 25–35.
5. (a) See p. 16, line 14.
   (c) See p. 18, lines 1–18.
6. See p. 16, line 40; p. 15, line 36.
7. See p. 16, lines 36–42.
8. See p. 1, 2(b); p.19, lines 1–6.
9. See 1 Cor. 1.23, 24.
10. See p. 9, lines 41, 43; question 6 on p. 13.
12. See Acts 8.12; 16.13, 14; Rom. 10.14, 17; 1 Thess. 1.5, 6.
13. (a) They had the Scriptures which prophesied Messiah's coming.
    (b) Christ was a Jew and preached to Jews.
    (c) Pentecost was witnessed by Jews from Rome and elsewhere.
    (d) The apostles went first to Jewish synagogues.

1.18–32

1. (a) examines; (b) heals. See p. 22.
2. See p. 24, 3.
3. (a) God is creator, God is powerful, God is eternal.
   (b)'They knew God' (v. 21); 'They know God's decree' (v. 32).
4. See Gen. 3.7, 14, 15, 21; 4.9, 15; 6.8, 18.
5. Wrath: vv. 21, 31, 33, 34, 58–67.
   Love: vv. 4–7, 12–16,20, 24–29, 38, 39, 42–55, 68–72.
7. (i) (b), (d)
   (ii) (a), (c), (e).

Special Notes A and B

1. Some illustrations may be found in Rom. 1.5, 11, 16, 17, 23.
2. Some examples might be:
   (i) (a) That human beings cannot save themselves.
       (b) That Paul and Barnabas brought a divine message.
       (c) That there was a true God whom they did not know.
   (ii) (a) That man-made idols can give protection.
        (b) That Paul and Barnabas were gods in human form.
        (c) That God actually lives in sacred places and can only be served there.

2.1—3.20

1. (a) (ii).
2. (a) remorse; (b) sorrow; (c) regret; (d) repentance.
3. (a) See pp. 36, 37.
   (b) See pp. 37, 38, Note on vv. 14, 15.
4. (a) See p. 35, lines 17–30; p. 37, line 13; p. 38, lines 38 to end.
   (b) See p. 35, lines 8–11; p. 36, lines 24–27; p. 37, lines 13–23; p. 41.
5. See p. 41, lines 9–12; p. 210, Law, 3.
6. See p. 35, lines 22–24.
7. (i) (b); (ii) (c); (iii) (a).
9. (i) (a); (ii) (c); (iii) (b); (iv) (d).
10. (a) See Gen. 17.1–10.
    (b) See, e.g., Gen. 17.7; Matt. 28.20.
11. Note words: 'the Israel of God'; 'the true circumcision'; 'say that they are Jews and are not, but lie'.
12. (b) None.
    (c) See Col. 2.11, 12.
    (d) See p. 204, 4–6; p. 34, lines 23–28.
13. See Jer. 7.4, 10, 14, 15.
14. See p. 37, Note on vv. 14, 15.

3.21–31

1. Pardon, remit. Overlook and ignore both mean 'to take no notice of'.
2. and 3. See, e.g., p. 209, lines 3–6; p. 210; p. 49; p. 59, Note on v. 25, 2(b).
4. See p. 47, Note on the righteousness of God.
   See 3.27–31 and p. 52, Note on these verses.

5. See p. 52, (b) and Note on vv. 27–31.
6. See p. 38, section C.
7. (a) See p. 52, Note on vv. 27–31.
   (b) See question 4 (b) on p. 43.
8. (i) (b);   (ii) (d);   (iii) (c);   (iv) (a).
9. See pp. 206, 207.
10. See p. 47, Note on the righteousness of God.
11. See p. 52, lines 25–35.
12. See p. 46, A.4.
13. God's action through Christ in giving life to the spiritually dead and in accepting the Gentiles.
14. (a) Compare p. 214, 2–4.
    (b) Compare p. 52 (b).
15. See Gen. 1.27; 3.19, 23, 24.
16. (a) (i) By His being subject to human limitations;
        (ii) By His taking a physical body and suffering temptation.
    (b) (i) Sinners;   (ii) Human beings subject to death.
18. (b) See p. 50, lines 17–19;   p. 51, last para.
19. See p. 46, A.5;   p. 49, Note on v. 23;   p. 52, Note on vv. 27–31.
20. (a) See, e.g., p. 205, 4;   p. 52, lines 25–29; p. 60, 4.

4.1–25

1. See p. 211, lines 1, 2. In v. 14 it means 'those who keep the law'.
2. See 4.11–13, 18, 19.
3. See p. 58, Note on vv. 18–25, 2–5; p. 59, 7.
5. See p. 60, 2, 3;   pp. 58, 59.
6. See p. 59, 7; p. 60, 4.
7. (i) (a), (c);   (ii) (b).
8. (i) Refs to both, in vv. 69, 70, and 73.
   (ii) (a) God regarded Abraham as His friend.
        (b) David was the sort of man God wanted as King of Israel.
9. They taught that a man had to become a Jew before he could become a Christian.
15. See Gen. 9.9–17; 17.4–14.
16. Grace, faith, righteousness, circumcision. See p. 57, Notes on vv. 10, 11a and 13–17.
17. See p. 46, A.5 and Rom. 3.27.

5.1–11

1. See p. 65, lines 1–8.
3. See p. 63, Introduction.
4. See p. 63 and 64, Introduction.
5. See p. 66, Note on vv. 5–8.
6. See p. 64, lines 4–13, and whole section 5.1–11.
7. See pp. 66 and 67, 2(b).
8. See p. 69, Note on v. 10.
9. See p. 66, lines 15–20; p. 68, last 3 lines; p. 69, lines 1–5; pp. 220–221.
10. See p. 69, Note on v. 11.

11. See Heb. 4.16.
13. (i)   (b), (d), (f), (g);
    (ii) (a), (c), (e);
    (iii) (b), (c), (e), (f);
    (iv) (a), (d), (g).
14. (i) (a);   (ii) (c);   (iii) (b).
16. See p. 213, 'Reconciliation'.
17. See p. 65.
18. See p. 66, lines 1–20;   p. 221, lines 1–16.
19. See p. 65, Note on vv. 3–5a.
20. See p. 66, lines 25–37.

5.12–21

1. See p. 74, lines 3–9;   p. 76, lines 16–22.
2. See p. 78, lines 1–20.
3. See p. 74, lines 1, 2 and 16–31;   pp. 78–79 (Special Note).
4. See p. 74, lines 3–6;   p. 76, lines 8–22.
5. See Joshua 7.1;   7.5,12;   7.11 (cf. 7.25).
6. (i) (c);   (ii) (b);   (iii) (a);   (iv) (d);   (v) (e).
7. See p. 75, last 5 lines. (i) (b);   (ii) (a).
8. Israel is God's chosen people: (a), (c).
   All men have a unity from God: (b), (d).
9. (a) Through prayer in His name;
   (b) in suffering;
   (c) through abiding in Him (i.e. faith and obedience) and bearing fruit.

6.1–23

1. See p. 85, lines 18–24.
2. See p. 81, 1; p. 82 (c).
3. (a) See p. 79, lines 1–11;
   (b) See p. 85, last 2 lines; p. 86, lines 1–21.
4. See p. 83, Notes on v. 6; p. 85, lines 25–42.
5. See p. 84, (a), (b), and (c).
6. See p. 82, 2 (vv. 3–5);   p. 202, 1 and 4.
8. See p. 86, 'Freedom and Slavery'.
9. (a) 1 Pet. 2.16;   (b) Rom. 3.8a;   (c) Rom. 3.31a.
10. Death: (a);   Resurrection: (b);   Ascension: (c);   Glory: (d).
11. See p. 85, lines 27–34.
    Point (a): verse (b);
    Point (b): verse (a);
    Point (c): verse (d);
    Point (d): verse (c).
13. See passages given and p. 88, lines 17–30.
19. (a) See p. 84, 4 (vv 8b–10);   p. 85, lines 1–4;   p. 85, lines 15–17 and 38–42.
    (b) See p. 85, last 2 lines;   p. 86, lines 1–14.

7.1–25

1. (i) See p. 208.
   (ii) First meaning given on p. 208: (a), (b); Second meaning: (c), (d).

2. See p. 99, Note on vv. 23–25; pp. 210–211, Law.
3. See p. 93, lines 1–3, 13–16; p. 98, Note on v. 6.
4. See p. 92, lines 10–14; p. 93, lines 32–36; p. 96, 'A Question', lines 1–5.
5. See p. 95, lines 1–21; p. 211, lines 11–17.
6. See p. 96, lines 1–12; p. 97, line 4.
7. See p. 99, lines, 27–34; p. 64, Note on v.1.
9. (i) He did not.
   (ii) He kept its commands in His life and bore its penalty ('curse') in His death.
10. See (a) 6.7; (b) 6.11; (c) 6.22.
11. See Gen. 2.16, 17; 3.1; 3.4–6; 3.7–10.
13. See p. 95, lines 8–13.
14. See p. 95, lines 22–33; p. 74, 4; p. 84, lines 1–5.
15. See p. 96, 'A Question', lines 6–11; p. 97, 4.

8.1–17
1. See p. 219. Man: (a), (d); Divine power: (b), (c).
2. (a) acquitted, justified.
   (b) See p. 95, lines 15–21;
   (c) See p. 93, 'The Teaching'.
3. See p. 211, 'Law' 4.
4. (a) See 5.15–21; 6.1–11.
   (b) Life (see p. 211).
5. See p. 93, lines 26–30; p. 219, lines 13–16.
6. See p. 92, last 4 lines; p. 93, lines 1–4 and 'The Teaching'.
7. See p. 103, line 4.
8. See p. 104, Note on v. 8; and p. 208.
13. See, e.g., examples on p. 1.
14. (i) See p. 89; p. 220, 1(c).
    (ii) Discipleship and eternal life.
19. See pp. 219 and 220, 'Spirit' 4 and 5.
20. See p. 107, (b).

8.18–39
1. See p. 111, 1(a), 2(a), and (b).
2. See p. 113, 4.
3. See p. 65, lines 1–8; and pp. 111–114.
4. See p. 117, 1.
5. See p. 115, lines 1–33; compare p. 107, (b).
6. See p. 117, 3; p. 11, Note on vv. 6, 7.
7. See p. 116, lines 6–17 (and pp. 116–118).
8. See whole section, but especially p. 113, last 8 lines.
9. See p. 220, 1 (c); p. 221, 2 (a), (b), (c),
10. (a) See Gen. 1.31; 2.8–15.
    (b) See p. 111, lines 2–8; p. 111, 1 and 2.
11. See p. 113, 3 (c); p. 105, Note on vv. 10, 11.
15. Like Christ—(d), (e); Not yet like Him—(a), (b), (c).
16. (b) See p. 111, 2; p. 113, 3; question 9 on p. 70.
19. See p. 118, lines 16–33.

Special Note F

1. (d) There are some ideas in question 6, p. 13.
2. (a) See, e.g., p. 97, 4.
   (b) See p. 98, line 1; 2 Cor. 4.16—5.8.

9.1–5

2. (a) See p. 131, lines 1–26. (i) glory; (ii) patriarchs; (iii) sonship; (iv) promises; (v) worship; (vi) covenants; (vii) law.
3. See Exod. 20.2.
4. See also p. 147, last 6 lines; p. 151, Note on v. 14.
6. See p. 131, lines 7–14 and questions there referred to.
7. See p. 130, 1.
8. (b) See p. 126, 3.
   (c) See p. 130, lines 18–24.
   (d) See p. 128, lines 19–23, 4 (c).

9.6–29

1. Sovereignty: control, rule, lordship; Responsibility: duty, obligation.
2. See p. 135, Note on vv. 6, 7; p. 57, Note on vv. 11b, 12.
3. (c) See p. 134, Note on vv. 6–13.
4. See, e.g., p. 38, section C.
5. See p. 135, Notes on vv. 14–18.
6. See Gen. 15.3–5; 17.15–21.
7. See p. 134, last 8 lines; p. 135, last 4 lines; compare also p. 116.
8. (a) See Isa. 45.1–5.
   (b) Isa. 44.28; 45.4, 6, 13–15.
10. See p. 136, 3.
11. See also Rom. 11.20, 22, 23; see p. 149, (a).

9.30—10.21

1. See 9.31; 10.2, 3, 6, 7.
2. See p. 142, lines 20–41.
3. See p. 142, lines 1–14; pp. 143–144, Note on vv. 3 and 4.
4. See p. 142, lines 1–5; p. 144, Note on v. 9.
5. See p. 143, Note on v. 33.
9. (c) See Special Note, p. 29.
10. See p. 34, lines 10–26; p. 38, section C.
12. (a) See p. 142, lines 20 to end;
    (b) See p. 143, Note on v.3; question 17 on p. 62.
14. See p. 144, Note on v.9.

11.1–36

1. Foreknew, remnant, chosen, elect.
2. See p. 204.
3. (a) See p. 151, Note on v. 15. Salvation of some Jews now through Paul's ministry; Life from the dead.
   (b) See p. 147, last 3 lines; p. 149, lines 1–12. Israel's unbelief and rejection; salvation for Gentiles; Israel's jealousy; Israel's acceptance.

4. See p. 151, Note on v. 18.
5. See p. 152, Note on v. 32;   p. 79, lines 12–18.
6. See p. 128, lines 1–23.
9. (a) Acts 13.46; 17.7; 18.6.
   (b) Acts 13.44, 48, 49; 17.4, 12; 18.8b, 13.
   (c) Acts 13.45, 50; 17.5, 13; 18.6, 12.
12. (a) See Acts 26.9–15;   Phil. 3.5–8.
13. See p. 151, Note on v. 14.
14. See p. 140, Introduction.
16. See p. 207, 5, 6, 7.
17. See p. 204, Election.

12.1–8

1. See p. 154, Introduction, para. 1.
2. Offer, present, spotless, consecrated. See p. 191, Note on v. 16.
4. See p. 155, 1 and 2.
5. See p. 154, last 9 lines; p. 155, lines 1–4;   p. 157, last 9 lines;   p. 158, lines 1–6;   p. 189, 1.
6. See Eph. 4.1.
9. See p. 157, lines 20–30.
10. (a) See p. 158, lines 4–8; compare p. 163, lines 3–10;
    (b) See p. 29, Special Note, para. 2.
12. See, e.g., 1 Cor. 12.14–26.

12.9–21

1. See p. 212.
3. See p. 212, 3(a) and (b);   p. 163, Note on vv. 19–21.
4. Every Christian: (b), (d);   particular groups: (a), (c).
5. See 3 John 5–10; compare 2 John 10, 11;   p. 163, Note on v. 13b.
6. (a): Rom. 12.20;
   (b): Rom. 12.14;
   (c): Rom. 12.18;
   (d): Rom. 12.17;
   (e): Rom. 12.9, 10.
8. (i) See p. 164, lines 1–9;
   (ii) Rom. 13.1–7: (b);   Rom. 1.27: (a);   2 Cor. 5.10: (c).
9. (i) (a): mercies;   (b): received;   (c): died for;   (d): forgiven, given himself.
   (ii) Respond: (a) and (c);   Imitate: (b) and (d).

13.1–7

1. See p. 168, lines 7–13.
2. See p. 218, p. 175.
4. See p. 168, lines 14–30; p. 171, 1.
5. See p. 167, 3;   p. 170, lines 12–17.
6. See p. 168, Notes on vv. 2, 3, 4, and p. 170, lines 1–11, 18–41.
7. (a) John 19.11;

(b) Acts 23.5;
(c) 1 Cor. 2.8;
(d) Acts 4.29–31.
8. See p. 172, 5 (a) and (b).
9. See Jer. 38.4; 37.20.
10. See p. 167, 1; see p. 168, Note on vv. 3 and 4.
11. See p. 173, 7.
12. See p. 174, (b); compare p. 29.
14. See p. 174, (a), (b), (g).
15. Compare Acts 4.17–20.

13.8–14

1. See p. 178, Introduction and Notes on v. 8.
2. See p. 179, Note on vv. 9, 10.
4. See Rom. 12.1, 5, 19–21; 13.5, 8.
6. See p. 180, lines 4–8, last 3 lines.
9. At first Paul expected the Second Coming to be soon. Later, he thought it might not be in his lifetime.
10. (a) 1–6.
    (b) This is a discussion question!
11. See p. 179, lines 15–24. Compare p. 162, last 6 lines, and p. 163, lines 1–10.

14.1—15.13

1. See p. 184, para. 3.
2. See p. 185, Note on v. 14a.
3. See p. 185, Note on v. 14b and lines 34–37; compare Rom. 3.8.
4. (a) See p. 184, lines 1–10; p. 185, Note on v. 14a.
    (b) See p. 185, 4 (b).
6. (a) See Acts 15.1; 15.9, 10.
    (b) See Acts 15.20.
8. (a) See p. 184, lines 36–39.
    (b) See p. 187, lines 1–10.

15.14–33

1. See Acts 18.23; 19.1; 20.1–6, 13–15; 21.1–3, 7, 8, 17.
2. See p. 191, lines 14–18.
3. See p. 191, lines 30–33.
5. See Acts 25.11, 12.
6. See p. 191, last 7 lines, p. 192, lines 1–8; see Col. 1.6, 25.
7. See p. 194, lines 1–16.

16.1–27

3. See p. 197, lines 6–13.
5. See p. 198, lines 1–13.

Index

Note: This Index lists only the major references to the main ideas and subjects, and names of the most important people, mentioned in Paul's Letter to the Romans. Related subjects are grouped together under one entry, e.g. 'Law of God' and 'law of nations'.

New family, 163, 190, 200
New life, 102, 104, 201, 202, 211
New man, 88, 97, 99
'Now', 47, 69, 102, 123, 179

Obedience, 37, 74, 76, 78, 88, 93, 154, 191, 198, 213
Old self (old man), 83, 84
Old Testament, 39, 46, 92, 205, 215, 216
Order, 168

Paul, 6, 7, 12
Peace, 11, 16, 63, 64, 69, 70, 201, 214
Pharisees, 7
Plan, God's, 147, 149, 150, 212
Power, of God, 9, 10, 16, 135; of sin, 16, 83, 218; powers of evil, 111, 221
Prayer, 107, 114, 115, 118, 119, 170
Predestination, 117, 118
Privileges, 34, 36, 38, 131; see also Religious privileges
Prophecy, 158
Propitiation, 51, 205
Proof of character, 65, 158
Punishment, 25, 39, 41, 98, 111, 164, 167, 170, 175, 211
Purpose, God's, 85, 114–118, 125, 126, 128–130, 134–136, 204

Rebellion, 24, 31, 74, 75, 111, 114, 222
Reconciliation, 69, 70, 201, 213, 214
Redemption, 46, 50, 113, 122, 214
Rejection of God, see Rebellion
Rejoicing, 65, 66, 69
Religions, 31, 32, 205
Religious privileges, 35, 128
Remnant, 135, 143, 147, 215
Renewal, 158
Repentance, 35
Responsibility, 126, 138, 140
Resurrection, 10, 82, 84, 93, 105, 202, 221
Return of Christ, 150
Revelation, 60
Revaluation, 171, 172, 174

Right relationship (between God and man), 19, 22, 47, 49, 57, 64, 85, 117, 144, 205, 207, 209–211, 216, 220
Righteousness, 1, 15, 18, 19, 23, 29, 36, 39, 45–47, 52, 56, 57, 59, 93, 105, 122, 136, 142, 167, 210, 215–217; of God, 1, 18, 26, 29, 39, 45–47, 52, 142, 215–217
Risen Christ, 98, 105
Roman Christians, 3, 194, 196, 197; Roman Church, 192; Roman Empire, 129; Roman government, 174; Roman readers, 191; Roman rule, 68, 168

Sacrifice, Sacrifices, 46, 51, 52, 60, 103, 157, 191, 203, 205, 206
Saints, 10, 11
Salvation, 16, 18, 19, 35, 36, 47, 59, 64, 97, 116, 117, 122, 134, 135, 144, 150, 179, 180, 189, 216, 217
Sanctification, 88
Saving activity of God, 117, 215, 216
Second Coming, 138, 180
Servant (Paul's role), 6
Scripture, 9, 12, 18, 41, 49, 53, 55, 56, 92, 143, 198, 210; see also Old Testament
Sharing Christ's death, 202
Sin, 37, 39, 41, 45, 51, 52, 66, 68, 74–78, 81–84, 86, 93, 95–99, 102, 103, 111, 185, 200, 203–206, 209, 210, 213, 214, 218, 223
Slavery, 86, 88
Sonship, 9, 10, 68, 105, 107, 108, 113, 131, 218, 219
Soul, 98
Sovereignty of God, 126, 134, 138, 140
Special relationship, 23, 38
Spirit, 9, 93, 102–105, 107, 113–115, 118–120, 122–124, 189, 190, 211, 219, 220
Suffering, 65, 66, 97, 108, 110, 111, 113, 114, 116–118, 220, 221

Teachings of Jesus, 89, 163, 190